The politics of housing

MANCHESTER
1824

Manchester University Press

The politics of housing

Power, consumers and urban culture

Peter Shapely

Manchester University Press
Manchester and New York
distributed exclusively in the USA by Palgrave

Copyright © Peter Shapely 2007

The right of Peter Shapely to be identified as the author of this work has been asserted by him in accordance with the Copyright, Designs and Patents Act 1988.

Published by Manchester University Press
Oxford Road, Manchester M13 9NR, UK
and Room 400, 175 Fifth Avenue, New York, NY 10010, USA
www.manchesteruniversitypress.co.uk

Distributed exclusively in the USA by
Palgrave, 175 Fifth Avenue, New York,
NY 10010, USA

Distributed exclusively in Canada by
UBC Press, University of British Columbia, 2029 West Mall,
Vancouver, BC, Canada V6T 1Z2

British Library Cataloguing-in-Publication Data
A catalogue record for this book is available from the British Library

Library of Congress Cataloging-in-Publication Data applied for

ISBN   978 0 7190 7433 2   *hardback*

First published 2007

16 15 14 13 12 11 10 09 08 07   10 9 8 7 6 5 4 3 2 1

Typeset
by Helen Skelton, Brighton, UK
Printed in Great Britain
by Anthony Rowe, Chippenham

Contents

Preface

This book is concerned with the interaction of traditional politics, culture and voluntary groups, of local and national influences, of ideals and individuals. It looks at local government, social groups and housing policy in the twentieth century. Manchester is the focal point, providing the type of specific detail that only single-city studies can supply. Studying housing provides the most dynamic of all policy areas. Housing absorbed a huge amount of time, money and effort. It was influenced by conflicting ideologies, professional ideals and financial realities. This is a remarkable story of how these factors were interwoven to create and manage policy. Nothing like this had ever been attempted. It was a massive challenge to reshape Britain on an unprecedented scale – to demolish and build homes for millions of people.

It is a story of heroic reformers, sweeping success and spectacular failure. Finally, it is also a story of ordinary people and of how they benefited or suffered as a result of policies formed and implemented from above.

Acknowledgements

This book is the culmination of research carried out over the last five years. The post-war material was part of a joint project with Professor Duncan Tanner, Professor Steven Fielding (Salford University) and Dr Andrew Walling, the Labour Party and the Politics of Housing in Manchester and Salford 1945–87, funded by the Leverhulme Trust. The pre-war material was supported by a further grant from the British Academy. I am also grateful for the additional financial assistance provided by the Department of History and Welsh History at the University of Wales Bangor.

Librarians and archivists are always unsung heroes. I am especially grateful to the staff at the Manchester Central Library Local Studies Unit and Archives. Also, the Working-Class Movements Library provided further useful assistance. My thanks must also go the well-oiled machine that is the Public Records Office. Also, I would like to express my gratitude to Christine Raiswell at the Manchester City Council Housing Department who freely gave up her time to supply some important factual information. Thanks must also go to Councillor William Egerton and Gerald Kaufman who provided some very useful interviews and to Mike Brennan for his additional comments.

On a personal level, I would like to express my appreciation to Professor Duncan Tanner, Professor Pat Garside and Professor Mike Rose who have very generously given me a great deal of time, support and invaluable advice. Also, I would like to thank Dr Nick Hayes, Professor Alan Kidd and Dr Wil Griffith for their further help and guidance. A significant degree of administrative support has also been provided by Mrs June Hughes and Mrs Stephanie Dolben. Their kindness and patience have been much appreciated.

Introduction

The task of clearing Britain's slums and providing affordable subsidised housing dominated social policy for much of the twentieth century. Conflicting ideas about how to achieve the objective, together with a series of economic restrictions, meant that housing programmes stuttered across the period. The story of housing policy is fractured, not coherent. National governments constantly changed the framework within which local authorities operated. Councils were continually granted powers and money under one government, only for them to be reduced by the next. Local authorities themselves shifted policy, not only according to national government legislation, finance and the condition of the market but also depending on which party had control of the Town Hall. The different political parties had their own ideologically based solutions. Much of this has been well documented. However, this only partly explains the creation and administration of policy. A distinct cultural context provided the environment in which the decision-making process functioned. Civic culture was shaped by voluntary organisations, individual pioneering reformers, political idealism and the local press. Grand visions and schemes were produced which were designed simultaneously to improve conditions for the slum dweller whilst enhancing the status of the city.

What happened in reality was a mixture of partial progress and missed opportunities. There were a number of successes as the Victorian slums were slowly cleared and (some) quality homes were built. But there were also a number of high-profile failures. Local authorities faced a number of barriers, including limited finances and lack of available land. They had to take advice from government and professionals which was difficult to contest. Moreover, they had to face daily problems in delivering an adequate service. Tenants lived with the consequences of these policies. Until the latter part of the century, tenants had little say in the creation and management of policy. Both central and local government adopted a top-down approach to tenants, which had more in common with the charity–recipient relationship than with providing a service for the people. The tenant was a recipient of taxpayer's munificence. This was acceptable and understandable whilst society remained relatively hierarchical and while people retained faith in the council to deliver them from the slums. Yet from the late 1960s, the tenant was becoming increasingly frustrated at the apparent inability of the local authorities effectively to manage housing policy. Some began to adopt the language of consumerism and to become organised in ways which paralleled the US consumer action groups. Increasingly, the tenant became a part of the policy process. By the time of the rebuilding projects of the early 1990s, consultation and participation were central elements in the creation and management of policy. The discourse of politics had been partially changed.

Manchester provides the focus for this study. It highlights the significance of the individual urban context, of local politics, culture and society in reaching an understanding of policy creation and implementation. Housing was chosen for this study because it was the most dynamic policy area in twentieth-century towns and cities. It is where politics (local and national) interacted with culture and society at a local level to influence policy before, during and after its implementation. Unlike other policy areas, housing was not dominated by any single professional group. It attracted huge sums of money and the attention of a range of opinionated politicians, professionals and social reformers. This is important not simply because of what it tells us about policy and society, but also in what it suggests about the study of urban history, about the interaction of government, society and culture and about the local decision-making process.

The Introduction will look at how research into housing has developed. Although housing histories have examined a range of policy issues, few have considered the cultural context in which decisions were implemented. Also, the role of the tenant is too often relegated to the periphery. Consequently, the Introduction will consider the necessity of reasserting an understanding of civic culture, local discourse, social and physical barriers and the role of the tenant, to appreciate fully the dynamics underpinning the politics of housing. It will look at the 'structure of feeling', the cultural context in which the key players, the councillors and professionals, made their decisions. Moreover, it will argue that any consideration of housing must necessarily consider the role of the tenant and how they moved from being dormant recipients to active consumers.

Housing histories

Housing in modern Britain has attracted a great deal of interest amongst historians. It has been the focus for a series of studies examining welfare, social policy and government and governance. Research has looked at a range of issues, focusing on conditions, ideological solutions, the role of central government and professionals and local government. However, while there have been a series of valuable accounts of the development of housing policy, they all too often take the decision-making process out of the context in which it was implemented and managed. Local civic traditions are usually ignored. Some take local political discourse into account, but they fail to appreciate the wider cultural influences. Most also fail to acknowledge that tenants were a part of the picture. Although not as obvious as the role of politicians or professionals, they had their own discourse which became increasingly important in the latter part of the twentieth century.

Many studies, especially of the nineteenth century, focus on conditions, the role of the private landlord and counter-reactions to the slums. The Industrial Revolution brought with it huge changes to housing patterns. Britain became transformed from a rural society to a dense, urban nation fraught with building, health and social problems.[1] Urban housing conditions for the poor and working classes were grim. A new class of landlords emerged who were only interested in squeezing a profit in what was a difficult and largely unregulated market.[2] Although there were some improvements in the second part of the nineteenth century, these were sporadic and tended to benefit the more affluent working classes.[3] However, from the 1880s conventional attitudes which emphasised a laissez-faire approach were challenged by increasing demands for some government intervention.[4] Alongside this was the growth of a distinctly anti-urban group. A number of studies examine how the idea of creating planned working-class suburbs to replace the slums gathered support. Suburban idealism was most obviously advanced in Britain and America, though there were comparable developments in other parts of northern Europe.[5] These studies do not take into account the cultural preferences of the working classes or slum dwellers. They show that, in Britain, the movement came from above, led by the likes of Sir Ebenezer Howard, and socialist architects such as Raymond Unwin. They developed the Garden City Movement which became enormously influential in shaping attitudes towards house building from the late nineteenth and throughout much of the twentieth centuries.[6] The overcrowded, dense and polluted urban environment was rejected in favour of a rural idyll, a belief that all should enjoy the benefits of open spaces and green areas. The built form of contemporary towns was abandoned in favour of alternatives based on the village and the countryside. Henry Vivian and Ebenezer Howard promoted the idea of co-partnership housing at Brentham, Letchworth and Hampstead. Supporters of the movement believed that everyone would have a higher standard of living and that this would, ultimately, reduce class conflict without challenging existing social relationships.[7] The ideal of suburbia was not an exclusive reserve of the right wing, or of the middle classes.[8] There were a number of influences on the Garden City Movement emerging from the end of the nineteenth century, including left-wing organisations such as the Fabians and the Co-operative society.[9] Many prominent people from across British society shared the vision, including E. M. Forster, Thomas Hardy, Hilaire Belloc, G. K. Chesterton and Vaughan Williams.[10] Alongside this was the idea of suburban living for all classes. Victorian social reformers such as Octavia Hill advocated the spread of suburban living for the working classes as the best long-term solution to the problems of urban life.[11]

Increasingly, from the early twentieth century, government policy encouraged expansion into new suburban areas. In many of these studies there is an underlying assumption that the working classes would follow the middle-class model for living. In reality, they had little choice. Local authorities, faced with a lack of available land and a professional belief in out-county suburbs, built large new estates miles outside the traditional centres. A few studies acknowledge that there was debate about the impact of this movement from the city to the new suburbs. Some highlight the sense of loneliness, dislocation and 'suburban sadness' suffered by many, especially women. Others, however, have pointed to the long-term benefits brought about by better living conditions and the creation of new social networks and common interests.[12] The invasive intrusion into rural areas was not without its opponents. Some contemporaries, such as J. B. Priestley and H. J. Massingham, feared overdevelopment and the loss of the rural idyll.[13] But many local authorities, encouraged by government, did try to pay attention to the exterior appearance of houses and the entire surrounding area. Civic pride was important as some councils were keen not only to build vastly improved homes for the working classes but also to create a better, brighter city.

In many studies, civic culture has not received as much attention as other, largely political, issues. Understandably, the role of central government has been the primary focus for research. They highlight how, during 1890–1979, British governments became involved in the development of large new towns and estates, provided subsidies and rent controls and set building standards.[14] Accounts underline the central role of planners, designers and politicians. Few studies take into account the ambitions of the tenants. However, Meller and Garside highlight the way some small-scale developments, sponsored by women reformers and charities such as the Sutton Trust at the start of the twentieth century, showed an impressive level of understanding and awareness of tenants' own hopes and desires.[15] Sadly, this did not feed into mainstream policy. Voluntary-sector housing reforms were swamped by public-sector developments. Government was unquestionably the central power in creating and implementing policy across the twentieth century. Studies show that ideological shifts, economic factors and social pressures shaped central government policies throughout the period. However, many of these studies take housing policy out of the urban environment, providing an almost exclusively centralised political account of the creation of policy. After the First World War, for example, research into the motivation behind Lloyd George's working-class housing programme have focused on progressive Liberal ideals, fear of revolution, guilt and social conscience. Christopher Addison's 1919 Act has been seen as a means of satisfying the population's desire for higher living standards in order to avoid revolution from a disaffected army of returning soldiers.[16] Ultimately, the programme was a failure, leading eventually to a Conservative revisionist programme.[17] This reflected the continual ideological shift which took place in the 1920s, 1950s and 1980s when Labour and the Conservatives exchanged places. Although the Conservatives recast themselves to a degree after the First World War, reflecting changes in electoral support, the apparent reformist agenda was simple and pragmatic. It did not constitute a fundamental shift in their underlying orthodox values.[18]

Party politics and central government are the sole focus of these studies. They show how housing continued to be a major political issue throughout the inter-war period. Even when Stanley Baldwin denounced the 1933 by-election of East Fulham as a triumph for pacifism, the real issues in the campaign were in fact housing and poverty.[19] Housing was generally recognised for some time as an important subject for both individuals and the state, but after the Second World War it emerged as a central political issue.[20] Labour's election victory in 1945 has been attributed to a number of factors, including the fear of returning to 1930s unemployment, a belief in the efficiency of socialism and the promise of the welfare state. While the creation of the NHS was obviously crucial, housing was equally important. Labour was seen as the party to produce an effective housing programme, a perception which was reinforced by its 1924 Housing Act.[21] The electorate had an intense interest in housing issues, with 41 per cent of people stating it was their main concern in a 1946 opinion poll.[22] Even local elections and party newspapers were dominated by housing issues.[23] However, it was also an issue that attracted continual public dissatisfaction, a fact underlined by a public attitudes survey of 1956. Public disappointment increased in the 1960s and 1970s with high-rise developments and tales of corruption.[24] The post-war house-building programme produced limited gains. Some historians have even seen it as a disastrous failure.[25]

Although the promise of the welfare state, and of housing as a component of that policy, was accepted by both parties, there still existed ideological divisions which punctuated conceptions and impacted on policy.[26] There was no clear consensus emerging.[27] This was highlighted by Bevan's Housing Act of 1949, which emphasised the role of the public sector, and Harold Macmillan's 'grand design', which attempted to make the private sector the central element of policy.[28] The Conservative governments of the 1950s placed greater emphasis on the role for the private sector. They were successful in not simply changing policy but also in shifting the discourse, underlined by the fact that New Town development corporations came to embrace private development and ownership.[29] By the early 1960s, a further change began to emerge at the national level. Conservative policies became unpopular as rent and land prices increased. Following the Rachman scandal of 1963, the government was placed on the defensive. It was forced to retreat from supporting an unfettered market.[30]

Central authority studies do not only examine the partisan politics and politicians. Some look at the role of the civil service. Although the Ministry of

Housing and Local Government had traditionally seen its role in terms of supporting local government initiatives, Crossman gave it a more active role. Civil servants, such as the formidable Evelyn Sharp, the Permanent Secretary of the Ministry of Housing and Local Government during 1955-66, dominated the department and local authorities, whom she regarded as children worthy of constant rebuke.[31] Some studies suggest that central authority figures were squeezing the power and autonomy of local authorities. Consequently, in a number of studies the role of local government is often downgraded or ignored. For some, in the 1960s and early 1970s, local government was reduced to nothing more than an agent of the state in the provision of housing.[32] Central government funding, for example, became the most important factor in determining architectural choice and policy.[33] Local government played little more than a supporting role to central government. It was their financial policies and determination to increase densities that drove policy.[34] There existed an important national public housing nexus, consisting of central government, designers and the construction industry.[35] The Ministry of Housing had a huge influence over public housing construction policy through its control of legislation, subsidies, cost controls and loan sanction approval. Ministry architects wielded extensive influence over local government architects through cost controls while architects and planning departments had a dominant role in many cities.[36] During 1964–73 local authority architects were responsible for less than 60 per cent of public housing designs, with the remainder coming from private builders.[37] The large contractors dominated public housing construction, many of them enjoying close personal links with housing ministers. Keith Joseph and Geoffrey Rippon, for instance, had close family and business links with the industry, while McAlpine and Taylor Woodrow were major donors to the Conservative Party.[38] The links between central government and the building contractors became a central dynamic behind housing policy.[39] This was partly a result of the need to fulfil the assurances of the welfare state, to clear the slums and the accompanying poverty.[40]

Despite the dominant position of central government, these housing histories only give a limited account of the creation and management of policy. Orthodoxy continues to stress that central government's influence over policy continually increases after 1900. Davis argues that power at the local level reduced throughout the twentieth century as central government expanded its role.[41] This contrasts sharply with the independence enjoyed by local authorities in the nineteenth century. However, the death of local authorities is exaggerated.[42] Governments were often remote from the environment in which detailed plans were formed and implemented. Local authorities still had a role to play in the implementation of policy for much of the twentieth century. The power of local authorities was retained as part of a continual process of bargaining with central government. Urban government did change as local authorities competed for resources from national government and, increasingly, from the

European Union, but it did not disappear.[43] It has remained the most effective institution to implement policies and deliver services because of local expertise, knowledge and its enthusiasm to provide the best solutions for their areas. Central and local government worked together. Urban renewal in the Withington district of Manchester during 1962–83, for example, involved a range of different agencies or policy participants, including private development companies, the council, local amenity groups and community action groups.[44] Until the 1980s and 1990s, local authorities had total control over the allocation and management of housing.[45] A number of studies highlight the fact that the relationship between central and local government still allowed a considerable degree of freedom for councils. Housing committees formulated their own individual policies, choosing the design, the contracts with private developers and the choice of building system.[46] Any model of governmental relations must reach beyond simplistic ideas of the centre providing the lead with local government following.[47] The inter-war period, for instance, was a 'golden age' for local government.

Councils played a major role in shaping their communities.[48] Although government was certainly taking a lead, it was never the producer of mass housing. The bargaining process between local and central authorities evolved across the century. Local authorities retained a great deal of autonomy. With slum clearance, although the state provided the legislative framework and resources, it was local government which defined the houses and areas for clearance.[49] After the Second World War, local authorities enjoyed substantial independence in carrying out their functions.[50] Local authorities were still able to influence policy.[51] Councillors in Bermondsey and Southwark, for example, were heavily involved in policy details, even making decisions on the layout of the flats and the colour of the curtains in homes for the elderly.[52] The issue of resources was also instrumental in shaping individual local authority responses to housing, as the obligation on councils to clear and provide houses could be set aside if they were not satisfied that they had the resources, such as land, vacant properties and manpower, to tackle them.[53] In a number of areas, local authorities extended their powers up to the 1970s. For example, in Sheffield there was a large expansion in the role of local government in a number of services, including housing.[54]

Local authorities were responsible for the organisation and actual building of new homes, but this is not to deny the impact of other agents in shaping post-war housing policy, including architects, town planners, contractors and builders. Mounting pressures to clear the slums quickly, and build cost-effectively, meant that the building industry resorted to a series of innovative techniques. A number of studies have looked at the impact of architects and designers in creating a modern social experiment. Post-war Britain witnessed the most extensive series of innovations in its history, with high-rise emerging as the central design feature. These innovations completely changed the nature of what was still a

Victorian industry.[55] Planners and designers became key players in housing policy. The increasing pressure to solve the housing problem, compounded by the impact of the war, led to a rational solution based on new methods and techniques. Design professionals began to promote new factory-built systems as the most modern and efficient means of resolving the problem.[56] Both Churchill and Bevan encouraged modern techniques as the answer to labour and material shortages and a number of local authorities carried out their own experiments. Many still remained sceptical about the value of these techniques, especially older architects, some local authorities and tenants.[57] But urgent need, modern theory and a belief in the efficiency of industrial techniques meant that factory system-built methods were able to provide quick and easy solutions.[58]

However, the creation of large tower-block schemes was not only a consequence of the vision of architects and designers (along with central government policies), but also a result of decisions taken by councillors and local government officials.[59] The decisions, and the timing, which led to mass modern house building can only be understood in the context of both the national constraints and the particular circumstances of key municipal authorities.[60] It is not accurate to suggest that large-scale building projects were just a result of pressure from building contractors or central government. Local authorities carried out their own programmes and made independent decisions, leading to diverse policies across the country. In the 1960s, for example, multi-storey flats accounted for half of new council dwellings in Greater London, but 75 per cent in Glasgow.[61] Councillors were the main driving force. Across the country, the 'crusading councillors' set the pace of change.[62] Tower blocks became an expression of local municipal power, not simply a product of government and planning professional pressure. They were a means of keeping people inside their city boundaries at a time when the land trap had threatened to take even more tenants into new towns and overspill estates. The power exercised by councillors underlines the continuing importance of local government throughout the twentieth century.

By the late 1970s and early 1980s, the housing debate began to shift significantly away from a needs-based approach to a market-orientated view of what people could afford.[63] Debate has centred on the impact of Thatcherism, the assault on subsidised public-sector housing and the role of the council. Housing was a policy area both affected by and central to the Conservative government's economic and social policies. Privatisation, cutbacks, deregulation and competition provided the new policy framework.[64] During 1980–87, an estimated 750,000 council homes were sold to their tenants.[65] But housing policy was not just about selling council homes. From the late 1980s and throughout the 1990s, a number of local authorities came to see housing as part of inner-city urban regeneration. Several inner-city areas were transformed because of schemes built in conjunction with central government and the private sector. Parts of Salford, Newcastle and Cardiff, for example, were redeveloped with high-status housing projects replacing dilapidated riverside and dockland areas. City centres such as

Manchester (actively promoted by the council) have undergone a gradual yet significant change with a series of luxury apartment developments. However, while councils, often Labour dominated, have played an important if not pivotal role in these developments, they are private apartment blocks and deliberately expensive. They are not social housing projects. These high-cost housing programmes in both residential and non-residential inner-city areas did not replace housing for low-income tenants.[66]

While some of these studies of the role of local government and professionals in housing policy have redressed the balance with studies which focus on central government, many remain problematic because they take the key actors out of the urban environment in which they worked and made their decisions. The local–central government dynamic is vital in any understanding of the politics of housing, but it fails to appreciate the cultural context in which decisions were made. However, civic culture can not be ignored. Councillors, and professionals, were inextricably bound to their communities. Any understanding of the decision-making process must take this into account. Recent studies have shown that British politics is being transformed. Increasingly, organisations from central government to local councils, political and public institutions are no longer dictating policy but are responding to public needs and demands.[67] Tenant wishes are more important as they become recognised as consumers. Yet most housing histories do not consider the role of the tenant. For most of the twentieth century, the tenant ambitions were ignored. The very notion of choice was never a realistic consideration. Necessity reduced the idea of providing options to the sidelines.[68] With a few notable exceptions, housing histories have relegated tenants to little more than bit players.[69] This reflects the position of tenants in society. Most tenants in clearance areas across Britain were only partially consulted about slum clearance and rehousing programmes. They were treated as the beneficiaries of public-subsidised housing. They were not property owners.[70] Where plans were presented to tenants it was often in the form of a triumphant explanation about what was going to happen to them. Until the 1980s, most local authorities were unconcerned with the views of tenants in clearance areas. Some did enjoy a degree of indirect influence. For example, in the years immediately after the Second World War public opinion did help to shape post-war housing provision. Popular opinion intersected with architects and planners.[71] However, it was a limited exercise.

Although tenants have been recognised as a large consumer group in the nineteenth century, their relationship with local authorities in the twentieth century has never been considered in the same way.[72] They were no longer in a fluid and competitive market but were the recipients of grand municipal schemes. The relationship in the private sector is more obviously based on notions of the market and choice. Tenants were purchasing a product. Local authorities were different. They were providing a subsidised service. Tax and ratepayers were contributing to the well-being of the poor. Besides, the local authorities were seen as the only institutions capable of rescuing tenants from the misery of the slums. They were trusted to deliver a quality alternative. In the predominantly paternalistic society of the pre-1960s, people believed the council would eventually provide decent homes.

However, the creation of the welfare state and the gradual changes to society created a different attitude in the tenant–council relationship. The welfare state gave people the right to decent living conditions.[73] But there is a tension between the way they were perceived and treated by government (local and national) and the way they behaved and viewed the role of local authorities. Power lay with the council. The few links that existed between the council and community were made largely through the local Party rather than any formal organisation or representation.[74] However, policy and management failures in housing policy did bring a challenge to council authority. Some tenants began to challenge and influence management decisions from the late 1960s. Tenant action groups were not recent phenomena. A number of groups existed from the nineteenth century.[75] Public-sector tenants' movements were in Glasgow, for example, for over sixty years.[76] However, the 1960s were an important period in the development of tenant action. This was partly due to pressure from central government, but it was also a result of organised tenant protests. Public expectations, which had risen after the war with the welfare state and economic growth, were being frustrated, giving rise to a tenant backlash.[77]

The roles of the council and the tenant underline the necessity of considering the urban context in which housing systems developed.[78] Besides tenants, this includes a discourse built around civic culture. Despite the extensive research into housing, there has been little recognition of the role of the tenant or civic culture in shaping policy. As Ravetz points out, the study of council housing has all too often been reduced to a history of national and local authority policy.[79] But policy did not emerge in a social or cultural vacuum and its impact on the lives of the tenants cannot be separated from the politics of housing. Council houses had a major contribution to working-class life and culture.[80] The effect of policy did not end with government directives. Councillors, backed by social groups, reformers and the local press, created policy within a distinct cultural context.[81] Local discursive culture, and the values emanating from civil society, provided an important framework in which policy was created and managed. The existence of local discursive cultures helps to explain why 'national' narratives did not always have an identical resonance across the whole country.[82] Although *national* discursive political traditions are important, so too is a culture constructed around local values.[83] Yet this also had to be played out in the face of local tenant problems and pragmatic issues. The land trap, for example, forced local authorities down certain policy pathways, either in the shape of overspill estates or tower blocks. The impact of the interaction of local discourse and immediate, often physical, problems can only be fully appreciated by focusing on each urban arena.

Civic culture – the structure of feeling

Housing histories highlight the need to consider the impact of civic culture and the role of the tenant on the policy-making process. In making their decisions, councillors were not operating in a social and cultural vacuum. Officials were part of an environment that had its own distinctive culture, shaped by social pressures, community groups, heritage, tradition and civic pride. Local cultural and historical 'structures of feeling' influenced local policy choices across the twentieth century. When councillors and officials became a part of the political framework, they entered a sphere of activity with its own cultural structures. Each city operated in the same framework established by central government. Many had shared characteristics, common features and made common claims. The Manchester story is not exclusive, but, like other cities, it is distinctive.[84] Every city also had different traditions. The distinctiveness of each urban context was highlighted by Taylor, Evans and Fraser's study of Manchester and Sheffield, *A Tale of Two Cities*.[85] The history and traditions of Manchester evolved from the late eighteenth century and throughout the nineteenth century when it became the first industrial city. A distinctive 'structure of feeling' was created, a culture whereby officials in the city saw themselves as being part of a bigger world with a larger set of opportunities, rather than simply an old industrial northern city trapped in a series of labour stereotypes.[86]

Civic culture constitutes a central element in the operation of government and governance at the local level. Civic culture transcends traditional politics. It provides a network of unspoken values, norms and patterns of behaviour. Local politicians have a shared sense of identity, of belonging to the same community with its distinctive history and traditions. This creates a series of codes and filters, giving meaning to actions and objects, to policies and politicians.[87] Cultural structures provide a framework, guides and motivation. They legitimise action and can open up possibilities.[88] Civic culture gives form to both structure and agency behaviour in the urban environment. In particular, it underpins local government discourse, aims and ambitions. This does not exclude other influential factors. In many policy areas, there were problems at the local level which defied the 'ideal'. Also, there was more than one discourse. Nevertheless, civic culture did provide the context in which local officials tried to create and implement policy.

While the nineteenth century has been seen as a zenith for local government and civic culture, its character changed but its relevance did not disappear in the twentieth century. The substantive value of civic culture in providing the norms and filters through which local government operates is highlighted by Manchester's political, social and economic leaders who not only embraced a belief in the city's status as an important international city, but actively promoted it (and continue to do so) at any opportunity. This was reflected in its Victorian past. The creation of Manchester council was a symbol of the aspirations and ambitions of the emerging middle classes. Initially, the council was a vehicle for some of the city's rich and powerful. However, from the late 1840s the city's urban aristocrats began to take a back seat. In the second half of the nineteenth century competing groups of ratepayers and reformers vied for control of the council.[89] This battle between those who demanded economy and retrenchment and those with a grander vision dominated local politics. Nevertheless, a sense of civic pride began to emerge. The more progressive elements on the council promoted some of the bigger schemes in municipal intervention. Once the council did take public action it could be bold and dynamic. It liked proudly to promote itself as a city of firsts. When, for example, it banned back-to-backs it was keen to point out that it was the first local authority in the country to do so. The council showed it could take a lead and even a risk throughout the century. This was highlighted by its support for the Ship Canal, the Thirlmere viaduct and even the huge £1,000,000 Town Hall.

Although the nature of local government changed in the twentieth century, civic culture continued to provide the context in which local government attempted to create policy. In Manchester, this was underlined with the Olympic bids, the Commonwealth Games and its successful bid to be the European City of Drama in 1994. Other developments such as the tram system and the airport also became an extension of the city's sense of civic culture. Manchester's leaders have continued to embrace the idea that it was a city of 'firsts', whether it was as the first industrial city, the first to adopt a new and modern tram network or even the first to declare it a nuclear-free city.

Manchester was not the only city to make such proud boasts. Other cities make similar boasts. Glasgow and Liverpool still make reference to their having been regarded as the 'second city of the Empire', Birmingham revels in the title of 'second city' while Leeds boasts about it being the 'capital of the north'. Manchester would, of course, contest some of these. Many cities promote themselves as pursing exclusive policies which reflect their own particular dynamism.[90] However, while elements are common to many cities, individual urban narratives became personalised and particular to each urban arena. Outcomes and points of emphasis vary according to each place, different inter-pretations and time.[91] In Manchester, a grand narrative was created in which members of the council, supported in the public sphere by the local and some of the national press, gave structure to the notion that it was an important inter-national centre capable of producing the very best, whether it be in industry and commerce, music, sport and leisure or housing. Proud boasts about Manchester's status have become deeply embedded in local culture with 'history' being used as evidence of its status. Housing was an extension of this ideal. Influenced by key reformers such as T. R. Marr, T. C. Horsfall and Ernest Simon, Manchester's civic culture was framed by a commitment to build high-quality cottages, to be bold and imaginative. Wythenshawe, built in the 1930s, was claimed to be the finest development of its kind in the country. After the war, Manchester proposed to build the biggest and best overspill estates in Europe. Flat building was rejected as a part of this civic culture. But even when flat developments could not be avoided, the council boasted it would be the best in the country. In a typically robust example of civic jingoism, the Lord Mayor Mrs E. A. Yarwood claimed in 1967, "we have some of the finest examples of [housing] in the country and when the Hulme redevelopment is complete it will be one of the finest examples in Europe". This rebuilding of Hulme (like other grand schemes from the past, such as Wythenshawe) was a part of the city's cultural discourse. The system-built units, the flats and especially the multi-deck access crescents, were heralded as part of a new dawn, which would see Manchester emerge as the new Bath or the new Bloomsbury.[92] Similarly, in the 1990s, the rebuilding of Hulme was again proclaimed as an example of the city's civic pride. As will be seen, a discourse developed around civic pride and jingoism, an ambition to develop the biggest and the best, and a desire to build cottages rather than flats, which was to have a significant impact on housing policy across the twentieth century.

The tenant as consumer

While the modern system-built developments were heralded as high-status projects, most proved to be a disaster. Manchester council had been reluctant to use the factory systems, but local circumstances pushed it into using the designs as the only solution to its continuing problems. Although it had a grand local discourse, a series of problems meant that the council was not always able to achieve its ambitions. The reality of many housing policies points to a picture of fracture, frustration and dislocation. Ordinary tenants had to live with the consequences of these policies. Many housing histories ignore the fact that this is an obviously significant part of 'housing policy' – not simply the creation but the implementation and management of policy and the impact it had on people's lives. Some tenants became increasingly angry and frustrated at policies and administration. Local discourse reflects growing disillusionment with policy, the council and the local Labour Party. This is the discourse of the tenant. Tenants constitute one of the most unrepresentative groups in housing studies. They had little direct influence on the creation of policies in the 1950s and 1960s. That is not the point. Studying tenant groups reveals much about the tensions between political parties and the people. From the late 1960s, groups of tenants began to act and to view themselves as consumers. Tenant groups came to use the language and some of the characteristics of the wider consumer movements emerging from the 1950s. Narrow definitions of consumerism centre on a strict producer-consumer relationship in a free market. Tenants were not operating in an environment structured by a free market. But this is not to deny the influence of consumer language or of the consumer movement in understanding the reactions and organisation of tenants, especially from the late 1960s. Tenant discourse absorbed and transcended traditional political discourse, providing an alternative model for understanding the shifting political landscape of the closing decades of the century.

Histories of consumption have moved into a range of areas other than the purchase of material goods.[93] Twentieth-century consumer movements were not only concerned with the protection of individual rights in the market place; some discussed social rights and citizenship.[94] Many tenant groups rode on the back of the social consumer movement, the intellectual origins of which were in the USA. Even in the early Progressive era, a view emerged that saw the citizen as a consumer not simply of material goods but also of wider public services.[95] The 'citizen consumer' was a protective group responsible for campaigning to protect the rights of citizens. They sought government help to guarantee safety.[96] Consumerism, in this sense, was a form of civic responsibility, a means of improving living standards for the nation.[97] It was a political as well as an economic issue. In this view, consumption as opposed to class was the underlying factor shaping twentieth-century America. In the 1950s, a number of groups were created that were designed to support the social and political interests of citizens. Their structure, aims and objectives were designed to mobilise, inform, educate and support grass-roots tenant movements. Some were involved in political action, but many went beyond conventional political ideologies. Although associated in retrospective accounts with the radical left, a number challenged the emphases of left-wing organisations and some developed a consumer ideology that celebrated the citizen or were simply protective community organisations.[98]

Housing protest from the 1960s became an extension of consumer protests against state failures. Sporadic protests were evident during the early twentieth century, but these were few and far between compared with the period from the late 1960s. Inter-war society was more hierarchical and paternalistic. Besides, although tenants did show a willingness to make organised protests against local authority policies, there was an underlying belief that the council offered the best solution to the local housing problems. After the Second World War, and with the creation of the welfare state, society began to change. Gradually, citizens were more ready, willing and able to make a stand on civil, social and political rights. Citizens had also become more materialistic than during the pre-war period. The result was a consumer revolt against the policies and mismanagement of the council. A degree of power eventually shifted away from the centre and towards the tenants as the end user of the product.[99] This shift took place from the mid-1970s. It was pre-empted by the rise of consumer advocacy in the USA from the mid-1960s. By the late 1960s, there was official recognition in some areas of the US government of the desire by citizens to be more directly involved in planning processes. Some government programmes for urban development included the poor in the decision-making process.[100] Under the leadership of Ralph Nader, consumer groups were created to protect the rights of individual citizens against large corporations. Activists fought to confront and expose injustices. The gathering and dissemination of information was central to their activities.[101] Nader believed that to counter corporate power it was necessary for citizens to get actively involved in campaigns at a local level. Any challenge to the power of those producing goods and services needed the consumer to organise and confront them in the market arena.[102] This confrontation was linked to a decline in the legitimacy of the business or institution providing the goods or services. When this legitimacy suffers then a climate is created which is favourable to consumers. It allows them to mount popular political campaigns.[103] There are clear parallels with this and the council and housing policy. As housing problems unfolded from the late 1960s, the legitimacy of the council to provide a quality service fell into decline, providing a climate for tenant action.

Politicians could not ignore consumer pressure. There were too many potential votes at stake. Consumerism became politicised, though the elasticity of consumer language meant that it could never be monopolised by any single party. At the national level, there was an attempt to hijack the notion of consumerism by both major parties. The Tories claimed to support the idea of protecting the rights of the individual in the marketplace, while Labour embraced the idea of social consumerism, which stressed the idea of a fair deal for the public and protection of the weak and vulnerable members of the community.[104] Consumer protection became associated with citizenship, with educating and informing the weak, with empowering them and, therefore, with enabling them to be full and active members of society. Citizens were urged to participate in industrial decisions, local planning choices and public services such as health and education.[105] In planning, for example, a number of reports were produced after the war, culminating in the 1968 Town and Country Planning Act, which required local government to consider the wishes of residents affected by proposed plans. The idea was reinforced the following year when Skeffington's Committee on Public Participation on Planning published their report, *People and Planning*.[106] Also, student protest and participation in the late 1960s, consultative committees for nationalised industries and the later creation of Community Health Councils, further promoted the idea of consultation and participation. The Labour Party was openly pro-participatory by 1969, even running a political campaign on this basis.[107] The language of consumerism and consumer action was framed on a collective basis. However, by the 1980s there was a clear shift to the language of individualism and, with it, ideas of partnership and reciprocity.

Rising expectations meant that people were less prepared to accept substandard services.[108] Groups were formed over a common cause because citizens felt powerless and excluded. Effective participation was prevented by local government's centralised administrative system of control and decision-making.[109] While political parties at the national level promoted consumer ideals, it was only a partial development. The political 'producers', especially local authorities, took time to change. Their power and authority were at stake.

Political struggles in Manchester show a continual process of pressure from tenants and at times grudging adaptation by the council. By the early 1970s, the language of consumer protection had entered the arena of public services, including education, welfare, health and housing.[110] In the 1950s and 1960s local government was in a strong position. Tenants trusted them to sweep away the slums and build a brave new world. Sadly, what many received was a concrete nightmare. The horrors of these projects became rapidly apparent in the 1970s. Local government was the focal point for complaints. Their legitimacy as a provider of quality homes declined. T. Bendixson, speaking at the Town Planning Institute in 1971, pointed out that people were growing in confidence and were increasingly prepared to "knock on the door of the Town Hall and say 'look, we don't like the way things are going now and we would like it done differently'".[111] At an earlier meeting in 1968, held at the National Council of Social Service, M. Broady claimed that people were reacting against local authorities because all too often town councillors were "inadequate to deal proficiently with public affairs".[112] Council tenants across the country complained at the lack of information, consultation and level of involvement in housing management.[113] The tenant action groups that emerged paralleled the US consumer groups. They were established at a grass-roots level and attempted to defend the interests of tenants in the face of poor housing conditions. Also, they collated and disseminated information and led popular campaigns which challenged the power of the council. Eventually, they helped to change both short-term policies and long-term attitudes in the relationship between the council and its tenants, with consultation and quality assurance becoming central features.

In a number of areas, participation schemes involving tenants and local authorities were fostered from the 1970s. Some housing departments in London began to show a genuine interest in developing schemes that would allow tenant participation in managing housing policy.[114] Local council officials began to appreciate the value of establishing a participation scheme that would enable them to obtain and provide information to and from tenants. Following the 1974 local government reorganisation, the gap between tenants and council officials increased. Participation schemes were developed which allowed this gap to be bridged. Increasingly, tenant organisations became seen as performing a legitimate role in urban politics, holding authorities to account.[115] Whilst it may be right to argue that many organisations were ephemeral or unrepresentative, prone to internal conflicts and quick to fade away, it can also be claimed that their lack of coherence, diversity and limited life spans, were part of their underlying strength.[116] Moreover, it would be wrong to assume that only long-lived organisations with offices in London are significant. The campaigns that developed during the late 1960s and throughout the 1970s forced a change in attitudes within urban societies, forcing governments and local authorities to rethink the role of participation. Traditional political discourse and class- or group-based identity were gradually challenged by the language of consumerism.[117] Studying this moment, and the way in which parties responded at the local level, can play an important part in appreciating the (partial) shift in political values and rhetoric that took place in the later 1970s and 1980s. For, however much national government policies and legislation dictated attention to consumer interests, what mattered to the tenant was how far rhetoric was translated into reality.

Outline

This book is divided into three sections, providing it with a structure which highlights the overarching narrative and key themes. The first section will look at some of the main aspects of national policy and legislation across the twentieth century and how these were then interpreted by different local authorities. It shows that while central government provided a lead, encouraging a common approach, this was only ever generalised. Cities continued to produce policies specific to their own areas, highlighting the continuing importance of locality in studying the decision-making process. Part II examines the rise of municipal housing in Manchester, looking at the creation and influence of civic culture on the council. In contrast, although Part III considers the continuing influence of civic culture on policy after 1960, it also highlights the decline of municipal legitimacy from the late 1960s. It looks at how tenant frustration gave rise to angry outbursts and organised protests, leading to a challenge to council authority and forcing a change to the decision-making process.

Each section is divided into relevant chapters to explore specific issues. Chapter 1 examines the constantly shifting context. Economic restrictions, the nature of the housing market and political ideologies determined policy at the centre. However, the different political housing philosophies did not always apply at the local level. Although there was a move from limited intervention to building homes for heroes and then to cuts in subsidies, this was largely a reaction to the changing ability of the private sector to deliver affordable homes for the working classes. Moreover, legislation allowed local authorities considerable autonomy. Economic restrictions did have an obvious impact. From the 1930s, both parties broadly supported slum clearance, though, again, this faltered because of the Depression. The interventionist dreams were revitalised in 1945, only for economic pressures again to put the brakes on the grand Labour vision. In the 1950s, the Conservatives moved back to a mixed approach, turning to private developers and home ownership as well as limited municipal expansion. The market was much stronger and the demand for private houses was growing amongst the working classes. This government was more successful in reaching its targets, but problems over rent reforms and racketeering brought an ignominious end to its policies in the early 1960s. By the time Labour returned to power, the emphasis had again shifted back to slum clearance, high completion rates and, to achieve this, the introduction of large-scale system-built schemes. However, it also recognised that the housing market and working-class demands had changed. By the end of the decade it was clear that the costs, both economic and human, were too great, and policy shifted towards modernisation of existing stock. For the first time, there was also a greater role for the tenant. By the 1980s, tenant choice had become a central part of government policy. Now, however, the Conservative government was to change the very role of local government, as council houses were sold off and the local authority was reduced from being the producer to the enabler.

Despite the fact that central government gave general direction to housing policy local authorities were still able to interpret, react and implement policies according to their own specific circumstances. Civic culture, developing working-class suburbs, slum-clearance programmes, building flats, overspill, tower blocks and tenant frustrations were all common features of housing politics across the country. However, policy choices and points of emphasis were not always the same. Chapter 2 looks at how these key policy features played out in other areas. Cities had their own traditions, created their own discourse and produced policies specific to their own problems. While, for instance, some cities came to embrace flat building in the 1930s as a solution to their problems and a sign of modern thinking, others rejected and resisted them into the 1960s. Equally, while some shared a belief in overspill estates, others saw them as a dilution of their power and authority. Although commonality also existed, locality is still important as it reveals the diversity and complexity of the decision-making process.

It was against this backdrop that Manchester city council created and implemented its own policies. It started the century as it ended it, not as a major producer of houses but as a basic enabler of policies designed to improve the environment. In the nineteenth century, it passed occasional byelaws, produced reports, reconditioned some houses and pursued a policy of limited slum clearance. However, the first three decades of the century witnessed a complete transformation. Chapter 3 looks at the change from minimal local authority intervention to extensive council involvement during 1890–1929 and some of the key influences behind it. Progressives inside the council, backed by prominent social reformers and voluntary groups, battled with the local Tories, who still held the market with veneration. Leading figures such as T. R. Marr, T. C. Horsfall and E. D. Simon campaigned tirelessly for widespread municipal action to replace the swathes of Victorian slums with quality new homes. Its vision became a part of Manchester's civic culture. It was proud of the achievements of the nineteenth-century city fathers and wanted to extend this into housing policy. Its vision (and it *was* Manchester's), was based on new working-class suburbs, a garden satellite town and the demolition of the crumbling inner-city housing stock. A local discourse emerged. Flats, from the outset, were at best to be rejected and, at worst, to be kept to a few low-rise inner-city developments. This was ideal for the tenants and a reflection of the proud legacy of the city. The people were not consulted. The paternalistic culture of the nineteenth century pervaded council attitudes. There was an underlying assumption that tenants would be grateful for what was provided. From the outset, the council adopted an attitude towards its tenants that mirrored the relationship between the philanthropist and the recipient. Whilst understandable, it became so engrained into civic culture that it was to create problems later in the century as the council struggled to adapt to a changing society, placing strains on council–tenant relations. Civic pride, fuelled by ideological beliefs, formed the points of reference in the creation of policy.

The main outcome of the efforts of reformers inside the council was the development of a large new estate in the 1930s at Wythenshawe. It was a grand plan designed to meet the general needs of the working classes, not the average inner-city slum dweller. Travel costs and rents meant it was beyond their means. In the 1930s, however, governments pushed councils into focusing on slum clearance and replacement. Chapter 4 looks at how the council struggled to clear the slums and build sufficient replacement homes, especially given the backdrop of the economic crisis and the pressing problem of land availability. Sweeping plans were produced. It identified a large section of the city for clearance and then attempted to rehouse the people by filling in gap sites or by moving them miles away on to new estates. This would allow the slums then to be demolished. Given the size of the task, the council's approach was understandable, but it did not always have plans for the redevelopment of the cleared areas and it never bothered itself with the encumbrance of meaningful consultation. This was never a part of political culture before the welfare state, but it did leave a lasting legacy throughout the century. Besides, most were happy at the prospect of moving to a new home, though some expressed reservations. Voluntary organisations produced a range of surveys that highlighted the extent of the problem and revealed that a number of slum dwellers wanted to remain a part of the community. For the council under pressure, this was not a serious consideration. It had the big plans which tenants would eventually appreciate.

These plans became much larger after the Second World War. Chapter 5 looks at how Manchester council's determination to create a new world of leafy suburbs for its citizens drove it to embrace the policy of developing overspill estates outside the city boundaries more than any other authority. It continued to reject flats, which would only be built as a last resort. Cottages in new towns and estates around Cheshire and Lancashire would solve all its problems, ending congestion and overcrowding, improving the lives of ordinary people and leading to the creation of the city beautiful. It aimed to build 40,000 new homes around the outskirts of Greater Manchester. This would fulfil the dreams of Marr, Horsfall and Simon. It was a central part of its civic culture. Besides, the number of Victorian slums in the city, together with the lack of available land, meant it had little choice. Yet it was to discover that 'choice' was even more restricted. Neighbouring local authorities, especially Cheshire, were willing to accept limited developments but provided fierce resistance against the larger plans. Manchester's civic culture, its vision for the creation of a new world, was not shared by Cheshire. Local discourse could only go so far. Once it met a brick wall of resistance it was essentially rendered meaningless. A series of bitter struggles seriously stunted the council's plans. In the end, it was only able to build half of its original target.

By the early 1960s, the council was finding itself under increasing pressure to find a quick and affordable solution to its slum problems. The failure of its overspill programme placed an intolerable strain on its ability to move people into new houses and then clear away the inner-city slums. Pressure from tenants, government and the land trap meant that new solutions had to be found. Chapter 6 looks at the growing number of housing failures, tenant criticisms and the gradual slide away from municipal controlled housing. The pressure to produce more homes pushed some council officials finally to embrace modern designs, involving concrete tower blocks, maisonettes and multi-deck access systems. But even in accepting these new designs, the council was keen to trumpet them as a part of its local discourse, as prestigious schemes which would boost the status of the city as a modern European centre. Manchester's Crescents, for instance, were trumpeted as the new Bath. Unfortunately, they turned out to be a nightmare. Yet again, the heralding of a new dawn was to end in frustration. Tenants reacted with increasing anger. From the late 1960s, individuals and organised groups of tenants voiced their mistrust and bitterness towards the council. Initially, following the 1969 Housing Act, tenants started to organise themselves into pressure groups to influence council slum clearance plans. They wanted to secure resources under the General Improvement Area and Housing Action Area schemes. Other groups reacted against rent rises, but a few were responding angrily against conditions in the new developments. Some adopted the language and organisational structure of the consumer movements. As consumers of housing, as customers of the welfare system, they were offering a challenge to traditional political discourse. The council struggled to adjust to the demands of the shifting political climate.

This was the start of its troubles. Chapter 7 looks at how conditions deteriorated in the 1970s and throughout the 1980s. The underlying economic decline that had blighted the city accelerated, plunging the area into a depression. Moreover, from 1979 the Conservative government was determined to cut public spending and role back government. Added to this, during 1984–87 the council fell into the hands of the confrontational New Left. These combined pressures had a serious impact on the city's housing policy. The mounting problems could not have come at a worse time. Housing stock was either suffering because of the poor designs of the 1960s and early 1970s, or because it was old and needed renewal. To add to its problems, the Thatcher government forced the council to allow tenants the Right-to-Buy. As the new system-built developments crippled the city's finances, the human misery increased. By the early to mid-1980s, it was obvious that the only solution was demolition, even though they had only been completed for ten years. Yet, despite the doom and gloom, by the late 1980s the city was starting to recover. The New Left evolved into a moderate, New Labour council that was prepared to work with the government. Manchester was reinvented as an entrepreneurial city and the council adopted a more pragmatic approach to policy. This led to a successful bid for resources under the City Challenge scheme, enabling the council to demolish the Crescents at Hulme. Significantly, the council was no longer the producer but was now the enabler. Equally important, rebuilding now involved tenant consultation and participation. This was a difficult and problematic process for the council, but it did mark the beginning of an important shift in relations between it and the tenant, a change that also had implications for urban governance as politics moved from the conventions of party politics and council institutions.[118]

Notes

1 A. Wohl, *The Eternal Slum* (London, 1977); E. Gauldie, *Cruel Habitations: A History of Working-Class Housing 1780–1918* (London, 1974); M. J. Daunton, *House and Home in the Victorian City: Working-Class Housing, 1850–1914* (London, 1983); R. Rodger, *Housing in Urban Britain, 1780–1914: Class, Capitalism and Construction* (London, 1989).

2 D. Englander, *Landlord and Tenant in Urban Britain* (Oxford, 1983).

3 R. Rodger, 'Political economy, ideology and the persistence of working-class housing problems in Britain, 1850–1914', *International Review of Social History*, 32:2 (1987), 109–43.

4 A. S. Wohl, 'The 1880s: a new generation?', *Nineteenth Century Studies*, 4 (1990), 1–22.

5 T. Cooper, review of M. Clapson, 'Suburban Century', *Urban History*, 31:2 (2004), 300–1.

6 S. Heathorn, 'An English paradise to regain? Ebenezer Howard, the Town and Country Planning Association and English Ruralism', *Rural History*, 11:1 (2000), 113–28.

7 M. Swenarton, *Homes Fit for Heroes* (London, 1981), pp. 5–26.

8 M. Clapson, *Suburban Century, Social Change and Urban Growth in England and the United States* (Oxford, 2003).

9 A. Reed, *Brentham: A History of the Pioneer Garden Suburb, 1901–2001* (Brentham, 2000).

10 Ibid.

11 S. M. Gaskell, 'Gardens for the working-class: Victorian practical pleasure', *Victorian Studies*, 23:4 (1980), 479–501.

12 M. Clapson, 'Working-class women's experiences of moving to new housing estates in England since 1919', *Twentieth Century British History*, 10:3 (1999), 345–65.

13 R. J. Moore-Colyer, 'From Great Wen to Toad Hall: aspects of the urban–rural divide in inter-war Britain', *Rural History*, 10:1 (1999), 105–24.

14 S. Butler, 'Socialism and housing: the British experience', *Journal of Social and Political Studies*, 3:4 (1978), 311–32.

15 H. Meller, 'Women and citizenship: gender and the built environment in British cities 1870–1939', and P. L. Garside, 'Citizenship, civil society and quality of life: Sutton model dwellings estates 1919–39', in R. Colls and R. Rodger (eds), *Cities of*

Ideas: Civil Society and Urban Governance in Britain 1800–2000 (Aldershot, 2004).

16 M. Swenarton, '"An insurance against revolution." Ideological objectives of the provision and design of public housing in Britain after the First World War', *Bulletin of the Institute of Historical Research*, 54:129 (1981), 86–101.

17 J. Yelling, 'Homes fit for heroes', *Modern History Review*, 9:4 (1998), 7–9.

18 C. Macintyre, 'Policy reform and the politics of housing in the British Conservative Party, 1924–1929', *Australian Journal of Politics and History*, 45:3 (1999), 408–21.

19 R. Heller, 'East Fulham revisited', *Journal of Contemporary History*, 6:3 (1971), 172–96.

20 C. Keating, 'Housing', *Encyclopaedia of European Social History*, vol. 5 (New York, 2001), p. 469.

21 H. Pelling, 'The 1945 General Election reconsidered', *Historical Journal*, 23:2 (1980), 399–414.

22 R. Lowe, *The Welfare State in Britain Since 1945* (Basingstoke, 1993), p. 235.

23 A. Walling, 'Modernisation, policy debate and organisation in the Labour Party 1951–64' (PhD dissertation, University of Wales, Bangor, 2001), p. 263.

24 Lowe, *The Welfare State*, p. 235.

25 P. Dunleavy, *The Politics of Mass Housing in Britain, 1945–1975: A Study of Corporate Power and Professional Influence in the Welfare State* (Oxford, 1981), p. 2.

26 R. Lowe, 'Welfare policy in Britain', *Contemporary Record*, 4:2 (1990), 29–32.

27 L. R. Murphy, 'Rebuilding Britain: the government's role in housing and town planning, 1945–1957', *Historian*, 32:2 (1970); P. Taylor, 'British local government and house building during the Second World War', *Planning History*, 17:2 (1995), 17–22; H. Jones, '"This is magnificent!" 300,000 houses a year and the Tory revival after 1945', *Contemporary British History*, 14:1 (2000), 99–121.

28 J. Yelling, 'Public policy, urban renewal and property ownership, 1945–55', *Urban History*, 22:1 (1995), 48–62.

29 H. Jones, '"This is magnificent!"'; A. Simmonds, 'Conservative governments and the new town housing question in the 1950s', *Urban History*, 28:1 (2001), 65–82.

30 P. Weiler, 'The rise and fall of the Conservatives' Grand Design for Housing', *Contemporary British History*, 14:1 (2000), 122–50.

31 K. Theakston, 'Evelyn Sharp', *Contemporary Record*, 7:1 (1993), 132–48.

32 O. A. Hartley, 'The relationship between central and local authorities', *Public Administration*, 49: Winter (1979), 439–56.

33 G. Towers, *Shelter is Not Enough: Transforming Multi-Storey Housing* (Bristol, 2000), pp. 186–88.

34 Ibid.

35 Dunleavy, *The Politics of Mass Housing in Britain*, p. 9.

36 Ibid., p. 12.

37 Ibid., p. 13.

38 Ibid., pp. 20–2.

39 B. Finnimore, *House from the Factory: System Building and the Welfare State* (London, 1989).

40 Ibid., pp. 242–4.

41 J. Davis, 'Central government and the towns', in M. J. Daunton (ed.), *The Cambridge Urban History of Britain*, Vol. 3 (Cambridge, 2000), pp. 261–86.

42 See R. A. W. Rhodes, *Control and Power in Central–Local Government Relations* (Farnborough, 1981).

43 See, for example, M. Goldsmith and J. Garrard, 'Urban governance: some reflections', in Daunton (ed.), *The Cambridge Urban History of Britain*, p. 23; R. H. Trainor, 'Decline of British urban governance since 1850: a reassessment', ibid., p. 40.

44 G. T. Stoker, 'The politics of urban renewal in Withington, 1962–83' (PhD dissertation, University of Manchester, 1985), p. 7.

45 See, for example, A. Power, *The Crisis in Council Housing* (Suntory Toyota International Centre for Economics and Related Disciplines, 1987); A. Power, *Council Housing: Conflict, Change and Decision Making* (Suntory Toyota International Centre for Economics and Related Disciplines, 1988); C. L. Andrews, *Tenants and Town Hall* (London, 1979).

46 Finnimore, *House from the Factory*, p. 241.

47 J. B. Cullingworth, *Housing and Local Government* (London, 1966), p. 64.

48 N. Hayes, 'Civic perceptions: housing and local decision-making in English cities in the 1920s', *Urban History*, 27 (2000), 637–58; J. Gyford, S. Leach and C. Game, *The Changing Face of Local Government* (London, 1989), pp. 13–15.

49 J. Yelling, 'The incidence of slum clearance in England and Wales, 1955–85', *Urban History*, 27:2 (2000), 234–54.

50 M. Blunt and M. Goldsmith, *Housing Policy and Administration: A Case Study*, Occasional Paper (University of Salford, 1969).

51 S. Goss, *Local Labour and Local Government* (Edinburgh, 1988), p. 52.

52 Ibid., p. 55.

53 See, for example, M. S. Gibson and M. J. Langstaff (eds), 'Introduction' in *Urban Renewal* (London, 1992).

54 W. Hampton, 'Optimism and Growth', in C. Binfield, R. Childs, R. Harper, D. Hey, D. Martin and G. Tweedale (eds), *The History of the City of Sheffield* (Sheffield, 1993).

55 E. W. Cooney, 'Innovation in the post-war British building industry', *Construction History*, 1 (1985), 52–9.

56 Dunleavy, *The Politics of Mass Housing in Britain*.

57 N. Hayes, 'Making homes by machine: images, ideas and myths in diffusion of non-traditional housing in Britain 1942–54', *Twentieth Century British History*, 19:3 (1999).

58 Ibid.

59 M. Glendinning and S. Muthesius, *Tower Block: Modern Public Housing in England, Scotland, Wales and Northern Ireland* (New Haven, 1994), p. 2.

60 Ibid., p. 3.

61 Ibid., p. 4.

62 Ibid., p. 153.

63 C. Whitehead, 'From need to affordability: an analysis of UK housing objectives', *Urban Studies*, 28:6 (1991), 871–87.

64 D. Maclennan and K. Gibb, 'Housing finance and subsidies in Britain after a decade of "Thatcherism"', *Urban Studies*, 27:6 (1990), 905–18; D. Marsh and R. Rhodes, 'Implementing Thatcherism: policy change in the 1980s', *Parliamentary Affairs*, 45:1 (1992), 33–50.

65 P. Machon, 'The sale of local authority houses in Great Britain', *Geography*, 72:2 (1987), 169–71; M. Cook, 'Council house sales: the rights and wrongs', *Contemporary Review*, 248 (1986), 314–17.

66 S. Cameron, 'Housing, gentrification and urban regeneration policies', *Urban Studies*, 29:1 (1992), 3–14.

67 See for instance J. Lees-Marshment, *The Political Marketing Revolution: Transforming the Government of the UK* (Manchester, 2003).

68 Hayes, 'Making homes by machine'.

69 See Dunleavy, *The Politics of Mass Housing in Britain*, p. 31. One of the most notable exceptions is M. Clapson, *Invincible Green Suburbs, Brave New Towns* (Manchester, 1998).

70 Ibid., p. 29.
71 T. Tsubaki, 'Planners and the public: British popular opinion on housing during the Second World War', *Contemporary British History*, 14:10 (2000), 81–98.
72 J. Lewis, 'Consumer politics and housing', *Bulletin of the Society for the Study of Labour History*, 47 (1983), 67–9.
73 See T. H. Marshall, *The Right to Welfare and Other Essays* (London, 1981).
74 Goss, *Local Labour and Local Government*, p. 54.
75 R. S. Cuthbert, 'Tenant participation in public sector housing: a case study of Glasgow' (MSc dissertation, University of Stirling, 1988).
76 C. Johnstone, 'The tenants' movement and housing struggles in Glasgow, 1945–1990' (PhD dissertation, University of Glasgow, 1992).
77 Ibid., p. 2.
78 R. Dennis, 'Room for improvement? Recent studies of working-class housing', *Journal of Urban History*, 21:5 (1995), 660–73.
79 A. Ravetz, *Council Housing and Culture: The History of a Social Experiment* (London, 2001), p. 3.
80 Ibid.
81 Local newspapers promoted civic pride in their towns and cities across the twentieth century. See, for example, M. Bromley and N. Hayes, 'Campaigner, Watchdog or Municipal Lackey? Reflections on the inter-war provincial press, local identity and civic welfarism', *Media History*, 8:2 (2002); P. Shapely, 'The press and the system built developments of inner-city Manchester', *Manchester Region History Review*, 16 (2002–3), 30–9.
82 J. Lawrence, 'Class and gender in the making of Urban Toryism, 1880–1914', *English Historical Review*, 108 (1993).
83 F. Trentmann, *Paradoxes in Civil Society: New Perspectives on Modern German and British Society* (New York, 2000).
84 Urban identity in several British cities was based on notions of progressiveness and narratives of modernity. See H. Meller, 'Urban renewal and citizenship: the quality of life in British cities, 1890–1990', *Urban History*, 22:1 (1995), 74–84. See also H. Meller, *European Cities 1890–1930: History, Culture and the Built Environment* (New York, 2001).
85 I. Taylor, K. Evans and P. Fraser, *A Tale of Two Cities: Global Change, Local Feeling and Everyday Life in the North of England* (London, 1996).
86 S. Gunn, *The Public Culture of the Victorian Middle-Class: Ritual and Authority and the English Industrial City, 1840–1914* (New York, 2000).
87 R. J. Morris, 'Structure, culture and society in British towns', in Daunton (ed.), *The Cambridge Urban History of Britain*, p. 397.
88 Ibid.
89 Trentmann, *Paradoxes in Civil Society*, p. 52.
90 Mellor, 'Urban renewal'.
91 See also C. Geetz, 'Religion as a cultural system', in M. Banton (ed.), *Anthropological Approaches to the Study of Religion* (London, 1966), pp. 1–46; D. J. Monti, *The American City: A Social and Cultural History* (Malden, 1999).
92 Shapely, 'The press and the system built developments', pp. 30–9.
93 J. Lowerson, 'Leisure, consumption and the European city', *Urban History*, 30:1 (2003), 92–7.
94 Raymond Williams recognised that consumerism had moved into the public sector in 1976. See M. Daunton and M. Hilton (eds), *The Politics of Consumption, Material Culture and Citizenship in Europe and America* (Oxford, 1990), p. 31.

95 L. Cohen, *A Consumer's Republic: The Politics of Mass Consumption in Post War America* (New York, 2003), p. 13

96 Ibid., p. 18.

97 Ibid., p. 133.

98 See M. Frances, *Ideas and Policies under Labour, 1945–1951: Building a New Britain* (Manchester, 1997).

99 A. Nove, *The Economics of Feasible Socialism* (London, 1983), p. 225.

100 E. S. and J. C. Cahn, 'Citizen participation', in H. Spiegel, *Citizen Participation in Urban Development* (Washington, 1968).

101 Y. Gabriel and T. Lang, *The Unmanageable Consumer* (London, 1995), p. 160.

102 Ibid., p. 161.

103 J. Tiemstra, 'Theories of regulation and the history of consumerism', *International Journal of Social Economics*, 19:6 (1992), 3–27, cited in Gabriel and Lang, *The Unmanageable Consumer*, p. 171.

104 Gabriel and Lang, *The Unmanageable Consumer*, pp. 240–53.

105 See for example A. W. Richardson, 'The politics of participation: a study of schemes for tenant participation in council housing management' (PhD dissertation, London School of Economics, 1978), p. 11.

106 Ibid., p. 21.

107 See L. Black, *The Political Culture of the Left in Affluent Britain, 1951–64: Old Labour, New Britain?* (Basingstoke, 2003).

108 Ibid., p. 28.

109 G. Daniel, *Looking to the Future: Report of the Seventh National Conference on Social Welfare* (London, 1970).

110 Ibid., p. 250.

111 The National Archive, London (hereafter TNA), T. Bendixson, speech at a forum on 'Public Participation', unpublished transcript (London, 1971), p. 25.

112 M. Broady, *Planning for People* (London: National Council of Social Service, 1968), p. 117.

113 See for example L. Hancock, 'Tenant participation and the housing classes debate' (PhD dissertation, University of Liverpool, 1994), p. 317.

114 A. W. Richardson, 'The politics of participation: a study of schemes for tenant participation in council housing management' (PhD dissertation, London School of Economics, 1978); J. S. G. Rao, 'Power and participation: tenants' involvement in housing' (MPhil dissertation, Brunel University, 1983).

115 Hancock, 'Tenant participation'.

116 Daunton and Hilton, *The Politics of Consumption*, pp. 2–3 and 12.

117 The profound nature of this shift was suggested in Daunton and Hilton, *The Politics of Consumption*, p. 32.

118 Ravetz, *Council Housing and Culture*, p. 5.

Part I
The national framework

1 Government, local authorities and housing, 1919–87

No history of housing is possible without reference to the policies, finance and legislative framework developed by governments. Although this is a familiar story, it needs revisiting to understand the context in which decisions were made. This legislation underlines two central issues. First, despite increasing central government interference, local government still enjoyed different levels of autonomy. For much of the century, local government interpreted, implemented and managed housing policy. Across the century, policies were subjected to a roller-coaster ride, shifting according to financial restrictions, social pressures, the condition of the housing market and ideological imperatives. The main political parties had their own housing philosophies, but these did not always apply at the local level. Legislation passed by a Labour government, for instance, was not always immediately disregarded by the next Conservative government. Unsurprisingly, the strength of the economy and the state of the market were important determinants. Labour local authorities did not necessarily suffer because a Conservative government was in power. Second, the top-down approach to housing policy – the pivotal role of central government and local authorities – was, for over half a century, underlined by legislation passed from 1919. It was only in from the late 1960s that national legislation began to recognise the value of consultation and participation.

The changing nature of government policies was highlighted in the inter-war period. The vision for widespread reform came with the 1919 Addison Act. Even King George entered the debate on housing in 1919, claiming that the housing question had never been so important and that if crime, drink and social unrest were to be avoided then "decent sanitary houses must be provided".[1] The almost euphoric dream to build high-quality working-class homes did not last long. While all political parties aimed to provide reasonably priced houses for the working classes, they still had to react to the conditions of the market, the ability of the private sector to deliver an affordable product and the condition of the economy. By the early 1920s, financial realities meant that the programme had to be cut. In 1923, the Conservatives believed that market conditions had improved, but, although they placed greater emphasis on encouraging private-sector development, subsidies were only reduced over a period of time. For all governments, it was a continual balancing act between what they ideally wanted to achieve and what in reality they could accomplish.

By the end of the 1920s, it was apparent that while a great deal had been realised in building new homes for working-class families, and private sector houses for the lower middle classes, the inner-city slum dwellers had not benefited. The Labour government passed legislation in 1930 that empowered local authorities to sweep away the slums and replace all demolished homes with new houses and flats. The Greenwood Act, like much of the inter-war legislation, promised a great deal but faltered due to problems of interpretation by local authorities and, above all, economic restrictions. While the government wanted five-year plans to clear huge swathes of the inner cities, the cost of clearance and replacement at the time of the Depression limited its ambitions.

Nevertheless, central government was beginning to have an impact. Initially, the post-war Labour government under Bevan produced plans designed finally to clear the slums and build sufficient new homes for everyone. Hundreds of thousands of quality cottages would replace the dismal slums. Again, political and economic realities curtailed and embarrassed Labour's plans. The government fell a long way short of its initial targets. Significantly, it also failed to meet the growing aspirations of many skilled and lower middle-class workers who hoped to own their own homes. The structure of the demand side of the housing market was starting to change. The returning Conservative government was able to take advantage of the improving market conditions and to meet the growing demand for private home ownership. It was able successfully to meet its completion targets.

While both Labour and Conservative post-war governments drove the national house-building programme forward to new levels, both also continued to adopt the same top-down approach as governments in the first part of the century. Neither was especially concerned with the views of the tenants. Governments took advice from experts and were prepared to leave policy creation and implementation to local authorities, but until the 1960s there was no conception of consultation. However, increasingly from the late 1960s through to the 1980s, the role of the tenant in consultation and participation became a feature of both parties. The tenant was gradually given greater recognition and support, with local authorities being pushed into greater levels of consultation and, by the 1990s, actual participation. Furthermore, throughout the 1980s, the role of local government itself changed. Legislation eroded their position as major producers. The Thatcher government forced a painful and profound trans-formation. Councils had to allow tenants the opportunity to buy their homes and were continually being pressurised to transfer estates to housing associations or management groups. Tenant choice and consumer rights entered the language of legislation. Crucially, though, this did not mean an end to local government, but another reorientation of its role. Local authorities retained influence as new regimes emerged to create and implement housing policy in the local environment. This chapter will look at some of the main developments in this constantly shifting picture, highlighting some of the difficulties faced by governments when confronted with economic and market problems and the ramifications of government policy, legislation and finance on local authorities and tenants.

Pressure to introduce sweeping reform had started to intensify before the First World War. Market dynamics were creating problems. The rate of house building had reduced and the country was beginning to face a serious shortage, especially in family housing. Some reformers were demanding that low-interest loans should be given to local authorities to allow them to build houses for the poorest slum dwellers.[2] Legislation was framed, but the outbreak of the war meant it was lost. Demand increased, but building rates continued to decline during the war. By 1918, the housing shortage totalled an estimated 600,000, a figure that increased to over 800,000 by 1921.[3] Overcrowding and slum conditions, inherited from the Victorian period, were acute. The problem increased because of the war. With demand high and supply stagnated, rents began to rise. The Glasgow rent strike, and the threat of social unrest across the country, forced the government to pass the 1915 Rent and Mortgage Restriction Act. Landlords were forced to fix rents at their immediate pre-war levels. The situation remained largely unchanged after the war, so the Act remained. This created a further problem. Builders were not prepared to build cheaper houses only to be forced to charge rents at 1914 levels, especially as high inflation had led to rising costs.

Added to these problems were the rising expectations of returning soldiers and social reformers. Lloyd George's government recognised that housing reform was essential for a stable and prosperous post-war Britain. Reconstruction dominated the domestic political landscape during 1916–21. Politicians and officials from all sides pulled together in a new spirit of optimism.[4] Conservatives saw this as a necessary, albeit short-term, measure to secure affordable houses in the face of difficult market conditions. Radical politicians from the Liberals and Labour parties believed this was the start of a new dawn in social reform. Local government could not shoulder the burden entirely by itself. This was apparent from the start of the government's investigations. In 1916, the Reconstruction Committee asked all government departments to report back with ideas on housing and public works. The Local Government Board highlighted the limited powers and financial capabilities of local authorities. Central government had to provide a subsidy to local authorities. Seebohm Rowntree, a member of the Advisory Housing Panel, believed that the government, working in partnership with local authorities, should aim to build 300,000 new homes in the first year after the war. The government agreed and in July 1917 it established a new committee to develop plans for the reconstruction of working-class houses. The Chairman, Sir John Tudor Walters, published his report in November 1918. They had looked into a wide range of construction and design issues and concluded that every family home should have as standard three bedrooms, a bathroom, living room, parlour and scullery. Overcrowding would be avoided by building a maximum of twelve houses per acre. A variety of other suggestions were made about space and appearance. These were radical recommendations. They were based on a belief in the cottage style of housing, rooted in the rural idyll. However, the report also made it clear that final designs were a local issue. Local authorities were being pushed towards creating a new suburban space for the working classes. Although central government would interfere in areas which it found to be dilatory, and could be painfully fastidious on the detail of some plans, local authorities who co-operated would generally be allowed to decide on the design, location and timing of new developments. They looked into every aspect of house building and in 1919 published their recommendations in the *Housing Manual*. The Ministry of Reconstruction was also established with the aim of forming a national plan for large-scale house building after the war.

The government was determined to press ahead with the most radical housing reforms ever passed. The President of the Local Government Board, Christopher Addison, framed the new Housing and Town Planning Act in 1919. Central government would provide virtually all of the finance, meeting all losses over a penny rate. It aimed to build 500,000 houses in three years and would adhere to the high standards outlined in Tudor Walters's *Manual*. Local authorities were instructed to assess their needs and to formulate plans for large-scale construction programmes. Addison claimed that existing legislation did not go far enough, there was no compulsion and that it was necessary to "make it a duty of a local authority" to provide "what re-housing is necessary".[5] Plans required government approval, but it still left plenty of scope for local authorities to develop and implement a programme according to their own needs. This defined the role of local and central government for much of the inter-war period.

In relative terms, this attempt to transform working-class housing with the creation of a series of new estates has been seen as a mini revolution.[6] Yet, in real terms, the early hopes of the government's housing reforms proved far too optimistic. Although Addison was confident that sufficient sites existed across the country for 460,000 new houses, by March 1920 there had been approval for only 161,837 houses.[7] A second Housing (Additional Powers) Act was needed to provide a further subsidy to private builders in an attempt to speed up the building process. Only a third of the homes built under this extension to the Act were designed for the working class.[8] Spiralling costs, material shortages and economic problems meant that by 1921 only 214,000 houses had been approved. These included non-parlour as well as the preferred parlour houses. In January, the Cabinet agreed to cut expenditure on housing. Addison condemned the decision as a complete reversal of the post-war policy and as a betrayal by the government.[9] He again demanded that the government support the construction of 500,000 houses, but economic realities were forcing them down a different path.[10] Faced with an increasing financial crisis, there were to be no new schemes. In the end, a total of 213,821 houses were built under the Addison Act, with 170,090 being completed by municipal authorities.[11]

In 1922, a new Conservative government swept to power and with it came an important shift in emphasis. Neville Chamberlain, the Minister of Health, immediately set about framing a new Housing Act that would encourage more building by the private sector. It believed that market conditions had changed and that the private sector could start to take greater responsibility. This did not mean an end to public-sector housing or to subsidies. The 1923 Housing Act provided a twenty-year subsidy for either private builders or local authorities, but it was only available to local authorities if they could prove that they were better suited to carry out the development rather than the private contractor. Local authorities still had a vital role, but there was a gradual move from municipal house building to the private sector. Of the 438,000 houses completed during 1923–29, only 75,000 were built by local authorities. The problem of providing quality low-cost rented accommodation largely remained. Most of the private-sector housing was made possible through lower costs and the fact that more people than ever were in a position to buy their homes because of more easily available mortgages. The high standards demanded under the Addison Acts were also diluted. Grants were now made available for smaller houses and the requirement to build a parlour was abandoned.

Conservative cuts to subsidies were only gradual. The housing market was still in a difficult position. There also remained an underlying recognition that the government and local authorities needed to get involved in housing for the poor and working classes. Whilst political ideologies were important elements in shaping government policy, the overriding issue for all parties during the inter-war period was the perceived ability of the private sector to provide affordable working-class housing. This was determined by economic circumstances and not political imperatives. In 1924, the Tories were replaced by the first Labour government. The new Minister of Health, John Wheatley, quickly introduced another Housing Act that recognised the pressing need to build subsidised houses with affordable rents. The Act promised a fifteen-year building programme, with annual figures rising from 60,000 houses a year to as much as 225,000 a year. A forty-year subsidy would be provided for houses made available for rent, while the rents themselves were to be controlled according to pre-war arrangements. Later in 1924, the Conservatives were back in power and, although they felt the market was right for cutting subsidies provided under both the Chamberlain and Wheatley Acts, subsidies under the Act (together with those under the Chamberlain Act) were still responsible for building over 579,800 local authority houses by 1935.[12] Local authorities did not necessarily suffer because the Conservatives were in power. Only in 1929 did they abolish all subsidies under the Chamberlain Act. The Wheatley Act was retained and saved by the returning Labour government, though it was also finally wound down in 1932.

Most of the housing legislation passed in the 1920s was designed to meet the general needs of the working classes. A large number of new estates were built outside most of Britain's major cities. These drew on middle-class notions of suburban life. However, most of these developments had little impact on the millions living in the inner-city districts, the worst slum areas. Most of the tenants in these areas could not afford to move. Rents were far higher and the extra costs involved in travelling to work meant it was beyond their means. A national anti-slum campaign was conducted by a loose federation of organisations, including the Church of England and the National Housing and Town Planning Council. In 1928, it was estimated that there were still 1 million unfit homes and 2 million overcrowded houses across the country.[13] Immediately prior to the 1929 general election, Arthur Greenwood, Labour's future Minister of Health, promised to make slum clearance his priority. He acknowledged that most people were living in houses which were "unworthy of a great nation ... and a disgrace to humanity".[14] Greenwood boldly promised that under a new Labour government all slums would be cleared and that 2.5 million new homes would be built for slum dwellers by 1939.[15] He promised that Labour would "at whatever cost pursue its considered policy of house building with assistance from public funds".[16] Once again, a future government had made wholly unrealistic promises, creating a grand plan which it was never likely to complete. Certainly, legislation in the early 1930s was designed to address the slum issue. However, the Depression compounded the problem, resulting in obvious and serious financial restrictions. Nevertheless, in 1930 Greenwood passed another Housing Act which formed the basis of slum clearance in the 1930s. Previous legislation and housing programmes had barely scratched the surface of the slum problem. The new legislation introduced a subsidy for slum clearance with replacement housing. Local authorities were given the responsibility to submit plans to the Ministry of Health that would supposedly solve their particular problems within five years. Central authority again relied on local government to fulfil the aims of their programme. Subsidies were given according to the number of people being rehoused rather than the number of houses being demolished, giving local authorities more resources to find suitable replacement houses for bigger families. It all proved far too optimistic.

Some slum-clearance programmes were carried out immediately in the early 1930s, but as the Depression plunged the country into severe economic crisis, and as the government was replaced by a national government, the Act was not finally adopted until 1933. It finally put an end to subsidies for new general needs housing. Working-class house building was left to the unsubsidised private sector. Policies again depended on the efficiency and interpretations of local government. Local authorities with populations of over 20,000 were asked to create five-year plans. Yet plans were produced which included only 250,000 houses. Clear guidelines were needed to define 'slum'. Subsequent changes identified nearly half a million slums, but by the outbreak of the war only half had actually been demolished. Nonetheless, given the economic crisis of the 1930s, the achievements of the Greenwood Act should not be dismissed. Besides the demolition of a quarter of a million slums, around 255,000 replacement homes had been built and 439,000 had been refurbished. Further legislation was passed in 1935 and 1938. The 1935 Housing Act was aimed at addressing the problem of overcrowding. It needed greater financial provision to make replacement accommodation more affordable. The 1938 Housing (Finance Provisions) Act gave a forty-year subsidy to help combat the problem. Time, however, was running out.

The inter-war period was a mixed bag in terms of achievements. Rising expectations prejudice the actual achievements. During 1919–39, an estimated 3,998,000 new houses were built. Local authorities were responsible for 1,112,000 and the private sector for a further 2,886,000 (of which 430,000 were built with government subsidies). The wild optimism of 1919 was curtailed due to economic and market realities. Although there was an underlying ideological struggle between the Conservatives and both progressive Liberals and Labour governments, it is simplistic to view housing policy as a polarised partisan battle. All sides sought to provide affordable housing in a shifting economic climate. Also, the Conservative–Labour division at central level did not always apply at a local level. Although legislation compelled local authorities to take action, the fact remained that it allowed a great deal of independent action. Government did not formulate the plans, implement and manage them. This depended on the willingness and ability of local authorities. The success or failure of a local authority did not necessarily depend on whether Labour or Conservatives were in power at Westminster.

If the housing problem was acute before 1939, then it was even more intense after the war. Air raids had caused widespread damage in a number of British cities.[17] It was local government that had to rise to the challenge. An estimated 475,000 houses had been lost to the Luftwaffe. At the same time, the demands of the war meant that there had been no rebuilding programme. It was also estimated that 1.25 million new houses were needed to replace the slums, meet the crippling demand and satisfy the rising expectations of the population.[18] The ideals of town planning, which had gradually emerged in the early twentieth century, appeared to provide the best solution to the housing problems. Lord Uthwatt's report into the future of post-war development and planning led to the creation of a Ministry of Town and Country Planning in 1942. It called for a more extensive planning system to tackle the short- and long-term housing problems. The spirit of 'planning for progress', of community planning, was embraced by the 1945 Labour government and was to dominate much of the post-war housing programmes.[19]

In 1945, Aneurin Bevan was appointed Minister of Health with a firm commitment to developing public-sector housing. As in 1918, there was an emergency in housing. This was reflected in the Conservatives' election campaign which promised a policy that embraced both the public and private sectors. They recognised that "in the first years of peace, the provision of homes will be the greatest domestic task", and that this would only be achieved by local authorities. They wanted subsidies for local authorities and for private enterprise alike.[20] This mixed approach was not shared by the radical Labour government. Houses were to be built to meet general needs, with local authorities again being given the central role. Labour promised to forge ahead with a housing programme with the maximum possible speed until every family had a good standard of accommodation.[21] Bevan's policy was very ambitious. Local authorities were to be given sole responsibility in order to maintain what Bevan described as the "essential psychological and biological one-ness of the community".[22] As in 1919, minimum standards were raised. Subsidies were doubled and, although Bevan accepted that only 15,000 houses would be built in the first year, he promised that this would rise to 150,000 in the second year. Eventually, the Labour government pledged to build 750,000 houses, enough to meet the immediate post-war demands. It intended to control the costs of construction through the Ministry of Works, and local government would be able to raise extra finance from the Public Works Loan Board. The Housing (Financial Provisions) Act 1946 was just the start of a brave new world that would eventually lead to slum clearance and large-scale urban renewal. However, as in 1919 and 1929, the hopes and dreams of the Labour government proved wildly optimistic. The housing programme became dogged by a series of market problems, including material shortages, rising costs and the financial crisis of 1947. Coupled to this, demand was continuing to rise. Between August and September 1947, Bevan was forced to make a number of cutbacks to the housing programme. Although the government had promised 750,000 new homes in its first term to meet the immediate demands created by the bombing, the fact was that, apart from 1948, it had failed to meet its targets.

As part of the drive to speed up house building, the government turned to developing new towns and overspill estates. These were the central features of public-sector housing policy up to the 1960s. As early as 1940, the government was looking to build new estates outside existing population centres as a long-term solution to the inner-city slums. The Barlow Commission on the Distribution of the Industrial Population recommended a phased and planned policy of overspill.[23] It called for the decentralisation and dispersal of people and industry from congested urban areas and increased development throughout the regions. The findings of the Barlow Commission formed the basis of the 1943 and 1947 Town and Country Planning Acts, which brought all planning under governmental control. It was also the foundation of the 1946 New Towns Act. The Labour government established Development Corporations to plan and build a series of new towns across the country. This, it was hoped, would finally ease the overcrowding and congestion, provide a new environment and free up space for inner-city redevelopment.

Although the Labour government was unable to deliver on its promises, it left important legacies for the future Conservative government. First, housing was moved from the Ministry of Health and the Ministry of Town and Country Planning to a new Ministry of Local Government and Planning. Second, the New Towns Act was the first piece of legislation designed to move people from the slums into new estates outside the congested cities. This became regarded as best practice in the ensuing years. Again, policy cannot be seen in terms of simple polarities. The future Conservative Housing Minister, Harold Macmillan, acknowledged that this was a "wise and profitable venture".[24] In the last few months of the Labour government, the Minister of Local Government and Planning, Hugh Dalton, drew up plans for a Town Development Bill that would allow towns and cities to buy land and build their own houses on a series of overspill estates. This was more cost effective than building new towns. When Macmillan became Minister, he used it as the basis of the 1952 Town Development Act. Now, local authorities could pursue their own policy of overspill. Crucially, unlike the New Towns Act, this could not be imposed by any authority but could only be achieved, according to Macmillan, by "orderly and friendly arrangements", by "agreement and co-operation" between local authorities.[25] Although it seemed to give local authorities the power to decide their own policy, in reality it was, at times, to prove almost impossible to implement successfully.

Despite its support for municipal overspill, in reality the Conservatives were able to change the emphasis back to private-sector developments. With the Conservative's election victory in 1951, the private sector was again to play a more prominent role. Both the demand and supply sides of the market were predisposed to home ownership. Conservative housing policy was far more ambitious than Labour. Labour claimed that more than 1,300,000 new houses had been built since the war and made an electoral promise to complete a further 200,000 new houses a year, most of which would be for rent and not for sale. The Conservatives, however, raised the bar. They promised to build 300,000 new homes every year. This contrasted with the apparent failures of Labour's programme. Most of these would be completed by the private sector, but this was more in line with the growing aspirations of the skilled worker. While there would be no reduction in the number of houses and flats built for rent, there would now be more freedom given to the private sector. Its aim was a property-owning democracy, because it believed that "the more people who own their homes the better".[26]

Harold Macmillan, who described his time as Minister as "three of the happiest years of my life", was given the task of delivering on these promises.[27] Controls on the building industry were relaxed to help stimulate growth and more licenses were given to the private sector rather than public house building. Under the 1952 Housing Act, the licensing system for private builders was relaxed and owner-occupation was encouraged. Initially, Macmillan faced huge problems as the nation's economic fortunes continued to flounder and the balance-of-payments crisis went from bad to worse.[28] He faced considerable pressure in 1952 to downgrade his housing plans.[29] However, as the economy started to improve, and Macmillan found the Treasury no longer opposing his housing plans, he was able to unveil his famous 'Grand Design'.[30] He now had the support of the Prime Minister and Cabinet, who recognised that housing had to be placed high up on the scale of the political programme, and was determined to fight his corner and "if necessary, back my demands by resignation".[31] The Ministry was reorganised and forged closer links with other government departments responsible for housing production, including the Ministry of Works. He also created Regional Housing Boards to help improve efficiency in the house-building programme. His 'Great Housing Crusade' had a number of obstacles to overcome, including shortages and bottlenecks, but Macmillan approached his policy with the zeal of a social war. Steel, timber and bricks continued to be in short supply, but productivity and confidence in the building industry slowly began to rise.[32] More controversially, Conservative policies encouraged the sale of council houses to tenants and a gradual reduction in subsidies. This seemed to represent an assault on local government autonomy, but local authorities were not forced into large-scale sell-offs, and the numbers actually sold remained limited.[33] From late 1953, Macmillan was ready to move on the white paper, *Houses: the Next Steps*, designed to lead to a programme of improvement of existing houses and to relax rent controls. As the market slowly improved, Conservative policy was moving towards the removal of rent subsidies. By the time of Macmillan's departure, the Conservative government had encouraged the growth of home ownership, reduced stamp duty and provided loans to building societies whilst continuing with some municipal building. From the middle of 1953, figures for completion rates showed a steady increase. Targets were actually exceeded. Completion rates rose from 318,779 in 1953 to 336,000 in 1954 and 382,000 in 1955. Public-sector housing was dominant, with an estimated three-quarters of all completions coming from local authorities, housing associations or new town developments. However, private-sector completions rose from only 22,551 in 1951 to 133,000 in 1955. By 1957, a total of 2.5 million new homes (including flats) had been built.[34] When the Tories gained power in 1951 only 29 per cent of the population were homeowners, but when they left power in 1964 this had dramatically risen to 45 per cent.[35]

Besides stimulating growth in private housing, the Tories returned to power in 1955 with a promise to focus on slum clearance. They boasted that there had been only one full-scale slum clearance drive in British history, and that was when they were in office in the late 1930s. Now, they promised to increase the pace of slum clearance whilst also rehousing at least 200,000 displaced slum dwellers a year. With Duncan Sandys taking over as Minister for Local Government, the Conservatives implemented its Housing Subsidies Act in 1956, with the aim of ending the general needs subsidies and of shifting funds towards replacing or at least improving slum housing. Rent subsidies for new homes were cut. When Henry Brooke became Minister, the government began to challenge the wider rent subsidies which were defended by Labour local authorities. However, in 1961 it recognised that serious problems were emerging in the provision of affordable rented homes. Troubles appeared for the Tories. Homelessness was becoming a major issue. More than 600,000 slums continued to blight the country's major urban areas. Yet, the government had cut back on subsidised public-sector house building and low-cost rents. Brooke and his successor, Keith Joseph, recognised the need to increase slum clearance and public-sector house building. In 1962, it proposed a large escalation in the slum-clearance programme, with the four giants (Sheffield, Birmingham, Manchester and Glasgow) being its priority.[36] The government established a Northern Housing Office to help local authorities in the north and midlands to increase their slum clearance and redevelopment programmes.[37] However, it was in many respects too late. It would take time to increase the programme. Slum clearance rates were the same as in 1936, while the total number of slums in 1965 was the same as in 1955.[38] Compounding its problems was the scandal created by the private landlord Peter Rachman. His unscrupulous management of slum proper-ties was linked to the Conservative Rent Act of 1957, which had freed over two million houses from rent controls. Rachman, and others, were blamed for the increase in homelessness. Higher rents and forced evictions became a damaging indictment of Conservative free-market housing economics.

Labour exploited public perceptions of Conservative failings in housing, despite the obvious successes of the 1950s. Housing remained a major political issue. At the 1964 election, both the Labour and Conservative party manifestos devoted considerable space to housing. The Conservative government trumpeted its achievements, claiming that one in four families were living in a new home built under its government, 800,000 homes had been refurbished and it had cleared half the slums.[39] It promised much of the same, with even higher comple-tion rates, greater levels of home ownership and the successful end to slum clearance by 1973. But the rent scandals had left their mark. Although it promised that no further steps would be taken to remove rent controls, it had lost a great deal of trust. The returning Labour government promised to repeal the notorious Rent Act and restore security of tenure to those in already decon-trolled rented flats and houses.[40]

With Labour back in power, the emphasis shifted back to public-sector building, but not at the expense of the private sector. The market had changed and there was a growing realisation that many members of the working classes aspired to become homeowners. What Labour hoped to do was to clear the slums and rehouse the poorer members of the community at affordable rents whilst avoiding any damage to private home ownership. In November 1964, the new Labour Minister, Richard Crossman, was confident that the government would be able to sanction the building of 400,000 houses (private and public) the following year unless it suffered a financial disaster or the building industry itself experienced a crisis. His plan was to concentrate all efforts on six or seven cities, including Manchester, Birmingham, Glasgow and London where, he claimed, the housing problems were so bad that "local authorities simply can't grapple with the job". Crossman was not entirely happy about the efficiency or effectiveness of local authorities. He felt that, as a Labour Minister, he should "impose central leadership, large-scale state intervention in these blighted areas of cities, the twilight areas which were once genteelly respectable and are now rotting away".[41] Crossman was confident that he could progress with the building programme. He told Evelyn Sharp that, following lunch with Harold Wilson, he was able to move forward with a public building programme for 150,000 completions over the following year, a figure Wilson himself had increased by 15,000. Crossman reflected that it was a "great thing to have a Prime Minister on your side".[42] When the housing programme was presented to the Cabinet he felt that Wilson "came out as a leader – a man who wasn't just content to sit back in the chair and see what happened but was prepared to make sure that things happened".[43]

The private sector was not to be neglected or ignored. Labour promised lower interest rates and 100 per cent mortgages to be made available through the local authorities.[44] The private housing drive of the 1950s, which had significantly increased the number of homeowners, could not be ignored. Neither could it disregard the aspirations of many Labour voters who now either owned or aspired to own their own homes. Again, partisan politics were not the only factor influencing housing policy. Essentially, Labour developed the same programme that it had inherited, though municipal house building was to have a greater role. Crossman's white paper proposed to build 250,000 council homes, half of the overall annual target of half a million completions up to 1970. This meant another large increase in municipal house building. The main focus switched from new towns and overspill estates. Now, far greater attention would be paid to the inner-city slum areas. To achieve his ambitious targets, Crossman urged local authorities to adopt the new system-built programmes, the industrial developments, that it was hoped would allow them to increase completion rates. This had been made a manifesto pledge in 1964. Labour had made it clear that it would increase completion rates by securing the "more rapid use of the new techniques of industrialised building".[45] Crossman told the Cabinet that they were now building fewer houses than the previous Labour government, and that public-sector housing was lagging behind the private sector despite the desperate need of cheap houses to rent. Through use of industrialised building methods it could move forward. Using system-built designs, Crossman argued, would avoid extra costs and prevent any undue strain on the building industry. It would allow them to produce another 12,000 houses, and, although the proposal was opposed on cost grounds by the Chancellor, Wilson intervened to support the plans.[46] They were not pioneers. The Conservatives had already started to encourage these new methods and had also made a pledge in 1964 to introduce new techniques to increase productivity. Crossman continued to promote the new building systems in the 1967 Housing Subsidies Act.

Local authorities could proceed with their house-building programmes secure in the knowledge that they could borrow at a maximum rate of 4 per cent from the government. If interest rates increased then the government would meet the extra costs. However, in many respects local authority autonomy had been undermined. Crossman and Sharp were exerting greater authority. They were being forced down a path that would mean adopting system-built designs, whether they liked them or not. However, although local authority choice was being restricted, they were still able to choose the designs, the areas to be redeveloped and the timing of the process. There was still plenty of scope for local choices. There were a large number of choices including different tower blocks, deck-access systems and maisonettes.

Central government was itself limited in what it could achieve. Once more, it fell short of its promises, hopes and ambitions. Economics again determined the extent to which policy could be implemented. Crossman and Wilson spoke in grand terms, making huge pledges, just as the Liberals had done in 1919. Yet economic realities severely restricted its scope for action. Despite the ambitious plans and hopes, all building programmes were subject to economic fortunes. From as early as the summer of 1965, government departments had been forced to make cut-backs. Local authorities were told to curtail all building programmes and mortgages, reducing them from £180 million a year to £130 million.[47] As Crossman realised, his housing programme was "at the mercy not of any cuts they (the Exchequer) may wish to make but of economic forces which are threatening and pressuring and bullying this poor government".[48] The battle with the Exchequer continued into 1966. He knew he was going to have a "tremendous fight in Cabinet" to get an extra 10,000 houses built. James Callaghan had already decided to cut back local authorities' borrowing rights without even consulting Crossman. He even accused Callaghan of taking an anti-local-authority and an anti-public-sector bias, and felt that Wilson was no longer giving him the support he needed. Ultimately, he was only able to secure an increase of 3,500 new houses.[49] The wrangle continued. With further cuts needed in the summer, Crossman had a "pitched battle" with Callaghan, while Wilson simply "stood aside". He understood that his campaign to get the extra 7,500 houses was part of a long-standing trend and that he was "having the row which every effective housing minister has with his Chancellor", including Bevan and Macmillan. The financial crisis of 1967 had a profound impact on Labour's ambitions. Devaluation led to a reduction in expenditure in housing from 1968 and it was unable to implement its plans to build 500,000 houses by 1969.

By the end of the 1960s a shift had started to occur in perceived solutions to the nation's housing problems. A number of issues influenced this change.

Besides the financial restrictions, it was believed that the immediate crisis in housing shortages had been met. Alongside this was a growing counter-reaction to the modern system-built designs. By the late 1960s, people were starting to question the desirability of the new inner-city developments. More importantly, a series of construction faults, highlighted by the Ronan Point disaster, and underlined later by a *World in Action* documentary, led to a general rejection of expanding further schemes.[50] The Labour government began to view improvement of existing housing stock as the preferred way forward. The 1969 Housing Act finally moved policy away from reconstruction and towards offering a series of grants to improve houses. Municipal authorities could acquire funds to support housing improvements. Resources were available for areas designated as General Improvement Areas. Government money could be used to improve streets, lighting, landscaping, paving and other aspects of the social fabric of the area.

Legislation in the late 1960s was also significant in that it finally began to recognise the rights of the tenants. Governments, central and local, had always adopted a top-down approach. There was an underlying assumption that tenants would learn to enjoy the benefits of public planning. If they had to be moved, then it was for their own benefit and for the good of the nation as a whole. There was no pretence of choice or consultation. The 1952 Town Development Act made it clear, for example, that tenants could be selected for the new overspill estates by local authorities from the housing list or by virtue of industrial selection. Tenants across most of the twentieth century were in a tightly controlled environment. However, the social and political landscape was changing by the late 1960s. The 1968 Town and Country Planning Act, for instance, obliged local authorities when making plans for an area to consider the wishes of residents. The Act stated that during the planning process adequate publicity should be given to planning proposals and that the public should be given the opportunity to make representations to the council.[51] In the same year, Frederic Seebohm's *Report on Local Authority and Allied Personal Social Services* called for greater involvement by consumers of the services.[52] The notion of consultation was strengthened in 1969 when Skeffington's Committee on Public Participation on Planning published its report, *People and Planning*. Skeffington made a number of recommendations regarding the ways in which public participation could be encouraged in the planning process. This was further reinforced by the Maud *Report on Local Government in England*, which stated that any reform should not restrict the growth in public participation in local affairs.[53] Also, the Ninth Report of the Housing Management Sub-Committee of the General Housing Advisory Committee, led by the influential J. B. Cullingworth, reported in 1969 that local authorities had to be far more aware and sensitive to the multifarious needs of their communities. It claimed that the country no longer had a single housing problem, but that it now had "a large number of local housing problems of great variety".[54] They had to think about changing family sizes, the elderly, single people, homelessness and race. This required a more flexible and responsive approach. The immediate result was limited. Despite this marking the beginning of a change in government attitudes, the fact was that even Skeffington failed to include tenants from slum-clearance programmes in his recommendations. When it came to clearing their areas, and moving to new districts, slum dwellers remained disempowered.

Besides, the early 1970s were characterised by large political and economic turbulence. By 1970, the Labour Party was in turmoil. It had suffered a series of embarrassing defeats at both the national and local levels. Labour councils were overthrown across some of their traditional heartlands.[55] In 1970, the Wilson government was defeated by Edward Heath. The Conservatives promised radical change. Like Labour, it promised to "house the homeless, concentrate on slum clearance and to provide better housing for those many families living without modern amenities".[56] This had been an objective since 1919, though their emphasis on the private sector had been traditionally more pronounced. Both municipal and privately rented tenants would receive a fair deal. In reality, this meant reducing subsidies. Throughout the late 1960s, the Tories had been formulating a market-led strategy towards housing. Heavily influenced by Keith Joseph, it wanted to encourage an expansion of home ownership. The first step was to reduce subsidies, bringing rents in line with market levels. Then it would encourage local authorities to sell off their housing stock to tenants and housing associations.[57] The role of local government would change. As soon as the Conservatives returned to office, the Ministry for Housing and Local Government was replaced by a new Department of the Environment. The Minister, Peter Walker, immediately set about changing the subsidy system. In 1972, the government produced the Housing Finance Act which was designed to keep subsidies to public housing in check by changing the distribution methods. The intention was to keep costs down by subsidising the tenants rather than the properties. Council expenditure would be subjected to greater checks and controls.

This was intended as the first step towards the new market-led strategy, but it was also the start of a more serious Conservative assault on local government power. As subsidies were reduced it was believed that rents would reach market level and, consequently, tenants would be encouraged to buy. Rents would be fixed along the same lines and principles as private-sector accommodation. Rent Scrutiny Boards were established to ensure fair rents would be set by local authorities, whether they agreed or not. Rent increases would be introduced gradually and a system of rebates would be paid from the local rates to help the poorer tenants. The new Act was met by an outcry across many traditional Labour districts. Threats of rent strikes and non-compliance were widespread. However, initial opposition from a number of Labour councils soon collapsed in the face of threats to use Commissioners to take control of local housing stock. Only Clay Cross in Derbyshire offered any resistance. A long and bitter struggle ended in 1974 when the district was absorbed into the new area of North Derbyshire.[58] But, despite its victory, the policy backfired on the government. Local authorities deliberately kept expenditure at a high level in 1972 because they realised that the government would calculate future subsidies on this basis. Consequently, expenditure on subsidies increased. The Tories also promoted the sale of council houses more vigorously than in previous years. Again, however, Labour councils proved constantly obstructive. By the time of the 1974 election, the government was complaining that the number of new homeowners would have been "still larger had certain councils not opposed the sale of council houses to those council tenants who were willing and able to buy them with the help offered by the government".[59] Future Conservative leaders were not going to leave the policy to chance.

Despite the confrontations, it is important to remember that relations between central and local government were not always characterised by ideological difference or similarities. The inter-war period highlighted the way legislation and subsidies were not simply passed by one government and removed by the next. In the post-war period, local leaders from across the party divide could enjoy good working relations with central government. The former leader of Manchester city council, William Egerton, admitted that in the 1970s Manchester was able to get most of the resources it needed for its housing policy from Labour and Conservative governments alike. He declared that "Manchester did very well with Tory Ministers", and that you "could actually go and discuss with Ministers and put a bloomin' good case every time and it was always accepted, I think it's always been accepted".[60] Cities like Manchester and Birmingham produced their own policies, within the broad framework established by central government, and enjoyed success in convincing central government to provide the resources. Egerton claimed that "Birmingham, like Manchester, got most of what they asked for", and that although "it may have took a good lot of arguing and maybe you did not get as much as you wanted, you couldn't do it as fast as you wanted, but eventually you got there".[61] This underlines the blurred relationship between central government, party politics, housing philosophies and the dynamics of the working relationship at the local level.

Economic fluctuations were an added complication. Mounting economic problems and growing industrial unrest brought the Heath government down in 1974. Housing remained a major political issue. Wilson returned to power promising to repeal the Housing Finance Act and restore the right of local authorities to fix rents below market values. Anthony Crosland took charge of the Department of the Environment, sweeping away the Rent Scrutiny Boards and the notion of bringing rents in line with the market. But there was to be no return to large-scale building programmes. The 1974 Housing Act increased the resources available for improvement grants, extended the GIA scheme and provided extra support for the creation of Housing Action Areas. Rents were frozen for eight months, though economic pressures meant this was reversed. Labour also continued to realise it was politically expedient to support home-owners. It promised to help home-buyers through a new National Housing Finance Agency, to assist first-time buyers and to stabilise mortgage lending.[62] Also, it proposed to allow local authorities greater lending powers to enable them to support house purchasers and keep down costs by supplying unified services for estate agency, surveying, conveyancing and mortgages. Like the Conservatives, it recognised that workers' aspirations needed to be supported and that the private market was capable of meeting their ambitions. Local government remained as the main agency in determining and meeting the needs and demands of the rented sector. Labour local authorities were also able to curtail sales of public housing stock to the tenants. Many Conservative councils, however, continued to promote council-house sales. Since the Conservatives introduced the Right-to-Buy under the 1957 Housing Act, there had been a very slow and gradual increase in the number of sales. In 1967, there had been only 3,200 sales, but the early 1970s saw a marked increase, with over 45,000 sales in 1972 and nearly 34,000 in 1973.[63] This was curtailed by Labour councils. When Peter Shore took control of the Department of the Environment he intro-duced restrictions to curb further sales. Labour, it was argued by their opponents, had again failed to react to the demands of the tenants who actually wanted to buy their own homes. The Conservatives were now to make this, along with the reduction of local government power, a central part of future housing policy.

Despite the broad ideological differences in housing, Labour and Conser-vative governments had, in reality, reached a broad consensus by the late 1970s on the need to support private home ownership, the role of housing associations and the need to reduce subsidies.[64] Nevertheless, the Tories returned to power in 1979 with a radical set of policies that would shake both housing policy and local government to their roots. Keith Joseph led the demand for reform in the mid-1970s. He claimed that rent control, slum clearance and municipal house building had "made the housing situation worse", because it had destroyed low-cost housing and increased homelessness.[65] Joseph believed that this was a moral as well as economic issue and that council housing had "wrought hard to the social fabric" of the country.[66] He argued that millions of people were seeking housing choice and an end to the post-war 'middle ground' consensus.[67] A new, ideologically based approach was created. Under Margaret Thatcher, and with Michael Heseltine as Secretary of the Department of the Environment, it set about changing the role of local government from service producer to service enabler. The Right-to-Buy was forced on local authorities in an unprecedented manner. Michael Heseltine claimed that the Right-to-Buy scheme was one of the core promises of the 1979 election and was the "most radical pledge" it had made.[68] The era of large-scale municipal-owned housing was over. It promised tax cuts to help potential homebuyers to get a mortgage, encouraged shared ownership schemes, a grant scheme to help first-time buyers and lower mortgage rates by cutting public expenditure. Tenants were promised a series of consumer rights under a new Tenants Charter. The private rented sector was also to be given greater encouragement and support. Labour, in contrast, was still promising a substantial programme of house building and home improvement and, in contrast to the Conservatives, made it clear that "local councils will continue to play a central part in meeting housing needs".[69] Yet, despite the old dogma, there were signs that a new consensus was emerging in other areas of policy. Labour agreed to give "a new deal to council tenants", which would include a series of rights such as security of tenure, the right to a written tenancy agreement and the right to improve the home". It even promised to "widen choice", by helping those who wished to buy their own homes.

The Conservatives kept their promises. Within six months of gaining power the government had produced a consultation paper on the Right-to-Buy.[70] All tenants were allowed to buy their homes without any form of local government resistance. The government described the Tenants Charter as a "far reaching and radical reform of the rights of council tenants".[71] By 1983, the government was boasting that, despite fierce resistance from Labour local authorities, at least half a million council houses and flats had been sold in the course of the previous Parliament and that in total there were now a million more owner-occupiers than there had been four years ago.[72] It promised to extend the scheme by increasing the discount to 60 per cent, and to develop the Tenants Charter by allowing tenants to carry out their own repairs and claim back the cost from the local authority. This was part of a wider struggle against what Heseltine described as inadequate local-authority management and, as such, an attempt to "introduce a better deal for those who didn't want to buy".[73]

The emphasis was on the right of the individual, on consumer choice. The 1980 Act brought a radical restructuring of housing policy based on classic liberal ideas concerning individualism and the primacy of the market. Heseltine boasted that it had produced a "comprehensive and radical reforming agenda across a wide housing horizon".[74] Critics claimed that this undermined the welfare state by increasing inequality and social divisions and by reducing the role of local government. Legislation was reinforced by the Housing and Planning Act 1986. By 1992, an estimated 1.5 million tenants had bought their homes. Conservative aims were ideologically driven as they were intended to create a capital-owning democracy. By the 1987 election, they boasted that "one million council tenants have become homeowners and another one and a half million more families have become homeowners for the first time".[75] It believed it was on course to making Britain the largest property owning country in the world. Heseltine described the policy as "epoch-making" and claimed that it had implemented a "quiet revolution" in property owning.[76]

But securing the tenants' Right-to-Buy was not the only aim of the government. It wanted to take all remaining homes out of municipal control and boost the private rented sector. The number of new homes built by local authorities declined rapidly. The very role of local government was changing from one in which it actually produced its own services to one whereby it enabled services to be efficiently managed. Diluting council power further was to be achieved by the transfer of municipal-owned houses to housing associations or private management companies. After the third and emphatic election victory of 1987, Nicolas Ridley unveiled an even more radical programme. The 1988 Housing Act was designed to stimulate the private rented sector and to free up the housing associations from local government influence. They were to act as independent bodies. The government was again claiming that it was increasing individual choice. Ridley's 1987 white paper stated that "the emphasis must be on greater consumer choice and more say for tenants".[77] The new legislation recognised that tenants were consumers of housing and that they should be given greater freedoms. Tenants who did not wish to buy were to be given the opportunity to choose their landlord, to transfer the tenancy from local government control to a private landlord. The Housing Corporation was formed to help tenants make their choices. The hope was that private landlords would take control over municipal housing. They would be able to offer greater investment, something from which local authorities had been systematically starved. The result, though, was a very limited uptake. Councils, however, did begin to respond to the needs of their tenants.[78] The idea that the tenant was consumer was starting to be recognised, at least at the national level. Labour had understood the shifting climate. In 1987, it promised to "maintain the right to buy", and to give remaining tenants a legal right to be consulted about rents, charges, repair and improvement programmes. It promised more consultation, claiming that tenants' associations would be given "representation in the decision-making structure and a say in spending budgets on their estates", while groups of tenants who wanted to take over the running of their homes would have the right to set up management co-operatives.[79]

Labour slowly recognised the changing demands of the tenants. But, for the Conservatives lasting change could only be secured by continuing the assault on municipal-controlled housing. Under the 1988 Act, local authorities were able voluntarily to transfer all their housing stock to housing-association control. Government pressures and financial controls threatened to squeeze local authorities into taking up this option, providing they also received tenant backing. However, yet again there was only a limited uptake. Nevertheless, the assault on municipal control of housing continued. Under the 1988 Act, the government introduced Housing Action Trusts. Local authorities could use private investment to refurbish their run-down estates. On completion, the estate would be transferred to either private or housing association ownership and management. Again, tenants were given the choice. Ironically, the tenants did make their voices heard. Tenant groups became organised in their opposition to the HAT proposals. They were so successful that all of the initial schemes identified for improvement under the HAT plans were abandoned.[80] This was later replaced by the policy of Large Scale Voluntary Transfer, which moved all local authority housing estates to a housing trust, though, again, it depended on tenant support.

More successful was the assault on housing finances. The 1988 Housing Act, and subsequent policies, represented a fundamental change to the entire structure of local government control over housing. All housing subsidies were now brought under central government control. It was able to have much greater influence over rents and council expenditure levels. Local authorities no longer possessed the level of autonomy they had enjoyed for much of the century. They could no longer subsidise their activities, including rent levels, through the rates. Added to this was that few new houses were being built, many tenants had bought their homes and there was a general lack of investment that was encouraging ever greater levels of private-sector involvement. It was clear that the role of local government in producing, owning and renting houses on a substantial scale was coming to an end.

But that did not mean that local government was finished. Instead, a new regime emerged in Britain's towns and cities, formed between central government, local authorities, private investors, non-profit making and voluntary groups as well as community groups. The Conservative government's use of the City Challenge scheme in the early 1990s involved all these agencies coming together to rebuild some of the nation's most dilapidated inner-city areas. Local authorities were invited to submit a scheme in a bid to win £35 million of government aid over five years to help redevelop some of the worst inner-city areas. They had to produce a type of business plan, giving details about the objectives, the strategy for achieving their aims, evidence of endorsements from community groups, teachers and the police and, inevitably, firm commitments from the private sector to increase the levels of investment. Michael Heseltine recognised that although the plans would be met with predictable hostility from the Labour Party, "one of the charms of local government is that in the end it has a simple understanding of the financial imperative".[81] He was aware that local authorities often transcended basic partisan allegiances, stating that if councillors perceived an "enlightened self-interest on behalf of their community then they go for it regardless of party politics".[82] If money was to be had, then local authorities would compete for their own area. Local government was far from finished. It had gone through another process of reconfiguration in its relationship with the central authority. Local authorities continued to take a central role in the bidding process and in the implementation of the policy. Although, throughout the twentieth century, governments had established the parameters in which local authorities worked, forcing reluctant Conservative local authorities to take action or reigning back more radical Labour authorities, the fact remains that local government was still given scope to interpret, create and manage policy. From 1919, all councils had to build new estates and from 1930 all councils had to produce plans for slum clearance. But every council was still able to determine the details, the designs, the locations to be affected and the time scales in which changes took place. Central government constantly changed direction according to ideologies, financial restrictions and political circumstances. Local government could not escape these realities. The state could, and did, severely restrict their ability to act. But, as will be seen, within these restrictions they were still able to influence policy and have a real impact on housing in their own urban arenas.

Notes

1 *The Times* (12 April 1919).
2 G. E. Cherry, *Town Planning, Britain Since 1900* (Oxford, 1996), p. 34.
3 M. Bowley, in J. Burnett, *A Social History of Housing 1815–1985* (New York, 1986), p. 221.
4 K. Young and P. Garside, *Metropolitan London: Politics and Urban Change, 1837–1981* (London, 1982), p. 143; P. Johnson, *Land Fit for Heroes: the Planning of British Reconstruction 1916–1919* (Chicago, 1968).
5 *House of Commons Parliamentary Debates,* Vol. 14 (1919), col. 1718.
6 Burnett, *A Social History of Housing 1815–1985*, p. 234.
7 Young and Garside, *Metropolitan London*, p. 153.
8 Cherry, *Town Planning, Britain Since 1900*, p. 35.
9 C. Addison, *The Betrayal of the Slums* (London, 1922), p. 15.
10 Ibid., p. 126.
11 Cherry, *Town Planning, Britain Since 1900*, p. 36.
12 Ibid., p. 40.
13 Burnett, *A Social History of Housing*, p. 243.
14 Arthur Greenwood, *The Labour Outlook* (London, 1929), p. 62.
15 Ibid., pp. 75–7.
16 Ibid., p. 75.
17 N. Tiratsoo, *Reconstruction, Affluence and Labour Politics: Coventry 1945–60* (London, 1990); J. Haesagwa, *Replacing the Blitzed City Centre: A Comparative Study of Bristol, Coventry and Southampton, 1945–50* (Buckingham, 1992).
18 K. Young and N. Rao, *Local Government Since 1945* (Oxford, 1997), p. 53.
19 L. R. Murphy, 'Rebuilding Britain: the government's role in housing and town planning, 1945–57', *Historian*, 32:2 (1970), 410–27.
20 Conservative Party manifesto, 1945. All post-war manifestos are taken from www.psr.keele.ac.uk/area/uk/manifesto.
21 Labour Party manifesto, 1945.
22 *House of Commons Debates,* Vol. 414 (17 October 1945), cols 1222/1223.
23 *Royal Commission on the Distribution of the Industrial Population* (London, 1940).
24 H. Macmillan, *The Tides of Fortune* (London, 1969), p. 418.
25 *House of Commons Debates,* Vol. 496, col. 725, cited in J. B. Cullingworth, *Housing Needs and Planning Policy* (London, 1960), p. 70.
26 Conservative Party manifesto, 1951.
27 Macmillan, *The Tides of Fortune*, p. 460.
28 Ibid., pp. 380–5.
29 Ibid., p. 388.
30 H. Jones, '"This is magnificent!" 300,000 houses a year and the Tory revival after 1945', *Contemporary British History*, 14:1 (2000), 99–121; A. Simmonds, 'Conservative governments and the new town housing question in the 1950s', *Urban History*, 28:1

(2001), 65–82; P. Weiler, 'The rise and fall of the Conservatives' Grand Design for Housing', *Contemporary British History*, 14:1 (2000), 122–50.

31 Macmillan, *The Tides of Fortune*, p. 395.

32 Ibid., p. 402.

33 Young and Rao, *Local Government Since 1945*, p. 65.

34 Figures from Young and Rao, *Local Government Since 1945*, p. 63.

35 Ibid., p. 66.

36 The National Archive, London (hereafter TNA) HLG 118/258, memo by E. A. Sharp 'Slum clearance drive', 9 April 1962.

37 TNA, HLG 118/258, memo from E. A. Sharp, 'Northern Housing Office', 23 October 1962.

38 Young and Rao, *Local Government Since 1945*, p. 69.

39 Conservative Party manifesto, 1964.

40 Labour Party manifesto, 1964.

41 R. Crossman, *Richard Crossman: The Diaries of a Cabinet Minister*, Vol. 1 (London, 1975), p. 44.

42 Ibid., p. 108.

43 Ibid., p. 169.

44 Labour Party manifesto, 1964.

45 Ibid.

46 Crossman, *Richard Crossman*, pp. 169–70.

47 Ibid., p. 266.

48 Ibid., p. 268.

49 Ibid., p. 506.

50 See below Chapter 3.

51 *Report of the Committee on Public Participation in Planning* (HMSO London, 1969).

52 *Report of the Committee on Local Authority and Allied Personal Social Services* (HMSO London, 1968).

53 *Report of Royal Commission on Local Government in England 1966–69* (HMSO London, 1969).

54 TNA, HLG 117/99, Ninth Report of the Housing Management Sub-Committee of the General Housing Advisory Committee, 1969, p. 118.

55 S. Fielding, *The Labour Governments: Labour and Cultural Change*, Vol. 1 (Manchester, 2002), pp. 199–210.

56 Conservative Party manifesto, 1970.

57 Young and Rao, *Local Government Since 1945*, p. 158.

58 Ibid., p. 162.

59 Conservative Party manifesto, 1974.

60 Author's interview with Councillor William Egerton, 25 January 2002 (University of Wales, Bangor).

61 Ibid.

62 Young and Rao, *Local Government Since 1945*, p. 167.

63 Ibid.

64 S. M. Cooper, 'English housing policy, 1972–1980' (PhD dissertation, London School of Economics, 1984).

65 K. Joseph, *Stranded on the Middle Ground?* (London: Centre for Policy Studies, 1976), p. 24.

66 Ibid.

67 Ibid., p. 30.

68 M. Heseltine, *Life in the Jungle* (London, 2000), p. 194.

69 Labour Party manifesto, 1979.

70 TNA, BD 107/21, 'The Right-to-Buy – a consultation paper', 11 October 1979.
71 Ibid.
72 Conservative Party manifesto, 1983.
73 Heseltine, *Life in the Jungle*, p. 194.
74 Ibid., p. 195.
75 Conservative Party manifesto, 1987.
76 Heseltine, *Life in the Jungle*, p. 196.
77 *Housing: The Government's Proposals*, paragraph 1.4. Cited in Young and Rao, *Local Government Since 1945*, p. 271.
78 Young and Rao, *Local Government Since 1945*, p. 272.
79 Labour Party manifesto, 1979.
80 Young and Rao, *Local Government Since 1945*, p. 276.
81 Heseltine, *Life in the Jungle*, p. 395.
82 Ibid.

2 National interpretations

Although local authorities worked within a common framework of national legislation and policy directives from the government, policy was also determined by local problems, council politics, the attitude of local authority officials and the distinct urban culture in which cities operated. Understanding the complexities of the policy process, appreciating the process of government and governance across urban society, underlines the importance of locality. This chapter highlights the significance of locality in the decision-making process by comparing and contrasting broad aspects of housing policy between different cities across the century. All cities faced huge problems and each had to react to government legislation and financial controls. This created an obvious element of commonality. Most local authorities had to build new working-class estates outside their borders, embark on slum-clearance programmes, build overspill estates and embrace system-built developments. Cities were influenced by similar and different pressures and political ideologies. Some were more innovative and receptive to new ideas than others. The issue also shifts over time. Local discourse was shaped by forces specific to each area. Moreover, local authorities faced physical and all-too-real problems which were often unique to their environment. There are general and even specific parallels to be drawn, but there were also clear differences.

The scale of the crisis in 1919 was daunting, with slum conditions and overcrowding common to all. Most British cities built working-class suburbs, inspired by Howard, Unwin and the Garden City Movement. Some estates were condemned as ugly and depressing. Others were praised for their building standards, designs and quality planning. Few really eased the chronic slum problems. Attempts to address the issues in the 1930s had varied rates of success. A few cities took an active interest in flats during the inter-war period. Liverpool was keen to build tenements in the inner-city area. London's architects were influenced by Le Corbusier and the Modern Movement while Leeds built one of the most outstanding examples of municipal flats. But most cities still frowned on them. After the Second World War, all cities were still affected by old Victorian slums, but for some the housing problem was made infinitely more acute by the German bombing raids. Prefabs were used to ease the more immediate problems, some of which remain in service. Long-term solutions were also sought. Labour's new welfare world promised a great deal for everyone. Initially, many cities believed that new towns and overspill estates offered the answer. Some receiving local authorities, such as Swindon, were keen to use overspill as a means to boost their economy, yet, as will be seen, few local authorities were willing to pursue overspill with the same vigour as Manchester.

While some slum-clearance programmes and inner-city redevelopment plans faltered, others achieved impressive clearance and completion rates. This was made possible by using new methods, including the tower block. A few cities were willing to build higher than ever before. Yet, the system-built developments left a dreadful legacy in most British cities. This, together with rent increases and the desire to influence slum-clearance plans and secure funds for refurbishment programmes, gave rise to a number of tenant protests. Some were more vociferous and successful than others. Many were small groups that achieved little. However, others did force a gradual change in perceptions. A few London local authorities were especially receptive to the idea of consultation and participation. For others, it remained a struggle. Yet the willingness of many tenants to voice their protests highlighted a gradual challenge to the traditional political discourse that had dominated, if not suffocated, community politics.

The rise of the 'Producer' council

By the start of the twentieth century, Britain's urban industrial centres were all suffering from slum conditions built up over the Victorian period. This inheritance proved the main problem facing local officials across most of the twentieth century. Although back-to-back houses had been banned in Manchester in 1844, they continued to dominate working-class housing in many cities. Manchester had a large stock, but it was not on the same scale as Leeds which had an especially bad problem with more than 78,000 back-to-back houses or 71 per cent of the city's total housing stock.[1] These were a major cause of overcrowding and subsequent poor health. National legislation introduced a gradually increasing degree of compulsion on local authorities. Following the 1890 Housing of the Working Classes Act, a number of municipal authorities attempted to demolish some the worst examples of slums. It was, however, a limited exercise, highlighting the different responses in different areas. Between 1905 and 1914, more than 1,600 slum houses were demolished in Leeds, but, like many others, the council remained deeply divided on providing subsidised housing.[2] Leeds council, with its strong Conservative presence, was reluctant to develop new municipal homes. Before 1914, it built a meagre thirty-six houses. Nationally, only 1 per cent of the entire housing stock was owned by municipal authorities.[3] Tynemouth council did not even discuss the 1890 Housing of the Working Classes Act until 1902, and then decided that one of its worst areas, North Shields, did not have a problem.[4] When it eventually gave in to pressure from the local Labour movement to discuss a proposal to build twenty experimental homes, it was comfortably rejected.[5] Local factors were at play. Out of the thirty-one council members, twenty had business connections in the building industry. Vested interests meant that it would be another decade before it began seriously to debate the issue. Newcastle was also slow to react. The Medical Officer of Health in the early twentieth century, Henry Armstrong, was criticised for his inertia. Despite there being an estimated 67,000 people living in overcrowded conditions, he had been unable, or unwilling, to do anything to improve the situation.[6] By 1917, the council had built only 455 tenements in six small schemes.[7]

This appeared to be in stark contrast with cities like Birmingham. Birmingham's progressive tradition, inspired by the Civic Gospel of Dale, Dawson and Joseph Chamberlain, meant it seemed to have a more interventionist approach, though in reality it barely scratched the surface of the problem. While improvements were carried out across the 'best governed city in the world', the programme lost momentum by the 1890s. The council accepted that it had a responsibility to provide houses for those displaced under slum-clearance programmes under the 1890 Act, but it did not show any particular enthusiasm towards widespread reform.[8] In 1914, it still had 43,366 back-to-backs in 6,000 courts.[9] However, progressive forces were at work in Birmingham. Like many cities, Birmingham was influenced by a number of prominent reformers, including Rev. T. J. Bass who published *Everyday in Blackest Birmingham* in 1898, and J. Cuming Walter, who highlighted the terrible conditions in 'Scenes in Slumland', published in the *Daily Gazette* in 1901. An ideological struggle was taking place in the city. Eventually, the council, still deeply divided, decided to form a Housing Committee. In 1905 it visited Berlin where it became convinced that the German model of town planning was the long-term answer to their problems. The successful model village at nearby Bourneville reinforced the belief.[10]

Other local authorities, such as Liverpool, showed a much earlier willingness to get actively involved. It built 1,895 new homes to replace cleared slums before 1919.[11] The city had also been affected by initial ideological objections to the idea of intervention, but these were overcome by the turn of the century and the council continued to show a commitment to resolve the problem.[12] It produced an energetic and coherent programme.[13] However, in stark contrast to cities such as Manchester, it was willing (even keen) to build tenements for slum dwellers. More expensive artisan houses were built for the affluent working classes. This two-tier system characterised policy in the first part of the century. Liverpool's council believed this would ease the problem of land cost and availability, a problem shared with many other cities. London had a similar, though much larger, problem. From 1900, the Labour county council built a number of estates and produced a few ambitious plans, though most had to be abandoned because of limited council power and local opposition.[14] Frustrated plans and continued demand meant that by 1920 it was estimated that London would need an immediate 75,000 houses. Birmingham was also faced with a severe shortage of land, but it was able partially to resolve the problem in 1911 by extending its boundaries, giving it 30,000 acres (24,000 of which was undeveloped land).[15] But the council continued to drag its feet. Although it had a reputation for bold civic action, the fact was that the Conservative Liverpool council had improved 11,000 houses, demolished 5,500 and built 2,322 by 1913, while Birmingham had reconditioned 3,311 houses, demolished 2,774 and built a meagre 165.[16] Even smaller cities like Swansea displayed a genuine zeal to develop new housing projects. By 1905, it had nine sites under consideration, though it tended to be small-scale infill areas.[17]

The inter-war period witnessed a huge growth in municipal-owned housing across the country. By 1945, 10 per cent of the population were living in council houses, with 90 per cent living on new suburban estates.[18] In the eighteen years between 1919 and 1937, an estimated 12 million people were successfully rehoused, around 1.5 million on new council estates.[19] The 1919 coalition government's determination to build homes for heroes led to a change in policy across all British cities. Local government remained the central agent for reform. Each acted independently. Local authorities produced their own policies and managed their own houses.[20] Central government acted as a good guide, but it did not have the administrative machinery to implement a monolithic policy across the country. Only the local authorities could perform this task. Each had its own discourse and each reacted to the specific problems in its own locale. Studies of Sheffield and Bristol in the inter-war period underline the influence of specific local conditions on housing policy. In Sheffield, the radical Labour council, which was in control from 1926, pursued municipal socialism with vigour. Housing reform was at the centre of this programme. In Bristol, Labour took office much later and its housing policy tended to be comparatively moderate, based on accelerating the building programme.[21] Similarly, Nottingham's progressive council stuttered towards creating a general consensus about the value of municipal house building. It was only by the late 1920s that a broad consensus emerged.[22]

While government instructed local authorities to build for the general needs of the working classes, or to pull down the slums, conditions in each city were different. Although the Garden City Movement was fundamental to design and planning in many cities in the first part of the century, policies were not always an ideologically driven attempt to build a better environment for the downtrodden masses. In a number of cities, the main reason for building outside the boundaries was because of land availability. Discourse had to adapt to real problems and barriers. Land values inside many cities, including Manchester, prevented local authorities from large-scale building inside their boundaries. This was a particular problem in London where the cost of land was so high that the London county council (LCC) turned to the development of new suburbs from as early as 1898.[23] At the turn of the century, the LCC was ahead of most local authorities. However, from 1907, when the Conservatives gained power, there was a greater reluctance to undertake large building schemes. Nevertheless, an important precedent had been established. Suburban housing, rather than redevelopment of cleared sites, became the dominant policy. It was, simply, much cheaper.[24] By 1914, the LCC had built 10,000 homes in new estates, including garden suburbs such as Norbury in 1902, White Hart Lane in 1904 and Old Oak Hammersmith. The size of these developments, however, was inadequate. London's problems were huge. It needed a more radical solution. Nearly 800,000 people were classed as living in slum housing. By 1919, it agreed to build a large new estate at Becontree to ease the problems in the East End. Initially, there would be 24,000 houses on the 3,000-acre site, which was meant eventually to house 120,000 people. A further 3,000 houses were to be built at Roehampton and Bellingham.[25]

The LCC was in competition with private developers for what were becoming increasingly scarce tracts of land.[26] More than most cities, this seriously affected its ability to build in sufficient numbers. After the First World War, the local authorities in London were responsible for 37 per cent of all new houses completed, while in Liverpool it was 80 per cent, Birmingham 70 per cent and Manchester 60 per cent.[27] In 1926, the LCC's Housing Committee estimated that it would need to purchase 1,000 acres a year to meet its targets.[28] Again, this meant building outside the city.[29] Estates were developed around the outskirts of Leeds, and, as with other cities, these were designed to meet the demands of general needs. In Birmingham, new estates were built in a series of working-class suburbs around the edges of the city. It aimed to build 10,000 houses, but this proved an ambitious target. Soaring costs seriously affected the programme, which in the end fell short by nearly 6,000.[30] As in cities across the country, the Geddes axe finally brought an end to building under the Addison Act in 1921.

Land was not the only problem. Like most British cities, the Becontree estate suffered due to lack of materials and skilled workers. By 1919, the building labour force was 45 per cent below its pre-war level.[31] In London, there was an estimated shortfall of 2,000 bricklayers.[32] Attempts to protect contractors from rises in wages and material prices, though not guaranteeing a profit, led to enormous difficulties in obtaining tenders, plunging the LCC into a housing crisis.[33] Labour shortages further compounded its problems.[34] Again, this produced a variety of responses across the country. The situation was so bad in Nottingham that although the council issued closing orders on all unfit properties in 1918, within three years many were being reopened.[35] In cities like Liverpool, shortages meant that private construction continued at a low level until the mid-1920s.[36] Central government encouraged local authorities to adopt non-traditional building methods to ease the problems in the building industry. Although government promoted the idea, it did little else other than to rubber stamp decisions made by the local authorities. Councils still enjoyed considerable autonomy.[37] Cities were able to innovate with designs, albeit out of necessity. Like many, Swansea's problems were so acute that in 1919 it discussed the idea of using 100 army huts, the purchase in 1920 of 100 wooden bungalows and further experimental purchases of concrete and steel-framed houses.[38] A local culture that was ready to try new methods already existed in a number of British cities.[39] Both Leicester and Nottingham relied on new building techniques. Manchester was so impressed with Nottingham's efforts that the Housing Committee sent a deputation to assess the value of its experimental houses. It used the Boot and Crane systems that incorporated pre-cast concrete slabs and used a greater degree of unskilled labour. Although mainly constructed after the immediate crisis in the later 1920s, Nottingham still built 3.4 per cent of houses in the inter-war period using new methods, while in Leicester it was as high as 16.5 per cent.[40]

These were a part of a particular set of responses to its housing problems. Central government remained on the periphery. But the government did become so concerned at the slow progress across all cities that it allowed the Office of Works, under the leadership of Sir Alfred Mond, to get directly involved in some of the larger projects. It was responsible for the 1,000 houses built at Woolwich and a further 4,000 houses developed across the country. However, central government involvement did not go much further. It remained the responsibility of local authorities to formulate and implement policy according to their own ambitions, traditions and physical circumstances. All British cities were forced to start building municipal houses, but reactions were varied according to the council and the circumstances. Some, like Swansea, showed genuine eagerness. By as early as September 1917, the Swansea city architect produced plans for 5,000 new homes.[41] This was an extension of plans developed in 1914, plans which were of such a high standard that it did not need to refer to the *Housing Manual*.[42] Similarly, York's pre-war plans to build 220 houses on the suburban Tang Hall estate were revived in 1918.[43] Much larger cities produced comparatively modest plans. Leeds council approved its first substantial scheme in 1918, agreeing to build 2,000 new houses.[44] Apart from two marked periods during 1927–30 and 1933–35, the Conservatives dominated Leeds council during the inter-war period. It still believed in the primacy of the market and even in the 1920s expressed misgivings at building municipal houses. However, the pressure of central government, and the sheer scale of the problem, forced them into becoming "reluctant collectivists".[45] By 1926, it had built 5,000 houses and a further 7,000 by 1930.[46] Again, the Garden City Movement was influential in the development of policy. Leeds preferred to build cottage houses in semi-rural locations. Before 1934, it tried to avoid flats. However, density levels in some inner-city areas meant that, eventually, building flats was unavoidable. It might not have relished the idea, but it had no choice. Initially, flats were low-level two-to-four storey buildings that maintained the appearance of semi-detached houses. During 1927–32, Leeds council built 1,572 units, but it temporarily abandoned all flat building in 1933.

Although all post-war housing schemes were floundering by 1921, subsequent legislation in 1923 and 1924 did allow further developments, albeit at a slower and fitful pace. Nevertheless, many cities expanded outwards during the inter-war period to create a new suburban landscape for both private homeowners and council tenants. In Leeds, 40 per cent of new houses were built by the council, creating more than twenty new housing estates outside the city. Estates like Gipton absorbed many of the ideals of garden suburbs, planting one tree for every house to "enhance the beauty of the estate",[47] creating open spaces, cul-de-sacs and crescents. It was trying to enhance the appearance of the city by using traditional designs from middle-class suburbs. London's estates were also meant to offer a "country environment", preserving natural features in what was essentially an anti-urban vision of the idyllic lifestyle.[48] Similarly, Swansea's Townhill estate was based on Unwin's Garden City principles.[49]

However, despite this well intentioned idealism, some of the new tenants did not appreciate the new environment but missed the shops and amenities they had been used to near the slums.[50] Many tenants in Liverpool struggled to adapt to life on the new estates in the 1930s. Besides rent and transport costs, they complained that the estates lacked the warmth and friendliness of the old slum districts and that they required essential amenities for many years.[51] There were even complaints about construction standards, maintenance and the drabness and monotony of the houses.[52] Liverpool council had received similar complaints about the small, comfortless, "ill designed and inadequate" tenements built before the war.[53] Some estates were condemned as complete failures. Becontree, the largest municipal housing estate in the world, was widely criticised as monotonous, ugly and resembling a concentration camp. Although other estates received similar criticism, some cities had taken greater care to build what they hoped were quality homes with open spaces and clean air. In pre-war London, the Old Oak estate was described as having made one of the "finest contribution(s)" to English architecture in the country.[54] Earlier developments at Norbury and White Hart Lane were also claimed to be models for suburban development.[55] Other cities were keen to incorporate traditional designs into the new estates. While the Wythenshawe estate in Manchester adopted Georgian style, Nottingham used Tudor designs.[56] Nottingham council believed it was part of its civic duty to create high standards for a better future.[57] In contrast, Becontree was badly planned. Although at first the LCC had wanted to build high-quality and low-density cottage homes, the estate was dogged by a lack of finance, leading to poor facilities.[58] It also struggled more than other estates to develop a sense of civic identity.[59]

Tenants were also unhappy about more practical issues. Many complained that rents were too high while the extra costs incurred through travel made them prohibitive for the poor. This was true of Becontree and other London estates such as Bellingham, which was purposely designed for "superior artisans".[60] Tenants tended to come from the more affluent members of the working classes. In one of the first post-war developments in Hull, only a quarter of the families who had moved in during the early 1920s remained by 1925, and these were clerks and cashiers.[61] They had been joined by plumbers, teachers, policemen and a merchant navy officer. In many estates across the country, the majority of new tenants were clerks, skilled workers and the wealthier semi-skilled in secure jobs. It was hoped that the filtering system in Liverpool would allow tenants to move up into homes with superior facilities while slum tenants would move up a level into the vacated homes.[62] The provision of facilities in Birmingham's new estates seriously lagged behind house building. Initially, it even failed to provide sufficient school places.[63] Only in 1929 did it begin to build shops for rent on the new estates. York council, however, deliberately sought to build houses for both the poor displaced slum dweller and the more affluent working classes at the Tang Hall estate. Yet increased demand, and pressure from the National Union of Railwaymen, forced the council to amend its plans, with the first 185 houses being built to larger designs to satisfy the demands of the more affluent sections of the working classes.[64]

Despite the costs and initial problems associated with community dislocation, many tenants were pleased with their new homes compared with the slums they had left behind.[65] The *Inquiry into People's Homes*, which was part of the Mass Observation of 1939, showed that 80 per cent of those living on the new working-class housing estates expressed satisfaction at the quality of their homes. Significantly, the vast majority also stated that their ideal house was the cottage design rather than a bungalow. Only 5 per cent preferred a flat.[66] But new schemes were not without opposition. Many existing residents voiced opposition. They resented the intrusion of the resettled working classes. In 1923, local residents objected to plans to buy the land for the Downham estate because it would "reduce the respectability" of the area, while in 1924 the LCC's attempts to buy land at Edgware was met with strong resistance from the locals.[67]

Despite the building programmes of the 1920s, slum housing continued to be a major problem in every British city. By the late 1920s, there was a growing realisation that the building programmes had little impact on improving the conditions of the poor.[68] There is an underlying problem in defining the 'slum'. Throughout the century, the term is amorphous. Where some believe homes were redeemable with building improvements, others saw them as beyond salvation. Although a slum could be defined as a unit that could not be salvaged because of the rotting structural fabric, it is not always clear if this applied to all homes across the country and throughout the period. Statistics from the 1930s, therefore, may not always be accurate and may be based on individual impressionistic interpretations. The same applies to later periods. Nevertheless, the figures do give estimates which reflect the scale of the problem. They suggest that London had an estimated 30,000 basement homes, Leeds still had a large stock of back-to-backs (33,000 of which were unfit for habitation), Sheffield had 60,000, Birmingham 38,000 and Bradford 30,000.[69] Ernest Simon's study of London in the 1920s and early 1930s highlighted the continued problems of high density levels, overcrowding and slum conditions which dogged all urban areas.[70] The problem in London was always greater than anywhere else because of its sheer size.[71] Despite the scale of Becontree, the estate did little to ease the chronic overcrowding problems in the East End. Initial plans had been cut in 1921 and, although the LCC had drawn up plans in 1919 to build 29,000 houses, it only succeeded in completing 8,799 under the Addison Act.

Simon thought that the main problem in London was the large number of families living in dilapidated large houses, just as it was in Manchester.[72] Construction of houses and flats during 1919–33 was barely sufficient to keep pace with the natural increases in demand and replacement homes for slum-clearance families. Some cities were more successful than others. During 1919–39, Leeds built more than 20,000 municipal homes.[73] In Leicester, by 1939, 35 per cent of the total 25,749 houses constructed were built by the local authority. Neighbouring Nottingham council developed 65.5 per cent of the 26,080 houses completed.[74] Birmingham built 40,000 council homes during the same period, even though it was much smaller than the capital. But Birmingham was still dogged with problems. In the mid-1930s, Simon and Inman pointed out that while Manchester had successfully abolished its courts and back-to-back houses for over a generation, Birmingham, which seemed to "have a gift of municipal publicity denied to Manchester", and which was "generally quoted as the city which showed the way in the reconditioning of slum dwelling", still had thousands of back-to-backs and courts.[75]

Slum clearance across the country was at first relatively slow. During 1919–32, Birmingham, Leeds, Liverpool, Manchester and Sheffield demolished less than 4,000 slums, even though they were able to build more than 100,000 council homes in the same period. Central government again gave a lead with the Greenwood Act, but local authorities still responded differently according to their own particular circumstances. Although some cities, like Nottingham, showed early enthusiasm for a slum-clearance programme (demolishing and replacing 3,600 homes by 1939), others faced large barriers.[76] While Tynemouth council eventually moved 9,000 residents from its notorious Bankside tenements to a new estate at Meadowell, the Housing Committee had a long battle against opponents from within the community and its own council.[77] Besides political opposition, there were more basic problems. Small towns like Tavistock were woefully inefficient. The Ministry of Health wrote to the Tavistock district council in 1934 ordering it to conduct a complete survey of housing needs. By 1936, the Ministry was again forced to write to it demanding details of all houses in its slum-clearance programme.[79] Later in the year, a government inspector visited the area and wrote back to the Ministry telling them that the Town Clerk was "exceedingly lax in every branch of local government", and that he was "distrustful" of him.[80] Bureaucratic inefficiency was not the only obstacle. As will be seen, Manchester dragged its feet over slum clearance because of basic practical problems. It had wanted to sweep them away in big, bold strokes, but stuttered because of the problems of building suitable and affordable properties for low-income groups. Grand visions could not always be implemented because of real, physical problems. Practicalities meant that the LCC condemned a mere 33,000 out of 749,000 houses and Newcastle only a meagre 1,000 out of 67,000 slums.[81] Hull managed to demolish only 1,058 out of an initial 3,445 houses because of its inability to build alternative and affordable accommodation.[82] The economic crisis of 1931 compounded the problem. Although the LCC had set itself a target of over 33,000 replacement homes in 1930, to be built over five years, it was only able to complete 118 by the end of 1933.[83] In Leeds, when the Conservatives returned to power in 1930, proposals to clear 3,000 slums over five years were reduced by a third, though they did promise to pursue a cheaper policy of reconditioning a further 9,000 homes.[84] This was barely scratching the surface.[85] Eventually, though, Leeds produced far more ambitious plans. The city adopted a radical approach when Labour regained power during 1933–35. It embarked on one of the most sweeping programmes in the country. A Housing Committee was finally created in 1934, fifteen years after Manchester and thirty-three years after Swansea. According to the Chair of the Housing Committee, Rev. Charles Jenkinson, housing was now "made the policy of the city".[86] Jenkinson was the Leeds equivalent to Manchester's Ernest Simon. The vicar of Holbeck, he took a keen interest in social reform. He was elected as a Labour councillor in 1930 and immediately began his campaign for housing improvements. Once in power, the Labour group promised to clear away 30,000 slums before the end of the decade, which, if it had triumphed, would have made it the most successful city in the country. In the end, it cleared only 11,132 houses by March 1940, leaving 64 per cent of the slums.

Grand plans showed vision, but cities were all too often faced by economic and physical barriers. Nevertheless, individual reformers offered drive and vision in some British cities. Herbert Manzoni, Birmingham's City Engineer and Surveyor, had a positive influence on housing policy from 1935. He was responsible for the large redevelopment of Duddeston and Nechells, a project unprecedented in its size and cost at around £6 million.[87] Similarly, under Jenkinson, Leeds thought in bold and ambitious terms. But discourse was rendered meaningless if it was unable to meet the challenges facing it. While Jenkinson maintained that "the cottage house is the best dwelling for the normal English family", the practicalities of the situation meant the council had no choice but to build flats. There was a fear that many tenants who lived near the city centre would be unable or unwilling to move to the new estates. Financial restrictions and land availability meant that flats were the only solution. These were the realities facing the council. While discourse played out on one level, with reformers and officials expressing what it ideally wanted to achieve, environmental factors restricted their scope for action. Leeds council eventually decided to build 6,500 new council flats by 1941. Although cities like Leeds, Nottingham and Manchester showed considerable opposition to large-scale flat building, several cities could not avoid the myriad of problems confronting them in the community. Flats still only constituted 5 per cent of the total number of homes built, but the inter-war period marked the start of a gradual change. Some local authorities welcomed the idea of flat building as a new and modern solution to their chronic problems. Newcastle had a long cultural tradition of housing tenants in what became known as the 'Tyneside flat'.[88] Liverpool and London led the way, building 60 per cent of all council flats between the wars.[89] By 1934, the London Labour Party agreed on a policy of discontinuing what it described as the dreary, monotonous and isolating cottages.[90] London was building more flats than houses by 1936. Initially, the Chair of the LCC's Housing Committee, Colonel Cecil B. Levita, had opposed flats, although he had given support to the earliest experiment at Ossulston Street in Camden. He was eventually replaced by Ernest Dence, who was willing to shift LCC policy away from out-county cottage estates towards building low-density flats and maisonettes in the inner-city areas.[91] By 1938–39, an estimated 76 per cent of all completions by the LCC were flats.[92]

The Modern Movement continued to gain influence throughout the inter-war period. A number of leading architects believed the Viennese workman's flats were a prime example of what could be achieved in British cities. This provided the inspiration for the Quarry Hill flats in Leeds. These were heralded as the best in the country, the most lavish of all flat developments.[93] Quarry Hill was the product of Jenkinson's reforming Labour council. Alongside him was the new Housing Director, R. A. H. Levitt, the man responsible for Manchester's Kennet House, a modest but, for Manchester, flagship development. The new flats in Leeds were built quickly and cheaply, using the Mopin system of concrete and pre-fabricated units.[94] It was a bold, modern and radical development of 938 flats, dwarfing the small-scale developments in cities like flataphobic Manchester. They were finished in 1938 and heralded as a great success. The flats were portrayed as an extension of civic culture, as 'an architectural ornament to the city' and as a testimony to Labour's radical housing programme. However, the euphoria did not last and the flats became plagued by vandalism and disrepair. They were eventually pulled down in the late 1970s, though they did last a great deal longer than many of the system-built developments of the early 1970s. Despite their success, nationally there remained an underlying reticence amongst many authorities and tenants towards flats. In 1938, the Mass Observation study showed that 60 per cent of tenants in London still preferred to live in a small house or bungalow.[95] Birmingham, backed by the Medical Officer of Health, continued to resist building flats. However, like Leeds and Manchester, land availability and costs meant that, inevitably, it was pressed into building a small number of developments. In 1930, the council sent a deputation to Germany, Czechoslovakia and Austria to look at working-class flats. The following year it finally agreed to build a prestigious development of 267 flats at Emily Street. The four-storey development was eventually completed in 1939, but, although it was followed by a few other developments, the number of municipal flats remained low. Unlike Glasgow, Liverpool and London, Birmingham shared Manchester's flataphobia.[96]

The problems of slum clearance and rehousing were also connected to the issue of affordable rents. Local authorities were able to exert considerable influence on rent structures during the inter-war period. Some produced radical schemes that were not always popular. Early in 1934, Leeds city council decided to consolidate all government subsidies available under different post-war legislation, and to provide rent rebates according to the income and size of each family. Unfortunately, the scheme proved not only controversial but a failure. Rents increased, tenants were means tested and only 10 per cent actually qualified for rebates.[97] The scheme proved so unpopular that the Labour council was defeated at the local elections, allowing the Conservatives back to power after only two years. Other cities attempted to follow the Leeds example. More than 100 councils had implemented a differential rent scheme by 1938, though they were more limited in scope than Leeds's over-ambitious programme which had offered free rent for the poorest families.

At the outbreak of the war, rents, slums and new houses continued to be a plague on all British cities. The housing reforms of the inter-war period fell a long way short of resolving the nation's chronic housing problems. There was a great deal of civic jingoism, of boasts about building the biggest and the best, but political differences, economic crises, low incomes and land availability provided serious obstacles. Although there is much to admire in the attempts by many local authorities to clear the slums and build new, often high-quality, estates, the underlying problem of inner-city slums remained. When they did build houses outside the inner-city areas, local authorities set the rents above the income levels of most slum dwellers. While the average rent for a slum house in Manchester was 7s to 9s, for the new homes it was between 13s to 15s. In Sheffield it was around 7s for the slum areas but 10s to 12s on the new estates.[98] Rent and transport costs also prevented the poor from moving out of Birmingham. New council houses cost 11s 4d as opposed to 4s 6d in the slums.[99] Rents on new houses were beyond the means of the poor. In Sheffield, a Survey Committee in the early 1930s looked at the reasons for people leaving the new estates and found that the vast majority of those who returned to the slum areas were driven back because of the high rents.[100]

Nevertheless, despite the problems, local government was instrumental in effectively institutionalising the whole process of suburbanisation for the working classes during the inter-war period. The war increased the hopes and dreams that local authorities would sweep away the slums and build quality cottages in semi-rural settings once it was over. Increased wartime expectations led to bold promises of reform, but, as in the inter-war period, economic and political realities were to lead to disappointment and frustration. By 1939, it was estimated that nationally, although 245,000 houses had been cleared, 472,000 slums still needed demolition.[101] After the war, the housing problem had been compounded in many cities because of the impact of bombing, though it affected some far more than others. While Manchester had suffered from a degree of bombing, it was relatively light compared with parts of London and the likes of Coventry and Portsmouth.[102] Reconstruction was a huge job, but it created a unique opportunity for planners and government. Local authorities produced plans of varying quality and substance, designed to give a vision of a bright new environment. Every aspect of the built arena was considered in these plans, though many were not actually a product of the war but were derived from inter-war plans. The land for the Woodchurch estate in Birkenhead was purchased in 1926, but plans produced for development were constantly shelved until after the war.[103] In other areas, post-war plans were not always introduced, and where implementation was successful it was often after decades of setbacks.[104]

While there had been some progress in house building immediately after the war, it was an understandably slow start for all cities. Nottingham, for example, was only able to build a meagre 179 houses by 1946, largely because of the labour and material shortages.[105] Like many cities, it had to erect 1,000 temporary prefabs, followed by over 2,000 steel houses. Birmingham and Coventry were the only cities to experiment with housing types during the war. It showed great willingness to consider a range of designs, including steel-framed and, after the war, system-built concrete houses. It did little to resolve its problems. By 1949, Birmingham council built an average of 1.39 new houses per thousand people, compared with the national average of 3.72.[106] The failure to increase completion rates persuaded them to use more non-traditional methods of construction. An initial 2,000 were included in the 1950 building programme.[107] But the problem was greater than just a shortage of materials. The pressing need to clear the slums, together with the continuing difficulty of limited land availability, led a number of local authorities towards supporting government new towns and creating their own overspill estates. Nottingham purchased the Clifton estate outside the city boundaries in 1946 and extended its boundaries in 1951.[108] The problem in Glasgow was even more acute due to severe overcrowding in its notorious tenement blocks. Even as late as 1964, it was claimed that it would still need to rehouse 500,000 tenants if it was successfully to reduce density levels from 400 per acre to 120 per acre.[109] It was estimated that 43 per cent of the entire conurbation's population lived at densities greater than one and a half per room, which contrasted starkly with the nearest conurbation, Tyneside, where only 19.8 per cent lived at the same density levels. This convinced Glasgow into adopting a substantial overspill policy.

Initially, there was considerable resistance to the idea of moving upwards of 250,000 people out of the city. Immediately after the war, East Kilbride became one of four possible areas for development, but difficulties meant it remained the only town to see concerted building. Glasgow, like several other authorities, did not embrace the idea of overspill with any enthusiasm. There was already a great deal of criticism for the inter-war estates. Many tenants, especially amongst the semi-skilled and unskilled inner-city dwellers, voiced opposition. When, in 1959, the LCC moved 1,000 residents from Paddington to a new estate in Slough, the hostility was so strong that even local members of the Labour Party began to question the policy. Inter-war observations and criticisms supported the belief that estates were remote and ugly. A 1958 television documentary claimed that Nottingham's Clifton estate, for example, was little more than a "grave with lights".[110] Moreover, established residents on neighbouring estates were not always welcome. Local homeowners in Cardiff, Oxford and Dartford divorced themselves from new council tenants by building a high dividing wall.[111]

Councillors in many cities shared the opposition, though not for the same reasons. Some feared that decanting thousands of tenants would result in a loss of revenue. In Liverpool, Councillor Shennan pointed out that "one of the great problems in replanning is the realisation that the city's corporate wealth is in its rateable value", and that this relied on the spending power of its own citizens. For this reason alone, it was essential that people and businesses were "retained within the city's boundaries".[112] Similarly, members of Glasgow city council wanted to keep the tenants, and the revenue, inside the city, even if it meant building on some of the green belt land. In 1950, Bailie Patterson, the Chairman of Glasgow's Housing Committee, agreed that overspill could be avoided, but only if it built large multi-storey blocks, a proposal that was turned down because it was too expensive. Expansion of neighbouring towns provided Glasgow with a cheaper and less controversial policy.[113] It was also hoped that it would speed up the process of clearing the city's slums. Glasgow city council was faced with a number of growing problems, including the same land trap that affected cities like London and Manchester. In 1953, the Secretary of State for Scotland claimed that by 1960 there would be no more building land available inside Glasgow. It was decided to develop land at Cumbernauld, chosen partly because it was thought that this would avoid any wrangle about the loss of valuable agricultural land. The plans were delayed as, unlike other English cities, Glasgow was less willing to make substantial contributions to the building programmes.[114] Yet the pressure on land, coupled with its ambitious slum-clearance programmes, meant it had to make a contribution. It was being pushed by the Scottish Office, which had decided that, in order to meet demand, it would have to encourage overspill as well as high-density building around the city.[115] Although Glasgow council had been reticent about the financial implications of overspill, for it, and other local authorities across the country, worries about the impact of overspill were not simply about money. They were also about power and control. Overspill was an erosion of the city's status. There were also a number of political struggles. Feuds broke out across the country. In the West Midlands, Birmingham had a number of overspill estates at Droitwich, Tamworth, Redditch and Daventry, but these were an inadequate solution to the city's huge slum problems. There was a complex series of struggles not just between Staffordshire and neighbouring urban authorities, such as Wolverhampton and Birmingham, but also between the town and city councils who were competing with each other for overspill land.[116] In the 1950s, Wolverhampton made an initial agreement with Staffordshire to build over 10,000 new houses, but, due to Staffordshire making agreements with other neighbouring authorities, this was eventually reduced to fewer than 4,000.[117]

Not everyone was against overspill. Many estates were built because the receiving authorities could see social and economic benefits. In 1952, following active lobbying from Swindon council, it was agreed to expand the town to enable it to receive tenants from Tottenham. It hoped to boost the local economy and provide much needed workers for local companies such as Vickers.[118] But Swindon was only in favour of overspill while it suited its needs. There was no altruism involved. Local economic demands dictated the pattern of house building. As the economy slowed down, so did the need for houses. The pattern was repeated in the 1960s. In 1962, Pressed Steel expected a boom in car production and, therefore, the need for a bigger workforce. It asked the council to increase its house building to 1,000 per year, but as the car industry went into recession the need for new houses declined.[119]

If a receiving authority could see the benefits, then introducing overspill was relatively easy. However, if the sending authority was the only one lobbying for a new estate then it could prove extremely problematic. In some cases, it could force plans through, but, in general, the policy of overspill and slum clearance proved difficult to implement. Local authorities across Britain became frustrated. In April 1956, seven of the country's biggest cities sent an ultimatum to the government demanding action on the related issues of overspill and slum clearance. Alternative policies and solutions had to be found.

Tenant frustration and the decline of municipal legitimacy

Low completion rates and stuttering slum-clearance programmes forced cities such as Nottingham, Sheffield, Manchester and Glasgow to look for suitable alternatives.[120] By 1964, Glasgow had successfully made fifty-seven agreements with other local authorities for overspill estates. This seemed impressive, but targets for new houses fell short of the original aims. Natural depopulation, together with a large multi-storey flat building programme, rather than overspill, were largely responsible for its successful slum clearance plans. New building systems appeared to offer cities an ideal solution. Although central government policies and subsidies pressed local authorities into adopting new concrete systems, local authorities were able to influence the decision-making process. System-built designs offered a reasonable amount of choice for local authorities. One size did not necessarily fit all, and contractors provided a number of alternatives to suit different local authority preferences. The problem of the land trap, together with the urgent need to achieve higher production figures, led many local authorities to turn to modern building techniques. For many, this meant widespread use of the tower block. Some continued to resist. Manchester's flata-phobia was shared by many across Britain. Norwich's city architect, David Percival, struggled to persuade the Housing Committee to build four-storey maisonettes.[121] Percival, like many professionals, had come to see modern designs as a real step forward. The architectural press showed a strong interest in modern methods in the 1940s. Designers, building interests and some government architects promoted the ideas.[122] Post-war governments, committed to efficiency through modernity in social and economic developments, were receptive to new techniques. Some local authorities became keen on the idea in the 1950s. Tynemouth council proposed to build flats in the east end of North Shields in 1950 and started to develop five-storey blocks in 1956. It regarded flats as the only answer to its general needs and allow further slum clearance.[123] But this was nothing new. It had been planning to build multi-storey flats since before the war. Nevertheless, some members of the council perceived new designs and techniques as a sign of a modern way of thinking.[124] However, despite this, and post-war shortages, elsewhere there continued to be scepticism towards modern ideas.[125] Most local authorities were reluctant to introduce new designs, even into the 1950s. The cottage and the principles of the inter-war *Housing Manual* remained dominant.

Attitudes began to change in the mid-1950s. By 1955, a number of larger cities had started to embrace the principles of the Modern Movement, Gropius and Le Corbusier. Birmingham and Liverpool took the lead outside London. They had little choice but to innovate given the shortage of land and aversion to overspill.[126] Additionally, changes in government subsidies were actively encouraging local authorities to build tower blocks and other system-built designs. During 1955–75, an estimated 440,000 flats were built, 90 per cent in urban districts, with the majority of tenants coming from slum-clearance areas.[127] The choice of building types was left to the local authorities. Indeed, in the mid-1950s, the introduction of subsidies for multi-storeys was a result of pressure from local councils. Some welcomed it, others ignored it.[128] Again, local culture and heritage played an important role. Cultural traditions made some more receptive to new methods. The first steps towards flat building were taken by Leeds and Liverpool, two cities that had experimented with flats in the 1930s.[129] Besides the associations with modernity, high blocks offered a quick and easy way to fill small gap sites. Cultural traditions were important, but large blocks meant high output.

From the late 1950s, Liverpool was one of the first to use tower blocks as a means to increase production, resolve the land trap problem and avoid overspill. Birmingham, Glasgow and London followed. Each had its own particular reasons, such as sectarian divisions, which help to explain the choices made at the local level.[130] Undeniably, high rise was sold by government, design professionals and construction companies as a technological shortcut to social change. Studies of Newham, Birmingham and Bristol suggested that large construction companies placed pressure on central and, through them, local government into accepting new building methods. This was the central dynamic explaining the high-rise housing boom of the 1960s and early 1970s. Construction in these areas appeared to stress the importance of structural influences and not local factors.[131] However, while central government placed pressure on councils to increase output, ultimately local authorities embraced a range of different modern building techniques and designs which suited their particular needs. Furthermore, to a large extent, housing interests within central government in the 1950s followed local governments' lead.[132] The role of central government was concerned with administration, legislation and subsidies while local authorities created and implemented their own plans.

From the late 1950s, Birmingham intensified its flat-building programme. In 1952, A. G. Sheppard Fiddler was appointed City Architect. Like Manzoni, he was to have a profound impact on the city's housing policy. He believed that Birmingham's severe land trap could only be resolved through a policy of mixed development, a strategy he had first used at Crawley New Town. All developments included a mixture of large high-rise flats, low-rise houses and maisonettes. Sheppard Fiddler believed that the lack of suitable land gave them little choice.[133] From 1960, he embarked on a huge programme of tower-block construction. Falling production levels led Birmingham back to the high-rise option while progressive traditions meant that it embraced it as an example of a forward-thinking city. Birmingham was doing things big and bold, a reflection of its status as the second city and a centre for modern and progressive improvement. The mixed development at Kinghurst won a Civic Trust Award in 1963. It developed some of the biggest tower blocks in the country, including twenty-storey flats at Newtown and the thirty-two storey blocks at Lee Bank.[134] As late as 1965, 77 per cent of all completions were flats.[135] It built a total of 463 tower blocks, 14.6 per cent of which were twenty to thirty-three storeys high. Tower blocks accounted for 21 per cent of the total public housing stock, higher than Liverpool at 20 per cent and far greater than the likes of Manchester and Sheffield at 11 per cent.[136]

Other cities, such as Salford, eventually followed the same policy pathway as Liverpool and Birmingham. Although Salford initially embraced overspill, it was forced to reverse the policy partly because Cheshire failed to deliver on its promises of new homes and partly because of the loss of population at a time when it was already suffering from acute migration problems.[137] Its overspill troubles were compounded further by their unpopularity amongst many tenants. In 1953, Lancashire county council carried out a survey of residents in the Worsley overspill estate, three years after they had arrived. They found that 15 per cent had returned to Salford and half of those remaining claimed they would return if offered suitable accommodation. Higher costs and poor social facilities compounded the general sense of dislocation.[138] Moreover, like other neighbouring districts, it was worried about being swallowed up by neighbouring Manchester.[139] In January 1953, Salford's Housing Committee agreed to build a number of seven-storey flats in Liverpool Street.[140] The process was stepped up in the early 1960s because of the need to increase slum clearance, the pressure to complete high densities in a short period and the structure of government subsidies.[141] Yet, civic culture was also an influential factor. Local councillor, Joan Bryans, believed that tower blocks offered a new, innovative way forward, allowing Salford to set new standards and provide it with a modern image.[142] The idea that this heralded a new dawn for downtrodden Salford was highlighted by Clement Attlee's visit to open the first eight-storey block in 1956. The centrepiece was the huge Ellor Street-Broad Street site covering eighty-nine acres. When he was shown the plans, Eddie Hough, councillor and Labour Membership Secretary, remembered how "we all stood there and thought, 'marvellous' … the high rise blocks allowed space".[143] In an area notorious for overcrowding and a lack of space, this offered an exciting way forward. Discourse emphasised local civic pride, though first and foremost councillors were making decisions according to local needs and pressures.[144] The drive to build a high-status project was also an influential factor in Sheffield. J. L. Womersley was responsible for the city's major development at Park Hill. It received international recognition, and prompted one councillor, Harold Lambert, to comment that the new flats were "producing something of the fascination of the Italian hill towns".[145]

Despite the hopes, and the hype, the optimism of the mid-1960s did not last. By the late 1960s, some local authorities were quietly expressing reservations. In 1968, R. Metcalfe wrote to the Ministry from its Northern Regional Office in Newcastle informing them that, although approval was about to be given for a large new development at Killingworth, there was disquiet amongst officials. The new estate consisted of 1,450 flats and maisonettes and was to be built jointly by Newcastle, Longbenton and Northumberland councils. However, on the eve of receiving the government loan sanction, the Town Clerk of Longbenton telephoned Metcalfe in confidence to tell him that if the loan application was refused then his council would not object.[146] He feared that the new estate would be like a similar development in the town which had been designed to take tenants from Newcastle and which, he believed, was "certainly nothing to be proud of".[147] Metcalfe also listed other arguments against the scheme, including family preferences for houses over flats, high rents, expensive interest payments on construction costs, letting difficulties, a complaint that the contractor had "not been very successful" with other developments and a series of "technical imperfections to the plans".[148] Nevertheless, Metcalfe believed that the schemes had to go ahead because any delay "would be put firmly to our account".[149] He still expressed considerable reservations at what they were doing. Not only did he feel very "unheroic" about continuing with the scheme but he was also "haunted by the spectre of flats which may prove difficult to let".[150] Unfortunately, the costs already incurred forced them to continue, "despite all the risks it entails".[151]

Central government and local pressures pressed local authorities into adopting developments often against their better judgement. Doubts were soon to be well founded as schemes across the country revealed a series of faults. Problems were apparent even in the 1950s. The first government *Manual on Flats* was published in 1953 but was criticised by architects after only four years for being stale and not paying attention to external design, structural design, setting and landscaping.[152] They urged it to be more comprehensive and to encourage local authorities to build flats "intelligently and attractively".[153] The government reacted by asking leading architects to provide them with illustrations of future developments.[154] However, when the *Manual* was finally produced in 1958 the central theme was not design but "economy in building costs".[155] The emphasis throughout was on "savings". The Minister, Henry Brooke, commented that he liked the general plan, but confessed that he could not "pretend to have read the text right through" and that one of the civil servants had "took me round the photographs".[156]

Many of the new developments suffered from poor designs, inadequate materials and inferior construction. Bison designs, for instance, were afflicted with a series of problems. Their wall-frame system involved placing prefabricated concrete blocks together using a type of glue which, it was later discovered, was not designed to last as long as the panels or to cope with the damp British climate. The system was not adequately waterproofed. During 1965–66, flats built by the company in Glasgow revealed serious flaws.[157] One former construction worker described the standard of workmanship as "pathetic". The rubber seals were badly fitted and panels were used which were either the wrong size, chipped or cracked.[158] Chemicals were used which corroded the steel and the whole system was poorly fitted. The general level of supervision and workmanship was substandard. As early as 1964, warnings were given about a series of faults from its first development at Kidderminster. Even its low-rise projects were later shown to be badly connected. Thinner walls and wall-to-floor connections were built to cut costs, one of the problems that led to the Ronan Point disaster. Ronan Point was a twenty-two-storey block of flats built in Newham in the mid-1960s by Taylor Woodrow–Anglian using the Larsen Nielsen system. Only two months after its completion an explosion destroyed twenty-two flats, killing four people and injuring seventeen others. It was later found that the cause was a faulty brass nut connecting the cooker to the gas supply, leading to a huge explosion in one of the flats. The inquiry into the tragedy found that the explosion was nothing exceptional in itself, but it had blown out concrete panels which had formed part of a load-bearing wall.[159] These walls were so inadequate that the explosion led to the collapse of the south-east corner of the block. The inquiry recommended that all tower blocks using the same design should have their gas disconnected until the walls had been strengthened, all blocks over six storeys should be inspected by structural engineers and all future building projects and regulations should be amended.[160] This was the start of a series of revelations. In some instances, if the panels were difficult to fit then the workers would cut the steel ties holding them together. Bison had known about the design faults for years. Problems in developments at Glasgow, Kidderminster, Hillingdon, Oldham, Birmingham and Portsmouth were ignored. Panels had actually fallen off one development in Glasgow due to corrosion of the wall ties because of the chemicals used. In 1979, panels fell into the children's playground.[161] When the Chief Executive, Peter Jupp, was interviewed he openly admitted that he had done nothing because it would have cost between £18–24 million to correct the problems and that would have meant bankruptcy.[162]

Tenants

The result of slum clearance and factory-built homes was increasing unrest amongst tenants. From the late 1960s, tenant groups emerged in a number of areas. Some were broadly similar in aims, objectives and structures, though there were specific differences in the levels of achievement and participation according to time and place. A number of urban areas had a long and successful tradition of consultation between tenants and councils. Others did not. Although the late 1960s witnessed the start of concerted tenant activity, tenants' movements existed from the late nineteenth and across the twentieth century. In 1891, a rent strike in the East End had helped support the London Dockers Strike. Tenant action and organisation in Glasgow has been established for over eighty years.[163] Following rent increases in Leeds in 1913 and 1914, a number of tenants formed a Tenants' Defence League to resist what they claimed to be landlord exploita-tion.[164] From then until the outbreak of the war, the League's activities centred on a campaign to persuade the council to embark on a more extensive programme of municipal house building.[165] Tenant action was evident in Birmingham's new estates in the 1920s. Various groups were formed that encour-aged gardening, co-operatively buying seeds and plants, hiring out garden tools and books. Others arranged lectures and passed on complaints to the council. On one estate, tenant pressure led to a new telephone box and letter box.[166] Labour's radical rebate system in Leeds led to a further rent strike in 1934. In the late 1930s, there was a series of campaigns by unemployed workers' organisations against high rents and evictions. After the war, tenant associations were created on new estates and new towns across the country. This growth led to the creation of the National Association of Tenants and Residents in 1948. Further rent increases in the 1950s led to tenant action across the country. The United Tenants Association (UTA), for example, was formed in St Pancras to fight the Conservative council's differential rent scheme. One march on the Town Hall attracted 4,000 people, while a local petition had 6,000 signatures.[167] A long and bitter struggle ensued over the year and throughout 1960, resulting in a series of rent strikes, forced evictions and public disorder. The situation was so bad that the Public Order Act had to be invoked.[168]

Despite these examples of early protests, before the late 1960s tenants remained a largely passive group. Local authorities seemed to offer the only solution to their miserable slums and private landlord exploitation. There was little resistance or challenge to post-war reconstruction plans. One woman in Coventry explained that, whatever was proposed, "you sort of went along it zombie like fashion".[169] The situation changed as local authorities became the dominant landlord in the rental sector, as new policies became perceived as unpopular failures and society changed. From the late 1960s and throughout the 1970s, a sustained period of tenant action emerged across the country. In Sheffield, at least twenty-three groups were formed to protest about everything from the lack of recreation facilities to changes to rent-rebate schemes.[170] Public expectations, which had risen after the war with the welfare state and economic growth, were being frustrated, giving rise to a tenant backlash.[171] As in St Pancras, many groups were created because of proposed rent increases. Tenants throughout the country reacted angrily to the rises, leading to a number of bitter rent strikes in London, Glasgow, Sheffield and Liverpool.[172] Opposition to the rent rebate scheme in Sheffield dominated council politics from 1967 to the early 1970s.[173] Thousands of tenants joined the campaign, forcing the council to amend its scheme and leading to the retirement of many old council members.[174] Rent strikes were not the only cause of anger. By the late 1960s, residents in some clearance areas became organised in a bid to influence wider housing policy. In Sheffield, for example, plans for the redevelopment of Walkley led to the creation of the Walkley Action Group, which demanded partial rebuilding and improvement. The group, formed in 1969, gained a reputation for professionalism and political skill.[175] In the Beckton district of Newham in 1968, alarmed residents under threat of being rehoused in new high-rise flats joined together to form a petition against the proposals. They organised a fighting committee and within two days had collected 700 signatures. The council's town clerk was told in no uncertain terms that they flatly refused to leave their homes "for modern slums".[176] The council refused to have any dealings with the committee. Housing decisions were taken without any meaningful tenant consultation. Demonstrations and meetings were organised by the committee, but they were toiling under the illusion that the council cared. It had made its decision and was not prepared to make any changes.[177] In the summer of 1969, the council agreed to meet the committee, only to tell them that the majority of residents would be rehoused in three tower blocks. Members of the committee were furious, and vowed not to take up the offer. However, the tenants' committee became divided and fell apart. Tenants were faced with the stark choice of moving to one of the new flats or moving to another area.[178]

Ray Gosling led a similar campaign in the St Ann's district of Nottingham in the late 1960s. Gosling, and a very small group of friends, formed the Tenants and Residents Association. They began with a leaflet campaign to raise awareness and provide information to residents and then pressed the council to answer questions about plans for the area. Like other tenant groups, Gosling felt it was "madness to knock down good houses".[179] They campaigned for partial redevelopment alongside refurbishment. Although people wanted to get out of the slums they did not necessarily want to leave the area. Similarly, there was a great deal of animosity by tenants in many parts of Birmingham to plans to force them out of their communities. Long established family and neighbourhood networks were a problem which irritated the council, but which it found impossible to resolve.[180] In Nottingham, Gosling's group found that "there was an appreciation of cheap living … [tenants] enjoyed the shops, the variety of entertainment, the nearness to Granny and to town".[181] People were "as fearful, as sceptical of the new as we were", and they did not relish "crazy new housing schemes, higher rents, leaving neighbours for overspill estates and high rise blocks".[182] Gosling accused the council of being deliberately secretive and believed that redevelopment plans would only be revealed when it was too late for change. He accused them of behaving like "a dictatorship".[183] One resident remarked that she knew more about the "the avenues of the Kingdom of Heaven, than the planners streets". Yet the impact of Gosling's group was limited. While they raised awareness of the problems and the issues at stake, support was limited. They had expected an avalanche of mail in response, but it never materialised. Gosling was "heartbroken".[184] They had delivered 15,000 handbills over one cold weekend in 1967, but had only two responses. People believed that either the plans were not going to affect them, that it was a futile exercise because you could not win against the council or that they would be victimised if they so much as signed a petition.[185] They did, however, hold a public meeting which received large support and which rattled the local councillors who attended, leading some to condemn Gosling as a "devious, horrible little man".[186] In the end, however, new plans were implemented and the entire area was redeveloped. People wanted to be rehoused and the local authority was still the best way out of the slums.[187] The council sold its vision to the people. It opened an advice bureau and produced a glossy pamphlet with romantic images and "all New Jerusalem" inside.

With the return of the Conservatives in 1970, housing finance and the issue of rents again took centre stage. The Housing Finance Act of 1972 was meant to introduce the notion of 'fair rent', with greater emphasis on market values rather than the ability to pay. The National Association of Tenants and Residents organised a series of protests against the Act. Rent strikes and protests broke out across the country. In London, the new Act led to opposition from the Association of London Housing Estates. They claimed the legislation was undemocratic, inflationary and socially divisive.[188] However, just as Gosling had found in Nottingham, while they campaigned tirelessly against the Bill, tenants were unwilling to engage in a rent strike, undermining their efforts.

People were desperate for new homes and they still trusted the council to deliver. Besides, it was difficult successfully to battle with intransigent local authorities, many of which still looked down on their tenants with a dismissive air. Local authorities exercised enormous power over tenants. If Newham and Nottingham had made a final decision to move its tenants then it was usually irrevocable. The local authority could choose which tenants would live in which areas. Tenants were selected by local authorities according to their own criteria. Cwmbran council limited its housing allocations for people working outside the boundary of the new town to people employed in four factories (Royal Ordnance, British Nylon, Vanteg Steel and Pilkington's Glass).[189] K. G. Gunn, clerk of Cwmbran council, wrote to W. K. Morris, General Manager of the Cwmbran Development Corporation, denying accusations that it had shown preferential treatment to Llanwern steelworkers "to the detriment of other persons on the corporation's waiting list".[190] The same pre-war mentality towards tenants was evident across the country throughout the 1950s and 1960s. Tenants were faced with very little choice. If they refused an offer, they could be placed at the bottom of the waiting list or made increasingly worse offers, which would eventually have to be accepted because of the threat of eviction from their condemned property.[191] For families who did not qualify for immediate rehousing under a clearance scheme, the situation was even worse. People dealt directly with the housing departments and councillors, but they were lone figures and, as such, unable to organise and act.[192] Power lay with the council.[193]

Policies in the 1960s, however, undermined council authority. Mistakes were made which were met with a series of protests. Socio-cultural changes meant people were more aware of their rights and more willing to fight for them. Councillors often viewed tenant groups with scepticism and even hostility. Labour officials in Birmingham regarded local tenant associations as a nuisance.[194] This was partly because they feared losing votes and partly because a few groups offered a political challenge. Some organisations were overtly political. Left-wing groups used some tenant associations as a vehicle for partisan struggles with the council. In Liverpool during the early 1970s, for example, militants infiltrated the Tower Hill Unfair Rent Action Group.[195] Similarly, the rent-rebate scheme in late-1960s Sheffield provided a platform for left-wing students to get involved alongside local tenants.[196] These included members of the Communist Party, as well as the Labour left. However, even in Sheffield many tenant groups, such as the Shiregreen Association, were eager to steer clear of left-wing infiltration for fear of the "Communist smear".[197] A number of tenants became united over a common cause, irrespective of political persuasion. The

UTA, which had led the rent strike in St Pancras, had also been accused of being a front for communists, but they had been keen stress that there cause had "got nothing to do with politics".[198]

Although tenant groups were involved in a political struggle, it was not one which belonged exclusively to any traditional political discourse.[199] Tenants reacted to the circumstances in their own particular areas. In 1979, a dozen women from the South Wales Association of Tenants occupied council offices, barricaded themselves into a committee room, chained themselves to a radiator and remained in occupation for three days.[200] This was part of a campaign against damp homes, a basic demand for a decent service. Some local authorities recognised that protests were not necessarily an ideological issue and were much more aware of the possible benefits of developing participation schemes. From the late 1960s and early 1970s, some housing departments in London developed their own tenant participation schemes.[201] In the mid-1970s, government-supported research, carried out by Anne Richardson, led to the publication of a handbook on tenant participation in council-housing management. The handbook, *Getting Tenants Involved*, was designed to promote participation schemes across the country. P. R. Tindale, Director of the Housing Development Directorate, claimed the Department was keen to encourage greater tenant involvement in management as a means of improving the quality of life for residents of council housing.[202] The handbook was aimed at local authorities.[203] Richardson claimed that councils should form participation schemes because they provided the best method for regularly gauging tenant opinion and that the views of the tenant should at "all times be taken".[204] This was about reacting to the demands of the tenant as a consumer of a public service. She listed a large number of authorities who had, to varying degrees, involved tenants, either by holding discussion meetings, by including them on advisory committees or even granting them a place on the full housing committees. Twenty-three London councils had created participation schemes but only nine other metropolitan districts formed similar links. These included Leeds, Liverpool and Newcastle. Manchester was conspicuous by its absence.[205]

Some local council officials began to appreciate the value of establishing a participation scheme that would enable them to obtain and provide information to and from tenants. Following the 1974 local government reorganisation, the gap between tenants and council officials increased as local authorities were enlarged. Participation schemes were developed in a number of areas to bridge this gap. A few local authorities began to view tenant organisations as performing a legitimate role in urban politics. Tenant activity in Merseyside successfully gave rise to a series of complex participation arrangements with local authorities. These schemes allowed tenants to hold authorities to account. In Sheffield, the struggle over the rent-rebate schemes led the council to become more receptive to tenant consultation and participation.[206] There were a number of successes, with a series of local authorities forming different participation schemes from the late 1960s. In 1973, Bury council co-opted tenants onto the Housing Committee, Rushmoor council established two Tenant Liaison Committees and Middlesbrough council formed monthly discussion groups on eight estates. The following year, North Tyneside council co-opted tenants onto a sub-committee of the Housing Committee. By 1975, a total of forty-six local authorities had at least one tenant participation scheme, including 70.6 per cent of all London boroughs and 27.8 per cent of metropolitan councils.[207] Only eleven schemes had existed prior to 1970. Tenant action began to have an influence on housing policy. This was highlighted in the Netherley district of Liverpool, where tenants carried out a nine-year campaign to demolish and rehouse families on the same site. Their pressure eventually led the council to demolish all 530 system-built units on the estate.

Tenant consultation and participation has become an important feature of urban politics, long after the Left tried and failed to channel it. In the late 1980s, a series of campaigns was conducted against the Housing Action Trusts, leading to the creation of new tenant organisations. They were supported in 1989 by the new National Tenants and Residents Federation. These organisations did have an impact. Formal groups came and went, but the shift from a rigid and dogmatic approach to one that began to recognise the tenants' demands had left its mark. The former leader of Manchester council, Bill Egerton, pointed out that times had changed and that, unlike the past, "consultation these days is vital. Today you adapt to the wishes of the community."[208] The rebuilding of Hulme highlighted the extent to which consultation had become a central feature of tenant–council relations.[209] In 1998, B. Natton, the Chief Executive of Merseyside Improved Houses, revealingly compared housing service provision with the experience of shopping in a supermarket.[210] Tenants had become consumers.

The rise of tenant activity underlines the importance of analysing each locality. The politics of housing across the twentieth century involved an inter-action of different forces. While national governments gave local authorities policy directives, there was still plenty of scope for interpretations. Many local authorities created broadly similar policies in terms of building working-class suburbs or carrying out slum-clearance programmes. But there was also consid-erable variation in the detail and timing of policy choices. A myriad of other local factors also influenced policy in each urban arena. Civic culture, specific local problems, the different attitudes of key professionals and politicians and the influence of tenants combined with other political factors (national and local) to produce multifarious policies. While this section has provided an overview of the interaction of national and local housing policy and the variability of local responses, the following two sections will examine in detail how the decision-making process evolved by reaction to particular circumstances in Manchester, creating policies specific and understandable only within the context of the city.

Notes

1 A. Ravetz, *Model Estates: Planned Housing at Quarry Hill* (London, 1974), p. 19; R. Finnigan, 'Council housing in Leeds, 1919–38: social policy and urban change', in M. J. Daunton (ed.), *Councillors and Tenants: Local Authority Housing in English Cities, 1919–1939* (Leicester, 1984), p. 103.
2 Ibid., p. 103–4.
3 Daunton, *Councillors and Tenants*, p. 32.
4 *North Shields: Working Class Politics and Housing, 1900–1977* (North Tyneside CDP, Nottingham, 1978), p. 9.
5 Ibid., p. 10.
6 M. Barke and M. Callcott, 'Municipal intervention in housing', in W. Lancaster (ed.), *Working Class Housing on Tyneside, 1850–1939* (Whitley Bay, 1994), p. 23.
7 Ibid., p. 25.
8 C. Chinn, *Homes for People* (Birmingham, 1991), p. 9.
9 Ibid., p. 12.
10 Ibid., p. 22.
11 C. G. Pooley and S. Irish, *The Development of Corporation Housing in Liverpool, 1869–1945* (Lancaster, 1984), p. 36.
12 Ibid., p. 38.
13 Ibid., p. 52.
14 A. Olechnowicz, *Working Class Housing in England between the Wars* (Oxford, 1997).
15 Chinn, *Homes for People*, p. 25.
16 Ibid., p. 28.
17 N. Roberts, *Homes for Heroes: Early Twentieth Century Council Housing in the County Borough of Swansea* (Swansea, 1992), p. 2.
18 Olechnowicz, *Working Class Housing in England between the Wars*.
19 Ibid.
20 N. Hayes, 'Civic perceptions: housing and local decision-making in English cities in the 1920s', *Urban History*, 27:2 (2000), p. 214; J. Gyford, S. Leach and C. Game, *The Changing Face of Local Government* (London, 1989), pp. 13–15.
21 D. Backwith, 'The death of municipal socialism: the politics of council housing in Sheffield and Bristol, 1919–1939' (PhD dissertation, Bristol University, 1995).
22 N. Hayes, *Consensus and Controversy: City Politics in Nottingham, 1945–1966* (Liverpool, 1996), p. 26.
23 Olechnowicz, *Working Class Housing in England between the Wars*.
24 M. Swenarton, *Homes Fit for Heroes* (London, 1981), p. 164.
25 Ibid., p. 166.
26 K. Young and P. Garside, *Metropolitan London: Politics and Urban Change, 1837–1981* (London, 1982), p. 142.
27 Ibid., p. 154.
28 LCC Housing Committee minutes, 13 and 27 October 1926, cited in Young and Garside, *Metropolitan London*, p. 159.
29 TNA, RG 19/101, E. D. Simon, *The Anti-Slum Campaign*, p. 109.
30 Chinn, *Homes for People*, p. 40.
31 Hayes, 'Civic perceptions', p. 212.
32 Olechnowicz, *Working Class Housing in England between the Wars*.
33 Swenarton, *Homes Fit for Heroes*, p. 167.
34 Ibid., p. 169.
35 Hayes, *Consensus and Controversy*, p. 20.
36 Pooley and Irish, *The Development of Corporation Housing in Liverpool*, p. 41.

37   Hayes, 'Civic perceptions', p. 213.
38   Roberts, *Homes for Heroes*, pp. 51–5.
39   N. Hayes, 'Making homes by machine: images, ideas and myths in the diffusion of non-traditional housing in Britain, 1942–1954', *Twentieth Century British History*, 19:3 (1999), 282–309.
40   Hayes, 'Civic perceptions', p. 217.
41   Roberts, *Homes for Heroes*, p. 21.
42   Ibid., p. 34.
43   Swenarton, *Homes Fit for Heroes*, p. 178.
44   Finnigan, 'Council housing in Leeds, 1919–38', p. 105.
45   C. Grant, *Built to Last: Reflections on British Housing Policy* (Nottingham, 1992), p. 56.
46   S. Burt and K. Grady, *History of Leeds* (Derby, 2002), p. 217.
47   C. Jenkinson, *The Leeds Housing Policy* (Leeds, 1934), p. 26.
48   C. B. Levita, 'LCC Cottage Estates', *Spectator* (27 February 1926), cited in Young and Garside, *Metropolitan London*, p. 156.
49   Roberts, *Homes for Heroes*, p. 30.
50   Burt and Grady, *History of Leeds*, p. 217.
51   M. McKenna, 'The development of suburban council housing in Liverpool between the wars' (PhD dissertation, University of Liverpool, 1986), Chapter 6.
52   Pooley and Irish, *The Development of Corporation Housing in Liverpool*, p. 102.
53   Ibid., p. 41.
54   Young and Garside, *Metropolitan London*, p. 114.
55   Ibid., p. 154.
56   J. Burnett, *A Social History of Housing 1815–1985* (New York, 1986), p. 234.
57   Hayes, *Consensus and Controversy*, p. 27.
58   Olechnowicz, *Working Class Housing in England between the Wars*.
59   Ibid.
60   *Home Sweet Home* (LCC), p. 32, cited in Young and Garside, *Metropolitan London*, p. 155.
61   B. C. Skern, *Housing in Kingston Upon Hull* (Hull, 1986), p. 8.
62   Pooley and Irish, *The Development of Corporation Housing in Liverpool*, p. 42.
63   Chinn, *Homes for People*, p. 57.
64   Swenarton, *Homes Fit for Heroes*, p. 179.
65   Olechnowicz, *Working Class Housing in England between the Wars*.
66   Burnett, *A Social History of Housing*, p. 237.
67   Young and Garside, *Metropolitan London*, p. 158.
68   Burnett, *A Social History of Housing*, p. 240.
69   Ibid., p. 243.
70   Simon's influence on Manchester's housing policies will be examined below, Chapter 4.
71   Simon, *The Anti-Slum Campaign*.
72   Ibid., p. 107.
73   Finnigan, 'Council housing in Leeds,' p. 107.
74   Hayes, 'Civic perceptions,' p. 217.
75   E. D. Simon and J. Inman, *The Rebuilding of Manchester* (London, 1935).
76   Hayes, *Consensus and Controversy*, p. 27.
77   *North Shields: Working Class Politics and Housing, 1900–1977* (North Tyneside CDP, London, 1978), p. 35.
78   TNA, HLG 47/594, Ministry of Health Circular 1331, 20 March 1934.
79   TNA, HLG 47/594, Letter to A. Johnstone, 3 March 1936.
80   TNA, HLG 47/594, Letter to W. H. Howes, Ministry of Health, 26 November 1936.

81 Burnett, *A Social History of Housing*, p. 244.

82 Skern, *Housing in Kingston Upon Hull*, p. 14.

83 Young and Garside, *Metropolitan London*, p. 180.

84 D. Fraser, *A History of Modern Leeds* (Manchester, 1980), p. 420.

85 Finnigan, 'Council housing in Leeds, 1919–38', p. 109.

86 Jenkinson, *The Leeds Housing Policy*, p. 3.

87 Chinn, *Homes for People*, p. 73.

88 K. Pearce, 'Newcastle's Tyneside flats', in W. Lancaster (ed.), *Working Class Housing on Tyneside, 1850–1939* (Whitley Bay, 1994), p. 39.

89 Burnett, *A Social History of Housing*, p. 247.

90 Young and Garside, *Metropolitan London*, p. 187.

91 Ibid., p. 160. See also S. Pepper, 'Early LCC experiments in high rise housing, 1925–29', *London Journal*, 7 (1981), 45–64.

92 Young and Garside, *Metropolitan London*, p. 189.

93 Burnett, *A Social History of Housing*, p. 248; Ravetz, *Model Estates*.

94 P. Mitchell, *Momento Mori: The Flats of Quarry Hill* (Otley, 1990), p. 26; Ravetz, *Model Estates*, p. 19.

95 Burnett, *A Social History of Housing*, p. 248.

96 Chinn, *Homes for People*, p. 69.

97 Ravetz, *Model Estates*, p. 37.

98 Burnett, *A Social History of Housing*, p. 238.

99 Chinn, *Homes for People*, p. 61.

100 M. Fitzgerald, 'Problems of new housing', *Social Welfare*, October (1933), 68–75.

101 Ibid., p. 244.

102 N. Tiratsoo, J. Hasegawa, T. Mason and T. Matsumura, *Urban Reconstruction in Coventry and Japan: Dreams, Plans and Realities* (Luton, 2002).

103 L. Potter, 'The Woodchurch controversy, 1944', *Transactions of the Historic Society of Lancashire and Cheshire*, 150 (2000), 152.

104 P. J. Larkham, 'The reconstruction plans', in P. J. Larkham and J. Nasr (eds), *The Rebuilding of British Cities: Exploring the Post-Second World War Reconstruction*, working paper series No. 90 (University of Central England, 2004), p. 13.

105 Hayes, *Consensus and Controversy*, p. 42.

106 Chinn, *Homes for People*, p. 87.

107 Ibid., p. 88.

108 Hayes, *Consensus and Controversy*, p. 51.

109 R. Smith, 'The politics of an overspill policy: Glasgow, Cumbernauld and the Housing and Town Development (Scotland) Act', *Public Administration*, p. 80.

110 M. Glendinning and S. Muthesius, *Tower Block: Modern Public Housing in England, Scotland, Wales and Northern Ireland* (New Haven, 1994), p. 160.

111 P. Collison, *The Cutteslowe Walls: A Study in Social Class* (London, 1963), p. 17.

112 Ibid., pp. 160–1.

113 Smith, 'The politics of an overspill policy', p. 82.

114 Ibid., p. 86.

115 Ibid., p. 90.

116 Glendinning and Muthesius, *Tower Block*, p. 161.

117 Ibid.

118 M. Harloe, *Swindon: A Town in Transition* (London, 1975), p. 63.

119 Ibid., p. 206.

120 Hayes, *Consensus and Controversy*, p. 196.

121 Glendinning and Muthesius, *Tower Block*, p. 172.

122 Hayes, 'Making homes by machine', p. 283.

123 *North Shields*, p. 45.

124 Ibid., p. 46.

125 Hayes, 'Making homes by machine', p. 292.

126 N. Bullock, 'Designing for post-war reconstruction', in Larkham and Nasr (eds), *The Rebuilding of British Cities*, pp. 37–9.

127 P. Dunleavy, *The Politics of Mass Housing in Britain, 1945–1975: A Study of Corporate Power and Professional Influence in the Welfare State* (Oxford, 1981), p. 1.

128 Ibid.

129 Glendinning and Muthesius, *Tower Block*, p. 163.

130 Ibid., p. 162.

131 P. J. Dunleavy, 'The politics of high rise housing in Britain: local communities tackle mass housing' (DPhil dissertation, Oxford University, 1978), p. 1.

132 Glendinning and Muthesius, *Tower Block*, p. 174.

133 Chinn, *Homes for People*, p. 108. See also K. Newton, *Second City Politics: Democratic Processses and Decision-Making in Birmingham* (Oxford, 1976).

134 Ibid., p. 108.

135 Ibid., p. 115.

136 Glendinning and Muthesius, *Tower Block*, p. 259.

137 See for example M. Blunt and M. Goldsmith, *Housing Policy and Administration*, Occasional Paper in Politics (University of Salford, July 1969), p. 24.

138 A. Walling, 'Modernisation, policy debate and organisation in the Labour Party 1951–64' (PhD dissertation, University of Wales, Bangor, 2001), p. 270.

139 Glendinning and Muthesius, *Tower Block*, p. 257.

140 Walling, 'Modernisation, policy debate and organisation', p. 269.

141 Ibid, p. 272.

142 Ibid.

143 Ibid, p. 273.

144 Ibid, p. 274.

145 W. Hampton, 'Optimism and growth', in C. Binfield, R. Childs, R. Harper, D. Hey, D. Martin and G. Tweedale, *The History of Sheffield 1843–1993* (Sheffield, 1993), p. 132.

146 TNA, HLG 118/79, Letter from R. Metcalfe to J. E. Beddoe, 15 January 1968.

147 Ibid.

148 Ibid.

149 Ibid.

150 TNA, HLG 118/792, Letter from R. Metcalfe to J. E. Beddoe, 24 January 1968.

151 TNA, HLG 118/792, Letter from J. E. Beddoe to R. Metcalfe, 29 January 1968.

152 TNA, HLG 157/21, Confidential note to the Ministry, 21 August 1957.

153 Ibid.

154 TNA, HLG 157/21, Letter to J. L. Womersley, 10 February 1958.

155 TNA, HLG 157/21, Memo on the *Housing Manual 1958*, 27 June 1958.

156 TNA, HLG 157/21, Appendage to Memo on the *Housing Manual 1958*, 27 June 1958.

157 *World in Action*, 'The System Builder' (Granada, 20 June 1983).

158 Ibid.

159 TNA, HLG 101/815, *Report of the inquiry into the collapse of flats at Ronan Point, Canning Town,* London, 1968, p. 61.

160 Ibid., p. 62.

161 *World in Action*, 'The System Builder'.

162 Ibid.

163 C. Johnstone, 'The tenants' movement and housing struggles in Glasgow, 1945–1990' (PhD dissertation, University of Glasgow, 1992).

164 See J. Grayson, *Opening the Window – Revealing the Hidden History of Tenants' Organisations* (Leeds, 1996) and Q. Bradley, *The Leeds Rent Strike of 1914* (Leeds, 1997) at www.freespace.virgin.net/labwise.history6/rentrick.htm.

165 Finnigan, 'Council housing in Leeds'.

166 Chinn, *Homes for People*, p. 38.

167 D. Mathieson, *The St Pancras Rent Strike* (London, 1987), p. 10.

168 Ibid., p. 24.

169 K. D. Lilley, 'Experiencing the plan', in Larkham and Nasr (eds), *The Rebuilding of British Cities*, p. 47.

170 P. A. Baldock, 'Tenants' voice: a study of council tenants' organisations, with particular reference to those in the City of Sheffield, 1961–71' (PhD dissertation, Sheffield University, 1970–71).

171 Ibid., p. 2.

172 See for example L. Hancock, 'Tenant participation and the housing classes debate' (PhD dissertation, University of Liverpool, 1994), pp. 146–7. For a detailed account of tenant action by the city's twenty-three different groups in Sheffield see Baldock, 'Tenants' voice', pp. 211–52.

173 Binfield et al., *The History of Sheffield*, p. 145.

174 Ibid., p. 146.

175 Ibid. For tenant action in Nottingham, see R. Gosling, *Personal Copy: A Memoir of the Sixties* (London, 1980).

176 Dunleavy, *The Politics of Mass Housing in Britain, 1945–1975*.

177 Ibid., p. 250.

178 Ibid., p. 252.

179 Gosling, *Personal Copy*, p. 164.

180 Chinn, *Homes for People*, p. 101.

181 Gosling, *Personal Copy*, p. 164.

182 Ibid.

183 Ibid.

184 Ibid., p. 167.

185 Ibid., p. 171.

186 Ibid., p. 176.

187 Ibid., p. 203.

188 J. Hayes, 'The Association of London Housing Estates and the "Fair Rent" issue', *London Journal*, 14:1 (1989), 59–67.

189 TNA, HLG 91/564, Population recruitment for Cwmbran.

190 TNA, HLG 91/565, Letter from K. G. Gunn to W. K. Morris, 5 May 1960.

191 Ibid., p. 31.

192 Ibid., p. 32.

193 Councils often displayed a condescending, negative and restrictive attitude towards tenants. See, for example, Ravetz, *Model Estates*, pp. 122–4.

194 Newton, *Second City Politics*, pp. 86, 202.

195 Hancock, 'Tenant participation and the housing classes debate', p. 155.

196 Ibid., p. 217.

197 Ibid., p. 219.

198 *St Pancras Chronicle*, 21 August 1959, cited in Mathieson, *The St Pancras Rent Strike*, p. 10.

199 See, for example, Hancock, 'Tenant participation and the housing classes debate' p. 320 and A. W. Richardson, 'The politics of participation: a study of schemes for

tenant participation in council housing management' (PhD dissertation, London School of Economic, 1978), p. 242.

200 'The South Wales Association of Tenants' campaign against damp homes in 1979', www.tenant2u.tripod.com/quotes.html.

201 Richardson, 'The politics of participation'; J. S. G. Rao, 'Power and participation: tenants' involvement in housing' (MPhil dissertation, Brunel University, 1983).

202 TNA, HLG 118/2642, P. R. Tindale, Director of Housing Development Directorate, *A handbook on tenants' participation in council housing management*, draft circular.

203 TNA, HLG 118/2642, A. Richardson, *Getting Tenants Involved*.

204 Ibid., p. 3.

205 Ibid., Table 4.

206 Binfield et al., *The History of Sheffield*, p. 146.

207 Richardson, 'The politics of participation', pp. 87–8.

208 Interview with Councillor William Egerton, 25 January 2002.

209 See below Part III.

210 Ibid., p. 323.

Part II

The rise of municipal housing

3 Civic culture, voluntarism and council intervention

Across the nineteenth century, Manchester city council's participation in housing was restricted to occasional byelaws, producing health reports and providing paving, street lighting and a clean water supply. By the end of the century it was gradually getting directly involved by reconditioning properties, limited slum clearance and building a small number of flats and cottages. However, although the case for municipal action in housing policy was being made, the council remained divided between two camps, the progressive Liberal and Labour members, who wanted greater levels of direct intervention, and the conventional, mainly Conservative members, who believed that ratepayers' money should be spent on areas that benefited everyone, not just the poor, and who still held the market in virtual reverence. This battle raged for nearly thirty years. But it was not confined to council chambers. Local voluntary groups and social reformers supported intervention. The traditional language of limited action was challenged by leading citizens in the community. Key figures emerged to influence the local housing discourse. Some, like E. D. Simon and T. R. Marr, were to cross the divide between the voluntary and municipal sectors, taking their vision and ambitions with them.

Their knowledge and experience gave them authority in the housing debate. They promoted the ideals of slum clearance, professional planning and creating new garden suburbs. In this grand narrative, people would live in idyllic cottages in green areas with clean air. Although this was part of the national trend towards Howard and Unwin's Garden City Movement, the council and social reformers developed their own ideas and created their own vision and policies based on what they believed was desirable. This chapter will look at the terrible legacy of the Victorian period, the constant struggle by reformers to produce a more active municipal policy, the practical difficulties facing the local authority and the determination by an active group within the council to impose their vision of a brave new world. Civic culture, with its shared sense of values and norms, underpinned the development of these policies. The vision of key individuals like Marr and Simon provided the guiding principles on which civic culture and policy evolved. After the First World War, cottages, large new estates, quality designs, and careful planning would all be features of the new vision.

Although improvements to the lives of tenants were the objective, they were not a part of the debate or planning process. This was never an issue in what was still a patriarchal society. Both political camps understandably believed that their knowledge and expertise allowed them to make decisions on behalf of tenants. There was never any serious attempt to engage with them, no culture of participation. The council's perception and treatment of tenants paralleled the nineteenth-century relationship between charities and recipients. Tenants, it was almost assumed, would be grateful for the policies created on their behalf. They were recipients of municipal benevolence, not paying customers. This created an attitude that characterised the twentieth-century relationship between the local authority and tenant. While the council was sensitive to the pressing needs of the slum dwellers (and what it set out to achieve across the century was often bold, ambitious and to be applauded), it was not sensitive to their specific fears, aims and wishes. Policy was influenced by other factors, by what was achievable and by civic culture – to be the biggest, the first and the best. This was reflected in the large new Wythenshawe estate. What it failed to do, however, was to take into account the fears and hopes of the slum dwellers. While this was understandable in the context of inter-war society, it was to be the source of tensions and problems later in the century.

The Victorian legacy: Manchester, shock city

As Asa Briggs pointed out, early Victorian Manchester became renowned as the 'shock city', the first industrial city where all the problems synonymous with poor housing existed. Contemporary writers produced a series of damning descriptions and reports. The city came to symbolise the very best and the very worst aspects of industrialisation and urbanisation. Contemporary observers like Dr J. P. Kay and Engels highlighted the growing chronic problems.[1] Engels described houses which had walls "as thin as it is possible to make them", and cellar walls which carried the weight of the ground floor and ceiling and which were "only one brick thick". Cottages across the city were described as "filthy … old and dirty" and generally in a "sorry state", while the ones in the Little Ireland district were "horrid little" slums that afforded "as hateful and repulsive a spectacle" as the worst houses in other districts.[2] Engels claimed that people lived in "dilapidated cottages, the windows of which are broken and patched with oilskin", while the doors and door posts were "broken and rotten".[3] He believed that an average of twenty people lived in each two-bedroomed house and that one privy was shared by 120.[4]

Large areas were dirty, damp, overcrowded and in desperate need of basic repairs. Manchester's housing represented the human cost of social changes across the country. Contemporary reports, literary accounts and newspaper reports conspired to construct an image of 'slumland' as a dark and dangerous place. The conditions, and the residents, were portrayed as immoral and menacing. However, as will be seen, while they were often dark, dismal and even dangerous places, these were often a misrepresentation of place and, more particularly, people.[5] Slumland was not simply a construct of middle-class culture. Nevertheless, cultural representations of the conditions permeated the national consciousness. Nineteenth-century accounts reinforced the impression that these were places and people to be avoided, to be contained and, eventually, to be reformed. Accounts such as Elizabeth Gaskell's *Mary Barton* gave readers a distinctly middle-class insight into another world. Writing about the area around Berry Street, close to the present-day Piccadilly Station, she described how it was "unpaved and down the middle a gutter forced its way ... as they passed, women from their doors tossed household slops of every description into the gutter; they ran into the next pool, which overflowed and stagnated". She vividly depicted how "heaps of ashes" provided the only stepping stones, while, in a cellar dwelling, three or four children rolled on the "damp, nay wet, brick floor, through which the stagnant, filthy moisture of the street oozed up".[6]

Although these accounts had obvious shock value, and served to structure impressions of slumland, it was the unsanitary conditions, rather than the actual housing stock, which led to municipal action. The council first became involved in housing as early as 1844. Under the leadership of Town Clerk Joseph Heron, the newly established council obtained its own Police Act, giving extensive powers to deal with a range of social problems, including banning the building of any more back-to-back houses. Little else was done except for one brief period in the 1850s when the council closed the unsanitary graveyards and demolished a few properties to create open spaces. In 1867, the council was successful in passing another local Act which allowed it to carry out effective reconditioning work on houses,[7] but it was only with the appointment of Dr Leigh in 1868 as the first Medical Officer of Health that a more sustained municipal interest in housing conditions emerged.

Although a gradual reduction in the rate of population increase, together with the enforcement of local byelaws, helped to contain the problem, they did little to actually cure it. Poor conditions were a blight on Victorian Manchester. In 1889, Fred Scott reported to the Manchester Statistical Society on *The Condition and Occupations of the People of Manchester and Salford*. He described houses where the "walls were saturated with animal exhalation" and which "reeked the polluted atmosphere". Scott claimed that conditions were worse than could be "found in the domicile of any other animal", and that while pig sties had their particular smells, they were not "as poisonous, or repulsive, or offensive as these". He believed that if you put a pig in one of the houses and fed him well for a year he would still "come out a lean pig".[8]

It was only in the 1880s that an effective reform campaign began to emerge. In 1881, Leigh presented a report to the council, in which he argued that the city's high death rate was mainly due to the high population-density levels in districts characterised by dark, narrow streets, courts and alleys, covered passages, old and decayed back-to-back houses, low ceilings, damp floors and walls, poor drainage and broken windows. Leigh produced other damning reports in 1883 and 1885. These, together with other reports from the Statistical Society and the Manchester and Salford Sanitary Association, raised public attention to the housing problem, helping to create a climate of demand for action.[9] In 1885, the council formed what was to become the Unhealthy Dwellings Committee, and instructed it to carry out a full enquiry into the city's slums. Meaningful reforms were finally underway. During 1885–1914, the council demolished an estimated 27,000 houses and merged a further 3,000 with adjacent properties to create bigger houses. Cellar dwellings, banned since the mid-nineteenth century, now virtually disappeared.

Two factors underpinned the drift towards direct intervention. First, in 1890 the government passed the Housing of the Working Classes Act. The Royal Commission Report on the Housing of the Working Classes, 1884–85, had highlighted the problem of overcrowding and deficient housing conditions but, despite its detail and recognition of the complexity of the issue, it still believed that individual moral reform and a market approach provided the best solutions. The new legislation, however, signified an important change. It forced local authorities to take more decisive action to clear the worst slum areas and replace demolished homes. In 1889, the new Medical Officer of Health, Dr Tatham, reported that one area of Ancoats was so bad that it should be designated an 'Unhealthy Area', unfit for human habitation and, as such, in need of total rebuilding.[10] This, together with the 1890 Improvement Act, compelled them to intervene. In 1891, the council obtained all the property, land, streets, courts and passages, demolishing 239 houses and displacing 1,250 people. Other schemes for Ancoats and Chip Town (Hulme) soon followed.[11] Second, change came as result of mounting pressure from within the community. In October 1896, the *Manchester City News* claimed that the slum-clearance programme had been "imposed upon them by the pressure of public opinion and the requirements of Imperial law".[12] The debate about how far the council should get involved raged both in the Town Hall and the community. One ratepayer, Henry Plummer, writing in the *Manchester City News*, claimed that the council's earliest development at Victoria Square was the first step towards municipal socialism.[13] He complained that while municipal action and policy were generally designed to benefit all members of the community, the flats provided "accommodation for but an infinitesimal section of the population, and every tenant therein is being housed largely at the expense of his fellow-citizens". This, he believed, benefited "the individual little, [while] costing the community much". Like many others in the community, and council, he did not believe that it was the duty of the local authority to interfere in the housing market by providing homes for the poor.[14] Individuals should take responsibility for their own homes, not the community. On the other side of the debate were those who supported intervention. One letter in the *Manchester Guardian* claimed that the "poor are entitled to homes", and that everyone had a right to a large living room, well-equipped kitchen and at least three bedrooms for the larger families.[15] The council was criticised for being dilatory and for its limited scope of action. He claimed that while it was deemed acceptable for the affluent members of the council to live in comfortable areas such as Victoria Park or on Kersal Moor, and to "give armchair legislation to Angel Meadow, Pott-street, or Pop Garden", the fact was that councillors would not like to live in those areas. He asked, "why, then, expect these poor people to live as we would not care to live?"[16]

This late-nineteenth-century debate underlined how the press enabled citizens to talk to each other.[17] Debates were often conducted through the local press. It performed an important role as a conduit for the formation of opinion in the community. Across the twentieth century, the local press orchestrated campaigns and attempted to direct opinion in housing policy. Newspapers like the *Manchester Guardian* and *Manchester Evening News* promoted and gave construct to ideas which were also a part of civic culture. This was evident, for example, in the 1920s and 1930s with the development of Wythenshawe and in the 1960s with the rebuilding of Hulme.[18]

By the late 1890s the issue of municipal involvement was being widely debated in public. In September 1896 a public meeting was held in Hulme to protest against the council's Sanitary Committee's proposal to build lodging houses for 1,000 tenants on land purchased to build workers' cottages.[19] Resolutions were passed which stressed the importance of slum clearance and building replacement houses. It was claimed that while Manchester city council was a powerful body, it was not committing itself to an effective housing programme. Although it was accepted that members of the council would not "willingly or knowingly oppress the people", they felt that they had to highlight the "hardships which were being inflicted on a section of the citizens". They wanted homes for the people who lived in Hulme and not lodging houses that were only fit for tramps.

The influence of the voluntary sector

Demands for housing reform increasingly permeated civic life. Reformers and voluntary groups had always taken an active interest in housing issues. In early Victorian Manchester, voluntary organisations were among the first to react to the poor conditions, and especially to the resulting outbreaks of cholera in 1832, 1849 and 1853. Individual reformers and charities formed an organised response. Dr J. P. Kay's report on the *Moral and Physical Condition of the Working Classes* was sanctioned by the Manchester Statistical Society as a result of the first cholera outbreak.[20] The growth of the sanitary movement in the 1830s, through to the 1850s, inspired the work and creation of organisations such as the Manchester Statistical Society, the Manchester and Salford Sanitary Association and the Education Aid Society. Over the following decades, social reformers and philanthropists raised awareness of the problems and attempted to educate the poor through house visits and public health lectures.

The housing reform movement grew in strength towards the end of the century.[21] Three prominent organisations emerged. In 1895, members of the university established a Settlement scheme in Ancoats.[22] The Settlement became the focal point for housing reformers. The movement was led by T. C. Horsfall, Thomas Robert Marr, Alice Crompton, Avice Trench and Hilda Cashmore who, in 1926, was appointed the first warden of the women's house. Besides the Settlement, two of the most influential societies to emerge at the turn of the century were the Ancoats Healthy Homes Society, established in 1888, and the Manchester and Salford Citizens' Association for the Improvement of the Unwholesome Dwellings and Surroundings of the People, formed in 1901. The group worked tirelessly in Ancoats, one of the worst slum districts in the region. They held regular public meetings at public halls, institutions and schools, even boasting in 1894 an aggregate attendance of 19,500, with an average of over 700 per gathering. A few meetings were so well attended that people were locked out.[23] All meetings were free to enter and covered a range of issues on health and sanitation, though some members of the audience may have been attracted by the accompanying musical entertainment.[24] Importantly, the influence of the Ancoats Healthy Homes Society was reflected in the list of serving officers for 1901. There was a clear cross-over between the voluntary sector and the council. It included the President, Alderman Birckbeck, and committee members Councillor Boyle, Alderman Grantham, Councillor Grime, Alderman Walton Smith and the Treasurer Councillor Howarth. It also included the prominent social reformers Fred Scott and T. C. Horsfall and the influential editor of the *Manchester Guardian*, C. P. Scott.[25] The voluntary sector, with its own values and attitudes, directly crossed over into the council.

The impact was two-fold. On the one hand, it influenced its relations with tenants across the twentieth century and became an engrained element of civic culture. The council viewed tenants as recipients of tax and ratepayers' benevolence. It was the ratepayers who were subsidising the construction of new homes and, later, the rents. Also, tenants lived in slums and, like the poor beneficiaries of charity, they needed to be educated in the virtues of moral education. This top-down approach viewed tenants as much in need of reform as the houses. Enlightened employers across Britain's industrial areas, including Ackroyd, Salt, Rowntree and Leverhulme, had built model villages for their workers, providing some of the highest living standards in a tightly controlled environment. Tenants were vetted and monitored. Adopting the right patterns of moral behaviour was vital. Similarly, charitable housing associations, such as Peabody and Guinness, provided quality homes but maintained strict rules. Queen of housing management, Octavia Hill, believed that all tenants had to be trained in moral behaviour. Even the Garden City Movement believed that creating the right environment and managing tenant behaviour were not mutually exclusive. Housing reformers assumed that both the house and the tenant had to be changed, controlled and carefully nurtured. Council attitudes were reflected in the first municipal flats. The new flats at Victoria Square were built without wooden skirting boards because it was believed that tenants would rip them out and use them as fuel. Iron pipes were used instead of lead because it was thought they would be pulled out and sold. Baths were also avoided because they were an expensive luxury that tenants had never enjoyed and so would never miss. The flats contained communal laundries, drying rooms, a communal lobby, sink and toilets. One member of the Sanitary Committee, Dr Simpson, assured delegates at a conference on public health, that "the habits of the people would be carefully watched" by the caretakers.[26]

Tenants had to be watched. Their moral habits needed to be monitored. Reformists and philanthropists assumed that while voluntary groups had a duty to poor tenants, the tenants also had a responsibility towards them. The charity relationship was a two-way process of moral obligations and responsibilities.[27] Attitudes were highlighted at a public meeting of the Manchester Housing Company Limited, a local organisation that was "conducted on the lines origi-nated by Miss Octavia Hill".[28] The idea was to produce small profits that would be pumped back into the properties. The hope was that it would serve as a good example to landlords and tenants across the city, with landlords looking after their properties and tenants "doing their duty to the landlord". Following the 'Octavia Hill model' entailed management and close scrutiny not just of the properties but of the tenants. If they were given decent homes then they had to reciprocate by adopting the right values, showing gratitude and accepting what was on offer without question. It was still a relationship based on the power of the donor over the recipient.

On the other hand, the voluntary sector was hugely influential in highlighting the city's housing problems and in promoting municipal planning and building as the solution to the slums. From the early twentieth century, Horsfall, Marr and women reformers like Avice Trench, Hilda Cashmore and Alice Crompton worked vigorously for over thirty years in collating facts, publishing graphic reports and campaigning for municipal action.[29] Horsfall, for instance, was acknowledged as a national leader in the housing debate.[30] He was recognised as the most prominent figure in promoting German town planning methods and it was claimed that the 1909 Town Planning Act was passed largely because of his energy and perseverance.[31] Marr campaigned tirelessly for reform through both the voluntary sector and the council. Not only did he conduct social investigations and lobby for housing reform, but he was also co-warden at the Manchester University Settlement. In 1905, he became Labour councillor for

New Cross, a district of Ancoats, where he was to remain until 1919. Horsfall and Marr were the driving force behind the Manchester and Salford Citizens' Association for the Improvement of the Unwholesome Dwellings and Surroundings of the People. Their aim was to "awaken public interest and to quicken civic action".[32]

Raising awareness was a central objective. If people knew the extent of the problem, then more pressure would be exerted on the council to produce solutions. Marr led a team of investigators to examine conditions in seven districts of Manchester and Salford. They looked at 2,000 houses, examining a range of issues such as sanitary conditions, density levels, prevalence of disease, tenant earnings and occupations. Amongst the narrow streets they found an absence of open spaces, density levels of 47 houses and 203 people to the acre (as opposed to 42 per acre for the rest of the city) and chronic overcrowding with three to six people occupying one room.[33] Marr published the report, *Housing Conditions in Manchester and Salford*, in 1904. His aim was to uncover the "unwholesome and degrading surroundings" in which many people lived and to raise public awareness because, Marr believed, people must be "ignorant of the facts, since such conditions are allowed to exist". If people knew the facts then there would be an increase in social consciousness that would, consequently, lead to reform. He claimed that 212,000 people were in a state of poverty and that, according to Rowntree's definition, more than 75,000 of these were in a state of primary poverty.[34] Many houses were badly built or in desperate need of repair. They were frequently damp, cold, old and dirty. Numerous houses were without a separate water supply, while between two and eight houses shared a closet. Marr described how "in many instances the closets are badly kept, and they are often so placed as to offend all sense of decency".[35] He detailed the large number of houses with dark rooms, poor ventilation, overcrowding and lack of open spaces and playgrounds.[36] Like so many in Victorian Britain, Marr believed poor housing to be responsible for many social ills. He blamed the slums for poor health, senility, drunkenness, sexual immorality, betting, thriftlessness, the decay of family life and lack of civic spirit.[37]

Charles Booth added his weight to the report and its findings. He believed that the organisation had been successful in acquiring expert knowledge and had done "much to awaken public opinion".[38] This was the *raison d'etre* for the report and the Association. They were not labouring under the illusion that the voluntary sector would be able to solve the slum problems and build new homes. This is not to deny that non-profit schemes emerged in the early twentieth century. In 1909, for example, a co-operative was formed to build a garden village, Chorltonville. Spread over a thirty-five-acre site, the development was built to high standards. Each tenant was a shareholder with at least two £5 stakes. They enjoyed good-quality houses, wide open spaces and facilities. However, with an annual rent of £23, these houses were designed for the lower middle classes rather than the inner-city slum dweller.[39] They wanted the "the right kind of tenants", which meant everyone from the "happy beginners in life to the busy city man seeking rest after toil and a healthy home for his family, and to the good friends who are looking for a nice quiet spot wherein to spend the eventide of life".[40] Other voluntary organisations developed their own building experiments. Later, in 1926, the Manchester and Salford Council of Christian Congregations formed a new society, Manchester Housing (1926) Ltd.[41] The society was designed to build and let houses for the city's poorer tenants. It followed a number of similar schemes across the country, including the Church Army Housing Limited and Public Utility societies. They recognised that new council homes and rents were only affordable for the better-paid members of the working classes. Neither the council nor the private sector was providing sufficient and affordable homes for inner-city slum dwellers.[42] They recognised that "the needs of the clerk and the artisan have to some extent been met, but practically nothing has been done for the labourer with three or more children".[43] Money was raised by donations, share capital (with a maximum dividend of 2.5 per cent) and loan stock. This allowed them to build houses and reduce the rents by up to five shillings a week. Again, local women reformers Hilda Cashmore and Marion Fitzgerald were prominent members, along with Canon Thomas Shimwell. In 1927, they built twenty-four three-bedroomed houses in Newton Heath, and in 1929 they started a further twenty-eight. Three women members and an experienced social worker selected tenants on the basis of the size of the family, level of income (and whether they could afford council housing), and the condition of their existing homes. For the first twenty-four houses alone, the society had 700 applications. Some local pioneer builders were members of the Seven Cities Housing Movement, a national organisation that attempted to build experimental low-cost concrete houses "for the poorest classes".[44]

Despite their efforts, by the early twentieth century most voluntary organisations recognised that they would never be able to solve the housing problems. A consensus emerged which understood that substantial reform would only be achieved through public pressure and municipal action. While some were trying to build homes and help a small number of poor tenants, they realised that their overarching aim was to increase public awareness of the problem and pressurise the council. The Manchester Housing Society pointed out that the "inauguration of such schemes and the publicity involved focuses public attention upon the housing problem", and that it was this publicity that was "likely to do a good deal towards creating a stronger public opinion, without which the housing problem can never be solved".[45] In his foreword to Shimwell's 1929 pamphlet, *Some Manchester Homes*, William Temple, the Bishop of Manchester, hoped that its publication would "help to fan the flames of that shame and indignation which will one day purge our slum areas and supply the driving power necessary to obtain the houses that are needed".[46] Shimwell admitted that the charity had been criticised as being wholly inadequate to meet the huge demand and that the problem was so great that "voluntary private effort cannot solve it". But this was missing the point. Shimwell understood that substantial reform depended on the "growth of a well-informed public opinion".[47]

Reformers realised that decisive municipal action provided the only solution to the city's long-term housing problems. Horsfall and Marr campaigned for a comprehensive policy. They believed that the council should take responsibility for demolishing all of the city's slums whilst also being given a statutory obligation to rehouse all tenants, providing a complete plan for the development of the districts, roads, streets and open spaces. New building byelaws needed to be passed and the work of the Sanitary Departments needed to be extended. More inspectors were required and local authorities should build "groups of working-class dwellings, exemplary in respect of size and arrangement of rooms and of pleasantness of exterior, and provided with adequate yard space and with small gardens". Marr urged the council to secure new powers from Parliament and, as the availability and cost of land was a major obstacle in providing affordable homes, it should acquire as much land as possible to build municipal houses.[49] Increasingly, the more radical reformers spoke in terms of a grand plan, a new vision to be designed and built for the people by the local authority. Marr argued that the council should be the agent of change because housing was an issue of civic pride. He claimed that "all these disease-haunting slums" should be cleared by "cities so strong in civic pride as Manchester and Salford".[50] Civic culture should, and did, shape housing policy.

Their inspiration came from other reformers involved in the Garden City Movement and town planning developments in Germany. At the 37th Annual Trade Union Congress, Horsfall moved a resolution in which he demanded that local authorities should be more active in preventing the development of new slum areas by controlling all planning for new housing areas and by obtaining parliamentary powers to enable them to acquire large estates. Horsfall wanted Britain to copy the example of many large German cities.[51] He believed the difference was startling. Although both countries had suffered as a result of industrialisation, urbanisation and subsequent overcrowding, he realised that German cities had been far more successful in reacting to and managing the problem. While British municipal authorities had to seek special permission from Parliament to purchase land, German cities were allowed to buy as much land as they wished, actively supported by the government. German cities were encouraged to rate land according to its actual selling value, were given extensive planning powers, were able to establish housing bureaus and had a thorough and continual system of housing inspection.[52] By adopting the German approach, he believed, British cities would create a new order based on broad, tree-planted avenues, strict imposition of house-building laws, regulated drainage and sanitation and slum clearance.[53]

Civic culture: the cottage solution and the drift towards intervention

A planned, orderly, modern programme, organised and implemented by the local authority, was seen by Manchester's reformers as the only long-term solution. Reformers had carried out their investigation, thoroughly researched and debated the issue. In making their recommendations, Manchester's housing reformers were convinced that flats were inadequate for most people and that cottage-style houses were infinitely superior. This was despite the council's first development, a block of new flats at Victoria Square. The flats reflected the dichotomy across the city. Some believed they were a progressive response to the dreadful problems in the area. They were cost effective and practical, but they also received criticism for being cold, ugly and uncomfortable. London architects were employed to design and build the flats, but it soon emerged that many were hostile to the idea of flats. The debate was conducted through the local press. Despite his letter urging the council not to get involved in housing reform, even Henry Plummer claimed that the "case of tenement is foreign to the spirit of Manchester".[54] In 1899, the council hosted a three-day conference on 'Sanitary Progress and Reform'. The chairman of Manchester's Sanitary Committee, Alderman Walton Smith, sympathised with the general public 'parrot cry' against the municipal flats at Victoria Square, agreeing that they were too high and simply inconvenient for young and old alike.[55] Walton blamed the Local Government Board, who demanded that people from slum-clearance programmes be rehoused in the same area. The council denied any blame. It had built perfectly good flats (so good they are still with us today), but Smith felt that flats were simply inappropriate. He was joined by another member of the Sanitary Committee, Dr Simpson, who felt that "he would rather see, if it were possible, each family living in its own little house".[56]

The council remained divided. The *Municipal Journal* described the clear "difference of opinion at Manchester" between those who believed the council should build flats and tenements and those who were committed to houses and self-contained cottages.[57] Some members of the Sanitary Committee believed that cottages were "more in keeping with an Englishman's idea of home that he should have a cottage to himself, and not occupy a portion of block dwelling rooms".[58] Others on the Committee believed that any decision made had to be grounded in firm business considerations and that tenements were cost effective. The Housing and Unhealthy Dwellings Sub-committee and the Education Committee were equally divided.[59] Eventually, the cottage lobby was successful, a decision which the *Municipal Journal* claimed "we shall all endorse".[60]

This was a momentous occasion. A decision had been made which became a central feature of civic culture. Although the cottage v. flat debate continued throughout the twentieth century, the dominant discourse (with the exception of a brief period in the 1960s) developed around a preference for houses. There was a continual tension between a socio-cultural preference for cottages and the pressure on land availability. It had a profound impact on shaping policy in the 1920s and again in the post-war period. Although the combined pressure of overcrowding and lack of suitable sites meant that the council was forced to build low-level tenements and flats at different periods, it was always with reluctance. Preferences expressed in local discourse could not always be translated into action. Nevertheless, the local authority always attempted to resist building flats. In 1928, for example, when the land issue was crippling its ability to build new homes, the council rejected a proposal to build flats over cottages. The Housing Committee was so concerned about proposals to replace some smaller houses with flats by one of its sub-committees, the Housing Special Committee, that it intervened to pass a resolution stating that it was "strongly of opinion that the provision of dwellings in the form of flats is undesirable and should be discontinued and that dwellings erected should be self contained houses".[61] At times, the preference for cottages almost became a mantra, an obsession that characterised the new estates in the 1920s, Wythenshawe in the 1930s and the overspill estates in the 1950s and 1960s. It even had an impact on the tenement and flat-building schemes of the 1960s, restricting the size and influencing the design of the programmes.[62]

Despite reservations and opposition about municipal house building, a few grand schemes were developed in the first part of the century. A more extensive redevelopment of parts of Ancoats followed the building of the Victoria flats. Yet these were relatively small, piecemeal projects. A much bigger scheme was needed. In December 1899, Alderman Walton Smith announced that the council had received an offer of 238 acres of land at Blackley.[63] The influence of Manchester's emerging civic culture was already evident as the land provided an ideal opportunity to build allotments and cottages with gardens. While plans were being drawn up for Blackley, other small-scale projects were planned. In February 1902, for example, the council agreed to build 150 houses on three inner-city areas. In 1904, it finally bought the land at Blackley.[64] However, the council was still divided about the extent of its role. Wrangling between the progressives and the traditionalists held back progress. By 1910, some members of the council wanted to use the land to build a 'garden city', proposing to spend £400,000 on the development, which would include a new tram system. However, Tory opposition delayed the proposals until after the war.

As the struggle continued between the two sides, other small and often experimental housing reforms were introduced. In 1906, the Sanitary Committee was given approval to build three blocks of three-storey tenements in the Barrack Street area.[65] Four years later it opened the country's first municipal lodging house for women. Inspired by the Sanitary Committee member, Margaret Ashton, the house was seen as a bold step, costing £313,000 and providing shelter for 220 women from the poorest backgrounds. The council could boast that it was the "first municipal enterprise of its kind in England".[66] Manchester liked to see itself as the 'city of firsts'. Ashton House continued to be a vital shelter for homeless women throughout the twentieth century. The shelter was part of an experimental phase in council policy. In November 1910, for example, it was presented with a proposal to experiment with providing furnished accommodation.[67] The Sanitary Committee recognised that while it could offer flats, many tenants were still unable to afford furniture. It hoped to provide some furnished flats in the short term and furnished houses later.

Laudable though these developments were, they had a limited impact. They did at least show that the council was slowly moving towards accepting responsibility for social housing. Its greatest triumph came in the reconditioning policy it adopted in the late nineteenth and early twentieth centuries. This proved to be the most successful aspect of Manchester's pre-war housing policy. During 1885–1906, an estimated 500 houses were reconditioned every year. When Marr was given responsibility for housing from 1906, the figure rose to around 2,000 per year up to 1914.[68] By the outbreak of the First World War, most of the back-to-backs and courts were either demolished or refurbished. Conditions improved, with more open spaces and the abolition of privies. Inevitably, the war brought things to a standstill. But the pre-war council did leave a legacy. Although central government had obliged local authorities to take more substantive action, it still enjoyed a great deal of autonomy in the decision-making process. Pressure had to come from within the community to secure sustained intervention. In Manchester, reformers had constantly pressured the council, highlighting the problem and promoting intervention as the only long-term solution to the city's chronic housing problems. They achieved some notable successes. The emerging champion of housing reforms, E. D. Simon, believed that pre-war policies were "by far the most effective and far-reaching piece of reconditioning that has yet been carried out in England", and that "really bad slums, which are still common in other cities, do not exist in Manchester".[69]

The inter-war housing programme

Despite its success and proud (though not entirely accurate) civic boasts, council divisions continued to impact on housing policy throughout the 1920s. There was still no consensus about how to resolve the many problems.[70] Most Labour members, and some progressive Liberals, wanted to expand the council's role through the creation of a direct works department. Most Conservatives, however, still believed the council should play a minimal role and that it should focus on assisting private builders by passing on central government grants. A third group advocated a mixture of both municipal and private-sector development.[71]

Nevertheless, the underlying trend was edging towards the progressives. In 1917, the council established the Housing Special Committee to develop policies for a post-war rebuilding programme. Plans were created to develop over 3,000 houses on four estates at a cost of £3,000,000.[72] Although this was a positive move, some recognised that it was still woefully inadequate. Dr Niven, the

Medical Officer of Health for Manchester, estimated the demand in 1919 was for 45,252 new homes, with a further 1,200 houses a year needed to meet the natural growth in demand. The council faced a number of problems. First were the continued divisions. Tory councillors such as Cundiff and Holt were obstructive. They were responsible for delaying Manchester's housing scheme at Blackley. Tory tactics had meant that only 203 houses had been built on the estate by 1914. Second, although the council finally established a Housing Committee in 1919, its members and staff lacked experience. Developing a professional and effective department took time. It was two years before all the staff were appointed. Progress was slow and Simon admitted that their achievements had been "lamentably disappointing".[73] This was partly due to the problems in the council, but also because basic policies needed the sanction of the Ministry of Health. Simon complained about how he had to battle with the Ministry which had refused them permission to fix towel rails as part of the bathroom fixtures on new houses. This was all time-consuming. Third, any new developments required large amounts of land, and Manchester found itself in a land trap. Not only was there little available land inside the city boundaries, but it was also encircled by urban growth from surrounding towns. The city policy-makers thought and talked in grand terms, but it was faced with a large physical barrier. This was a problem that frustrated council thinking and influenced policy up to the 1980s.

Following the 1919 Addison Act, the political atmosphere in Manchester became conducive to more radical action. Government was committed to high subsidies, Simon was in charge of the Housing Committee and Labour had made considerable gains in the local elections, leaving the Tories without an overall majority. The new Housing Committee searched for suitable land for purchase and development. When it met in 1919, it agreed to build 17,000 new houses in four years. As so often during the twentieth century, the council had the big vision and had increased expectations, only to see it all ending in frustration and disappointment. Targets proved wildly ambitious.[74] Besides the lack of staff, experience and organisation, it was faced with labour and material shortages.[75] It only appointed a Housing Director, Lieutenant Colonel S. Smith, in April 1920. Even then, it was not looking for someone with specific expertise in housing but rather a man of "good business ability and experience … a capable organiser and administrator".[76] In October, the shortage of skilled workers was so serious that the new Temple Estate had only twelve bricklayers, or one trowel per six houses.[77] The council was so desperate to attract builders that it agreed to give the first hundred houses completed as temporary lets to contractors for their workers.[78] Material shortages were so bad, and pressure so great, that it considered a number of different schemes, including timber-built houses.[79] Alternatives included an experiment with twelve McAlpine concrete houses.[80] However, while these innovations reflected a fresh, dynamic and progressive approach to the city's problems, the new designs were not going to provide long-term solutions. In 1920, the Deputy Town Clerk reported that 7,706 houses were to be built but that a further 17,724 were urgently needed and at least an extra 2,500 per year required to keep pace with demand.[81] Demand was so urgent that it even discussed buying forty-six army huts in Heaton Park to convert into semi-detached cottages.[82]

Despite looking at temporary solutions, the council was always keen to maintain high standards. It wanted to uphold the best housing standards and was prepared to debate issues in great detail. Discussion raged about the minutiae of housing plans, including the angle and pitch of the roof, the height of rooms and the use of bricks for facings.[83] It agreed to accept the high standards set by Tudor Walters for room sizes, facing bricks on the front and sides, 45 per cent angled rooms (30 per cent for slates) and minimum heights of eight feet for internal rooms and upstairs bathrooms.[84] The Women's Advisory Committee made its own series of recommendations, including modifying door panels, changing window hinges to make them easier to clean and make them draught and weather proof, changing toilet windows, parlour sizes and larger windows.[85]

Standards were important. New houses were to be a reflection of civic pride. But the overall impact remained limited. By 1921, it had built a mere 546 houses. The pressure was so great that the council decided to use subsidies to promote and stimulate private house building. In what became known as the 'Manchester Housing Policy', this was to become an integral part of Chamberlain's new Act.[86] The only problem was that it led to a temporary suspension in the municipal programme and it was only with the Wheatley Act in 1924 that the council was able to renew its building plans.[87] A number of problems had dogged the programme, including a dispute with the plumbers and a bricklayer's strike which lasted for nearly four months (by which time many of the bricklayers had found other jobs).[88] It had only managed to build 4,378 houses by 1925.[89] The era of broken promises and frustrated dreams had begun. It was to be a familiar story throughout the century.

A more realistic target of 10,000 completions was agreed in 1925. Steady progress was made throughout the mid-to-late 1920s, though, again, the programme was frustrated by strike action. In 1927, one Labour member of the council criticised the Housing Committee for failing to meet demand.[90] Councillor Westcott replied that union disputes over demarcation lines had led to a nine-month delay on 500 houses, while other strikes during 1919–24 had led to an aggregate delay of over ten months.[91] During 1927–29, the council managed to complete an average of 2,500 houses a year and by 1929 the Housing Director reported that, of the 10,000 target, it was now building 9,006 new houses on a number of sites, including Withington (2,042), Kingsway (1,392), Ladybarn (1,110) and Barlow Moor Road (1,404). The Housing Committee was so proud of its achievements that in May it agreed to pay for a memorial tablet to celebrate the completion of its 10,000th house on the Moat Withington Estate.[92]

Yet the underlying problem remained – lack of available land. The Housing Committee was so desperate that in 1929 it asked the Chair of the Sites sub-committee and the City Surveyor to search for any available plots of land of over five acres which it felt suitable for housing.[93] By August it had identified three areas at Chorlton, Briscoe Lane and Newton Heath.[94] But these were small extensions of existing schemes. The Medical Officer of Health, Veitch Clark, underlined the problem. In 1928, he reported that to meet natural growth in demand, and to carry out basic slum clearance, a total of 47,650 houses would be needed by 1936.[95] If the council successfully completed its targets for house completions, it would still leave a shortfall of over 37,500.[96] The city had to expand southwards.

Simon, civic culture and Wythenshawe

Throughout much of the 1920s, it was hoped that this expansion would come in the form of a huge new project at Wythenshawe, just outside Manchester's southern border. The city's progressives, led by Ernest Simon, his wife Shena and Alderman Jackson, were convinced that this was the answer. Civic culture provided the points of reference. They wanted to build the biggest and the best municipal housing estate in the country. Manchester would be the lead city and the council would be at the heart of the new development.[97] Simon emerged as the driving force behind the Wythenshawe project. Educated at Eton and Cambridge, Simon became involved in public life at an early age.[98] Municipal politics, housing and Manchester were his main interests. In 1912, he was elected on to the city council aged thirty-three. Simon and his wife became deeply involved in Manchester's circle of progressive New Liberals, which included the editor of the *Manchester Guardian*, C. P. Scott.

The city's housing problems were the main focus for their attentions. In December 1919, J. Luke, the City Surveyor, reported that Wythenshawe might provide the answer to the land trap.[99] Wythenshawe was ten miles from the city centre but would offer an idyllic location for a new suburbia for working-class tenants. He claimed it would "form one of the finest Garden Cities in the U.K.".[100] The Committee employed Professor Patrick Abercrombie from Liverpool University to report on the suitability of the land and, early in 1920, he confirmed that it would make a good site.[101] The only problem was that the owner, Lord Thomas Egerton of Tatton, was unwilling to sell. This, coupled with Tory resistance in the council, meant the scheme suffered a series of long delays. The progressive wing of Manchester politics became increasingly frustrated. In 1924, Ernest Simon was elected MP for Withington, restricting his ability to influence the scheme. But he, his wife and their supporters continued to campaign for the scheme. They were convinced that it provided the only viable answer to the city's chronic problems.

Moreover, it was an ideal platform to develop a greater sense of civic pride.

The two were inextricably linked in the minds of reformers. Slums were a shameful reflection of the city's failings. The new estate would be a shining example of its success. In a letter to the *Manchester Guardian* in 1925, Shena Simon called on the council to be bold and creative. Again the local press provided the vehicle for public debate. She wrote that there was only one chance of doing something "big and imaginative to ensure that at least one part of the city shall be beautiful for all time", and that now was the time to "begin a new and more imaginative policy".[102] Civic culture, history and tradition had established a framework for policy production. She claimed that their forefathers on the city council had shown "courage and imagination in financing the Ship Canal, in building the College of Technology, in going to Thirlmere for their water". Simon condemned the lack of action over the previous twenty years, claiming that it showed a deplorable "lacking in initiative", but that the council was now in a position to put it all right by taking a "broad and imaginative view of their duties".[103] The progressives believed Manchester's civic culture demanded that the council take the initiative, show imagination and be bold, just as it had done in the past. In a public meeting in February 1926, Alderman Jackson argued that he could "scarcely recall an instance where the big view, the bold policy and action, had proved to be wrong", and that the "whole history of local government was filled with the records of lost opportunity". Jackson boldly exclaimed that "Manchester had a reputation for doing big things", and that developing Wythenshawe would continue the tradition.[104] At times, the supporters of the scheme displayed a form of civic jingoism that bristled with pride. In the 1930s, Leonard Heywood, the Housing Director, described the scheme as "a courageous experiment and a model of forethought and planning to the rest of the world".[105] The drive, vision and passion of the progressives was underlined when the Simons tried to force the pace of change by purchasing 250 acres of Wythenshawe Hall and Park which they gave to the council "for the people of Manchester".[106] Simon believed that Wythenshawe was the most important example of town planning and of a garden satellite town in the country. He later described it as the "most imaginative and important enterprise" undertaken by the council, and that it was all conceived on "such a scale and has been so well planned that it is certainly the most important experiment in satellite-garden-town building which is now going on in England – and perhaps anywhere else".[107]

Civic pride determined that Manchester would build the best estate in England or "anywhere else". Social reform was important to ease the plight of the poor and the working classes, but civic jingoism was a vital driving force. Eventually it was agreed to build a satellite garden town, as opposed to a totally self-contained garden city, with a population that it was hoped would rise to 100,000. People would work in existing industrial centres such as Trafford Park, but this was to create a major problem. It added travel expenses on to the weekly working-class budget, pushing it beyond the means of the poorer slum dwellers.[108] Nevertheless, Wythenshawe's supporters believed this was the only way forward. It would provide working-class families with the same benefits that were enjoyed by the middle classes. During the Town Planning Exhibition and Conference held in Manchester in 1922, it was made clear that the inspiration for the idea came from one of the speakers, Ebenezer Howard. Simon had an almost utopian vision. He passionately believed that Manchester could build the biggest and the best housing development. Working-class tenants would move out to a new suburbia where they would enjoy "houses of a good standard", and "where they would get light and air".[109] A suburban ideal, with clean, fresh air, open spaces and high-quality cottage-style houses would set a new benchmark in housing, and it would be created by the council. Simon articulated his vision to the wider audience, though he acknowledged and appreciated the role of Alderman Jackson and other "enthusiastic and devoted workers" for their drive and ambition "in carrying this great project through to success".[110]

There was one basic problem with this idealistic vision, this grand discourse – it was not shared by others, either in the council, the city or the neighbouring districts in Cheshire. Neither was it necessarily shared by the tenants. From the outset, there was considerable Tory resistance to the idea of the council building such a large estate. Councillors expressed opposition to the Abercrombie report, claiming that there was sufficient land in the city boundaries to satisfy its needs, that the estate was not needed for years and that it was all too expensive.[111] Others were against the council developing its own direct works to build the new houses. Opposition and delaying tactics meant that the issue dragged on until 1926. Further support for the opposition came from the Conservative *Manchester City News*, the Manchester and District House Builders Association and the Manchester and Salford Property Owners and Ratepayers Association. Nevertheless, the council pressed ahead. In 1926, it finally agreed to purchase the estate. By now Tatton had died and his son, although initially reticent about selling, agreed to let the council buy the land, incorporate it into the city and develop it for new housing. Yet this was only finalised in 1929, and building only began in 1932. One of the problems faced by the council was the resistance of Cheshire county council and many of its residents.

Leading the Cheshire resistance were the county council, Bucklow rural district council and other local authorities. Dealings between the two sides became fraught and bitter.[112] As will be seen later, this became a familiar story in the relations between Manchester and Cheshire for much of the century and was to have a marked impact on housing policy in the post-war period. Some were afraid that Manchester was trying to expand its territory into north Cheshire. Worries were expressed in 1920 when a number of Cheshire authorities objected to various developments under the South Manchester Town Planning Schemes.[113] In 1926, Cheshire county council, Bucklow RDC and other local authorities combined to fight Manchester's plans to purchase and incorporate the Wythenshawe estate. In their petition to the House of Commons they listed the objections of ratepayers, again claiming that there was enough available land in the city, that the estate was unsuitable for working-class housing and that Manchester's real objective was to expand into Cheshire.

Despite the sustained opposition, the council was finally able to purchase the estate in 1926, though even this was not completed until the following year. In 1927, it applied to Parliament for an extension to its boundaries to include the three parishes covering the Wythenshawe area. Initially, Parliament rejected the request. But the issue was becoming ever-more urgent. Lack of land within the city meant that the existing building programme was slowing down. In 1930, it again applied to Parliament. This time it was successful. After approving the Bill, the Wythenshawe Estate Special Committee could finally press ahead. In 1928, it accepted a town-planning scheme for the development of the estate from Barry Parker. Parker already had an international reputation and was the central figure in the development of Letchworth and Hampstead Garden Suburb. His appointment reiterated the council's ambition to build the best housing development in the country. Of the 5,500 acres for development, 2,000 acres were set aside for agriculture, playing fields and open spaces. The remainder was to be used for houses, schools, shops, a civic centre and other facilities. In 1929, the Housing Committee agreed to build 10,000 houses at a cost of £5 million.[114]

Despite its lofty ambitions, the development of Wythenshawe was fraught with problems and disappointments. Civic dreams, and boasts, were often undermined by harsh realities. When it finally pressed ahead with the scheme, it proved difficult to meet its own targets. Building eventually began in 1932, but only 400 houses were constructed. By 1946 it had completed 8,145, around one-quarter of all completions for Manchester between the wars.[115] The estate did provide houses for the city's general needs. Yet this was barely sufficient to keep up with growing demand. In a letter to the Housing Committee in February 1931, Veitch Clark estimated that 42,100 houses were needed to meet demand by 1945.[116] Besides, many of the new houses, especially those in Wythenshawe, remained beyond the means of the thousands of inner-city slum dwellers. Subsidies were insufficient for lower-paid workers. The Housing and Town Planning Conference, held at the Town Hall on 17 April 1928, stressed that there was a "very serious shortage of houses which can be let at rents within the means of the lower paid wage earners", and that no more houses could be built "under the present economic conditions without adequate State assistance".[117] In September, the Housing Committee expressed concern about the increase in the number of unemployed builders due to a reduction in the number of houses being built. At the same time, it stressed that it was unable to build enough houses to meet demand.[118] Even subsidies for private-sector developments had been brought to a standstill during 1927–28 because of problems with government finances. The numbers employed in construction again fell from 3,829 in May 1928 to 2,740 in September 1928 and then steadily reduced further to 1,243 in October 1929.[119] The National Federation of Trades Operatives wrote to the

Housing Committee in September 1928, expressing its concerns that the number of workers employed in Direct Works had fallen by nearly a half over the year.[120] By the end of 1930, the number of employed workers fell to only 968 and by November 1931 it had dropped to an alarming 332.[121] The situation was dire.[122] Manchester was no different from most of the country. Unemployment in general was becoming a huge cause for concern. The national economic situation was deteriorating so rapidly that H. W. Francis from the Ministry of Health wrote to the council (and to all major local authorities) urging them to review their situation and to make every effort to build as many homes as possible. He asked them to complete 20 per cent of its total programme in one year in the hope that it would alleviate the unemployment situation.[123]

The reduction in the numbers employed in building reflected a change in policy direction. From 1930, there was to be a shift away from general needs provision towards slum clearance. Despite the problems in meeting its targets, finding sites and securing sufficient government funding, the fact was that by 1930 attitudes towards housing, towards solving the problems of the slums and overcrowding, together with a shift in the perceived role of the local authority, had transformed policy. In 1930, the Housing Committee was finally made a Standing Committee. It now enjoyed a greater level of autonomy. All building, letting and management powers were finally transferred to the Committee.[124] It had earned the recognition. The Housing Committee had been created from scratch and yet it had overcome many problems and tried to stay at the forefront of professional development. Besides hosting conferences, such as the National Housing Conference for Local Authorities in 1923 and the National Housing and Town Planning Conferences in 1928 and 1936, it also sent officers to the 12th International Housing and Town Planning Congress in Rome in 1929, provided material for an exhibition stall for the International Federation for Housing and Town Planning in Berlin in 1931 and played host to a number of visitors eager to learn from the Manchester experience, including Helen Hanning, the Chair of the Housing Committee for the communities of New York City and a housing sub-committee from Blackpool in 1928. The Blackpool delegation was so impressed that they wrote to the council praising them for the "scientific and statesmanlike way in which they have handled Manchester's housing problem". They even claimed that the city's housing projects were models of efficiency, while Cardiff's City Engineer stated at an earlier conference that Manchester was in "many ways leading the country".[125] The council was also willing to increase the professionalisation of its own workforce, approving a scheme for 'facilitating study amongst officials', in the Department's Tenancy Section.[126]

The council had made considerable advances since creating the Housing Committee in 1919. It had inherited a large number of slums from the Victorian period. From the late nineteenth century, debate had raged about the degree to which it should get involved. Social reformers and organisations had campaigned for direct intervention. They successfully influenced the discourse of civic culture. A few dynamic figures entered municipal politics, taking their campaign to the heart of the instrument they believed to be central to their dream for a brave new world. They promoted a discourse which stressed the ideal of quality cottages and of building on a grandiose scale. Disraeli had once described Manchester as being as great a human exploit as Athens, and people like Marr and Simon were determined to create a new urban model.[127]

The reformers left a significant legacy. First, the discourse of civic culture provided the framework in which policy evolved. Second, reformers came from a distinctly philanthropic tradition which transferred into municipal politics. The council's attitudes had an underlying assumption that tenants were recipients of municipal generosity. This was understandable in the context of the period, but it became engrained in council attitudes and was to have an adverse impact on council–tenant relations later in the century. Finally, while the local discourse on housing was often bold and ambitious, it was doomed to lead to frustration. Idealised visions were not always attainable. However laudable its efforts and ambitions, the creation and implementation of policy was riddled with problems. Not only was it constantly curtailed by government spending plans and legislation, but it was opposed by groups inside the city and in neighbouring districts.[128] An ambitious discourse emerged, but it was not always possible to achieve its aims. As the working classes moved out to new estates it was assumed that slum dwellers, who could not afford to move to areas like Wythenshawe, would filter up through the existing stock. The problem was that acute shortages and limited demolition meant that 'filtering' did not work as an effective strategy. Policy was about meeting general needs, leaving the inner belt of slums in need of special attention. The 1930s attempted to address this problem.

Notes

1 J. P. Kay, *The Moral and Physical Condition of the Working Classes Employed in the Cotton Manufacture in Manchester* (Manchester, 1969).
2 F. Engels, *The Condition of the Working Class in England* (Oxford, 1971), p. 68.
3 Ibid., p. 71.
4 Ibid., p. 73.
5 See below Chapter 4. Also, see A. Mayne, *The Imagined Slum, Newspaper Representations in Three Cities, 1870–1914* (Leicester, 1993). For a balanced (and robust) response, see also D. Englander, 'Review', *Urban History*, 21:2 (October, 1994), 309–10, and D. Englander, 'Urban history or urban historicism? A response to Alan Mayne', *Urban History*, 22:3 (December, 1995), 390–1. See also A. Mayne and S. Lawrence, 'Ethnographies of place: a new urban history agenda', *Urban History*, 26 (1999), 325–48; B. Doyle, 'Mapping slums in a historic city: representing working class communities in Edwardian Norwich', *Planning Perspectives*, 16 (January 2001), 47–65.
6 E. Gaskell, *Mary Barton* (Oxford, 1998), pp. 66–7.
7 Ernest Simon claimed that it was better than the national legislation in the 1920s. E. D. Simon, *How to Abolish the Slums* (London, 1929), p. 25.

8   F. Scott, *Transactions of the Manchester Statistical Society* (Manchester, 1889), p. 101.
9   *Housing of the Working Class*, City of Manchester pamphlet (Manchester, 1904).
10 Ibid.
11 Ibid.
12 *Manchester City News* (17 October 1896).
13 Ibid. (20 April 1895).
14 Ibid. (20 April 1895).
15 *Manchester Guardian*, Manchester Central Reference Library cuttings, 1896.
16 Ibid.
17 M. Bromley and N. Hayes, 'Campaigner, Watchdog or Municipal Lackey? Reflections on the inter-war provincial press, local identity and civic welfarism', *Media History*, 8:2 (2002); P. Shapely, 'The press and the system built developments of inner-city Manchester', *Manchester Region History Review*, 16 (2002–3), 30–9.
18 See below Chapter 6.
19 *Manchester Guardian* (9 September 1896).
20 Kay, *Moral and Physical Condition*.
21 M. E. Rose, 'Culture, philanthropy and the Manchester middle classes', in A. J. Kidd and K. Roberts (eds), *City, Class and Culture* (Manchester, 1985), pp. 103–14.
22 *Manchester University Settlement, Diamond Jubilee – Souvenir Brochure* (1954); see also M. E. Rose 'The Manchester University Settlement in Ancoats, 1895–1909', *Manchester Region History Review*, 7 (1993), 55–62.
23 *Annual Report, 1894–05* (Ancoats Healthy Homes Society).
24 *Annual Report, 1900–01* (Ancoats Healthy Homes Society).
25 *Annual Report 1901–02* (Ancoats Healthy Homes Society, Officers and Committee).
26 *Manchester City News* (27 April 1890).
27 P. Shapely, 'Urban charity, class relations and social cohesion: charitable responses to the cotton famine', *Urban History* 28:1 (2001), 46–64.
28 *Manchester Courier* (16 June 1911).
29 See below Chapter 4.
30 M. Harrison, 'Thomas Coglan Horsfall and the example of Germany', *Planning Perspectives*, 6 (1991), 297–314.
31 E. D. Simon and J. Inman, *The Rebuilding of Manchester* (London, 1935), p. 17.
32 *Municipal Journal* (May 1904).
33 Ibid.
34 T. R. Marr, *Housing Conditions in Manchester and Salford* (Manchester, 1904), p. 3.
35 Ibid., p. 4.
36 Ibid.
37 Ibid., p. 9.
38 C. Booth, *The Housing Question in Manchester: Notes on the Report of the Citizens' Association* (Manchester, 1904).
39 *Chorltonville, A Garden Village of Better Planned Houses* (Manchester, 1911), p. 5.
40 Ibid.
41 See also K. Skilleter, 'The role of public utility societies in early British town planning and housing reform, 1901–36', *Planning Perspectives*, 8:2 (1993), 125–65.
42 *The Woman Citizen* (15 July 1926).
43 *Manchester Housing 1926 Ltd*, pamphlet (Manchester, 1929).
44 TNA, BT 56/10, *The Seven Cities Housing Trust Limited*.
45 *Manchester Housing 1926 Ltd*.
46 W. Temple, Bishop of Manchester, 'Foreword', in Canon T. Shimwell, *Some Manchester Homes*, pamphlet (Manchester, 1929).
47 Ibid.

48   Marr, *Housing Conditions in Manchester and Salford*, p. 5.
49   Ibid.
50   Ibid., p. 9.
51   *The Times* (5 September 1904).
52   Ibid.
53   Booth, *The Housing Question in Manchester*.
54   H. Plummer, letter on 'The financial policy of the city', *Manchester City News* (20 April 1895).
55   'Housing of the Working Classes', Report from the Sanitary Committee (18 October, 1899).
56   Ibid.
57   *Municipal Journal* (6 May 1904).
58   Ibid.
59   Ibid.
60   Ibid.
61   Manchester Housing Committee minutes, 11 June 1928.
62   See below Chapter 6.
63   *Housing of the Working Class*, City of Manchester pamphlet (Manchester, 1904).
64   Ibid.
65   *Barrack Street Tenement Dwellings*, council proceedings (8 January 1906).
66   *Municipal Journal* (9 September 1910).
67   Ibid. (12 November 1910).
68   Simon and Inman, *The Rebuilding of Manchester*, p. 17.
69   Ibid., p. 18.
70   K. Brady, 'The development of the Wythenshawe Estate, Manchester: concept to incorporation, 1919–1931' (MSc dissertation, Salford University, 1990), pp. 47–62.
71   Ibid., p. 161.
72   A. Redford, *History of Local Government in Manchester*, Vol. 3 (Manchester, 1940), p. 226.
73   E. D. Simon, *A City Council from Within* (London, 1926), p. 203.
74   Ibid., p. 32.
75   Simon and Inman, *The Rebuilding of Manchester*, p. 24.
76   Manchester Housing Committee minutes, 12 February 1920.
77   *The Times* (16 October 1919).
78   Manchester Housing Committee minutes, 7 March 1921.
79   Ibid., 1 March 1920.
80   Ibid., 11 October 1920.
81   Ibid., 1 March 1920.
82   *The Times* (16 October 1919).
83   Manchester Housing Committee minutes, 1 March 1920.
84   Ibid., 22 March 1920.
85   Ibid., 13 December 1920.
86   *The Times* (17 March 1923); (26 March 1923).
87   TNA, RG 19/101, E. D. Simon, *The Anti-Slum Campaign*, p. 17.
88   Manchester Housing Committee minutes, 13 December 1920; *The Times* (27 March 1924).
89   Redford, *History of Local Government in Manchester*, p. 234.
90   *The Times* (4 January 1927).
91   Ibid.
92   Manchester Housing Committee minutes, 14 May 1928.
93   Ibid., 8 April 1929.

94 Ibid., 22 August 1929.

95 *The Times* (3 September 1929).

96 Manchester Housing Committee minutes, 22 August 1929; figures taken from Report to the Health Committee, 1 February 1928. In the minutes for 17 September 1929 they reported that Clark's estimate for extra houses was 40,795.

97 B. Rodgers, 'Manchester Metropolitan Planning by collaboration and Consent or Civic hope Frustrated', in George Gordon (ed.), *Regional Cities in the UK, 1890–1980* (London, 1986).

98 For notes on Simon, see Brady, 'The development of the Wythenshawe Estate'; B. Jones, 'Manchester liberalism 1918–1929: the electoral, ideological and organisational experience of the Liberal Party in Manchester with particular reference to the career of Ernest Simon' (PhD dissertation, University of Manchester, 1997).

99 Besides Brady's invaluable study on Wythenshawe, see also A. Kay, 'Wythenshawe circa 1932–1955: the making of a community?' (PhD dissertation, University of Manchester, 1993).

100 Ibid.

101 P. Abercrombie, 'Report to the Housing Committee', 10 March 1920, included in the Housing Committee minutes, 29 March 1920.

102 *Manchester Guardian* (29 December 1925).

103 Ibid.

104 *Manchester Guardian* (4 February 1926).

105 L. Heywood, '50,000 Houses below a reasonable standard of habitation', Manchester Central Reference Library cuttings, 1934.

106 *Manchester Guardian* (29 December 1925).

107 Simon and Inman, *The Rebuilding of Manchester*, p. 36.

108 See below, Chapter 4.

109 E. D. Simon, *How to Abolish the Slums* (London, 1929), p. 52.

110 Simon and Inman, *The Rebuilding of Manchester*, p. 42.

111 See Brady, 'The development of the Wythenshawe Estate', chapter 6.

112 Ibid., chapters 7–8.

113 *Manchester City News* (18 September 1920).

114 *The Times* (13 December 1929).

115 These figures were in stark contrast to London's major out-county estate, Becontree. See above, Chapter 2.

116 Manchester Housing Committee minutes, 9 February 1931.

117 Ibid., 14 May 1928.

118 Ibid., 10 September 1928.

119 Ibid., 9 September 1929.

120 Ibid., 20 September 1928.

121 Ibid., 8 December 1930, 18 April 1931, 10 November 1931.

122 Ibid., 10 November 1931.

123 Ibid., 8 June 1931.

124 Ibid., 30 October 1930.

125 *The Times* (24 September 1925).

126 Manchester Housing Committee minutes, 10 April 1933.

127 B. Disraeli, *Coningsby, or, the New Generation* (London, 1911).

128 The ad hoc and intermittent nature of housing policy from 1909 was highlighted by J. Sheail, 'Interwar planning in Britain: the wider context', *Journal of Urban History*, 11:3 (1985), 335–51.

4 Slum houses, slum dwellers and slum clearance

Wythenshawe was an impressive attempt to produce a bold solution to Manchester's problems. The city was trying to create a new, clean world for its workers. By 1930, Britain's cities were instructed to turn to the deep-rooted problems of the inner-city slums. In Manchester, the slums were concentrated around the inner-city belt and were characterised by poor maintenance, lack of the most basic amenities and overcrowding. However, the physical fabric of the houses was not the only issue. Rents for the new houses, and extra travel costs to work, were too high for the poorer tenants. The council selected tenants for its new estates and, in the first years, slum dwellers were not usually on the lists. Nevertheless, with the 1930 Greenwood Act, emphasis shifted towards slum clearance. Problems were acute, and the government was pressing local authorities to take decisive action. The council was eager to clear to comply, but it was faced with a myriad of problems. Clearing slum housing meant constructing replacement houses, but suitable building land remained in short supply.

The process of change was affected by a series of complex issues. On the one hand, the council wanted to build new homes, avoid flats wherever possible and identify and purchase an ever-diminishing supply of land. Coupled to this was a serious financial crisis. On the other hand, prospective tenants were not universally enthusiastic. A number of voluntary-sector surveys reflected the grim reality of life in the slums but also highlighted tenant concerns and wishes. These investigations served an important purpose in the crusade against the slums. Findings were disseminated through pamphlets and public meetings. Housing reformers were again influencing the local housing discourse. They acted as a pressure group, mobilised public opinion and supported the local authority, with which they broadly shared the same views and attitudes. Some Labour councillors resented what they viewed as middle-class do-gooders. But others supported them. They agreed that tenants should be managed in the 'Octavia Hill fashion'. Reformers believed that once removed to the new estates, tenants should be encouraged to adopt good habits. This reinforced the underlying attitude that tenants were not trustworthy and that their behaviour needed nurturing. The same attitude pervaded council thinking. Civic culture and liberal idealism were the guiding principles on which policy was developed. The council, and many reformers, wanted to do things big – sweep away the slums, destroy established communities and build large, new estates away from their old neighbourhoods. Tenant views were not part of the equation. Even so, groups of tenants did protest against some proposals and policies. While this did not constitute the type of sustained action that emerged from the late 1960s, it highlighted the engrained attitudes of the council towards tenants whilst also anticipating tenant discourse and conflict later in the century.

The inner-city slum

By the late 1920s, focus was shifting away from general housing provision for the working classes to the much bigger problem of clearing and replacing the inner-city slums. In Manchester, areas like Collyhurst, Ancoats and Hulme suffered from some of the country's worst housing conditions. They were notorious for poor building maintenance and a lack of the most basic amenities such as a toilet and running water. Overcrowding compounded the problems. In 1929, Simon commented that although over one million houses had been built across the country since the end of the war, the fact remained that "we have done nothing for the poorer workers".[1] Despite the promise of homes for heroes, slum conditions had actually deteriorated. While the government demanded action, local authorities struggled to build replacement houses before clearing the slum areas. As the nineteenth century had shown, failure to do so would simply increase overcrowding in other areas.

Nevertheless, the 1930 Act meant that from April 1931 the council's attention turned towards slum clearance. This was not just a reaction to central government policy. Pressure for radical changes mounted throughout the early 1930s from the city's housing reformers. The same people and organisations that had led the clamour for action from the late nineteenth century continued to pressurise the council throughout the 1930s. Although they were not at odds with the council, they acted as a pressure group, carrying out basic surveys which were then published at low cost.[2] Like the local press, the voluntary sector had an important role in keeping housing issues firmly in the public sphere. A number of organisations came together at a housing conference initiated by the Federation of Building Trades Operatives, held at the Albert Hall on 25 October 1930. This led to the formation of the Manchester and Salford Better Housing Council. The other prominent voluntary organisation to emerge was the Manchester and Salford Council of Social Service. This became involved in helping co-ordinate services, working with the public utility societies, the Better Housing Council, housing associations and the Federation of Building Trades Operatives and the Trades Council.[3] However, it was the Better Housing

Council that became the principal organisation. Members included the Manchester University Settlement (which carried out three surveys in Ancoats), the Manchester Housing Company, the Women Citizens' Association, the Federation of Building Trades Operatives, Manchester Housing (1926) Ltd, the Ancoats Local Housing Committee, the Social Service Group of the Auxiliary Movement, the St James' Birch Fellowship, and the Red Bank Survey Group. Prominent group members included Marion Fitzgerald, Simon's secretary, C. Pear, Avice Trench and Miss Remington.

The group aimed to co-ordinate all their activities and to educate public opinion. Like Horsfall and Marr, it believed that it was absolutely necessary for the entire community to have direct knowledge of the city's worst housing conditions because any hope of solving the slum problem depended upon the "driving force of a strong, well-informed public opinion".[4] Its extensive published surveys were aimed at educating local people, another attempt to raise a sense of community consciousness.[5] Some reports proved so popular that they quickly sold out. They gave graphic details of the human cost of the slums, showing how tens of thousands of men, women, children and the elderly were living in abject poverty.[6] The group was also determined to ensure the council continued its efforts to solve the slum issue, promising that any slacking by the local authority would force them to make direct representations with a view to securing amendments.[7]

The reports again highlighted the problems inherited from the nineteenth century. In 1931, a survey into Chorlton-on-Medlock, carried out by the Manchester and District Survey Society, revealed that all the houses investigated were constructed between 1794 and 1820 and that most were built without water supply, drainage, sanitation or ventilation. Some were reconditioned back-to-backs, converted by demolishing every third house or by removing the back section. Even these were described as "mean-looking ... ugly and deformed".[8] Despite the reconditioning, the houses were still in a poor condition due to lack of repairs, the continued existence of stone-flagged floors, doorways without steps to keep out the rain, bedrooms without doors, windows without cords, a general lack of washing accommodation, a total absence of hygienic storage places for food, overcrowding and a seemingly never-ending tide of vermin.[9] They showed that from 350 houses investigated only nine had baths, sixty-nine had no wash boilers, fifty-six shared yards and toilets, three had no sink, five had their own tap and sink in the yard, and 21 per cent were overcrowded.[10]

Conditions in Chorlton-on-Medlock were replicated in other surveys. In 1931, the Better Housing Council investigated the notorious Angel Meadow district.[11] It described the district as being unfit for habitation and claimed that it was so bad that "no blade of grass exists in the whole area".[12] In total, only four houses possessed a bath (one of which stood in the middle of the living room), 144 had no wash boiler, ten were without a sink and thirty shared toilets. Most were in a poor state of repair. The usual complaints were listed, including dampness, leaking roofs, crumbling plaster work, badly fitted doors and another army of rats and beetles. Some of the direst conditions were in rooms let as furnished. These were characterised by drab walls, broken plaster, dark stairs, broken windows, absence of any water supply (except for a tap in the yard), and water closets shared between four or five families (in one case two between over thirty people).[13] The surveys painted a grim picture. The Better Housing Council's investigation into the St Clement's Ward, carried out by the St Chrysostom's Housing Survey Group, found that only three houses out of the 595 inspected possessed a bath, seventeen had no tap inside the house and ten had ash closets, one of which was unusable.[14] The University Settlement survey in the Angel Meadow and Red Bank districts described how "the smells from the glue, rubber and gas works and from the polluted river Irk pervade the neighbourhood".[15] Their survey of the New Cross district of Ancoats revealed a similarly grim picture in which "almost all houses were worn out completely", lacking basic amenities for food storage or even for washing.[16] Again, the houses were over a hundred years old and, despite some council improvements in the late nineteenth century, the fact remained that "they scarcely achieved redemption".[17] Slums had not been removed; they had merely been patched up. The entire area remained "sordid and ugly", and over a quarter were still officially designated as overcrowded.[18] Slums were in danger of being overridden with rodents and insects. The survey found that 1,525 houses were affected, with 1,467 infested with bugs, 546 with beetles, 175 with mice and 12 with rats.[19] Perhaps most shockingly of all to contemporaries was the realisation that the inner-city circle of slums were not the only areas to suffer. This was highlighted in January 1933 when John Inman carried out a survey into conditions in Miles Platting. His study, conducted for the Economic Research Section of the University, revealed the same story of poverty, poor housing and overcrowding.[20] In an area thought to be working-class, the study revealed that 23 per cent of children were living below the needs standard.[21]

Reconfiguring the tenant

The reports portrayed conditions in the type of vivid, intimate and effective way that only came with first-hand knowledge and experience. In contrast, the council appeared to have little direct contact with the slum dwellers or even tenants on the new estates. In 1932, it decided to carry out its own survey. A questionnaire was sent to a number of households on the Anson estate. It did little else. There were none of the door-to-door enquires of the voluntary surveys. Of the 42 per cent who replied, it found that twelve out of twenty-eight families with sufficient income were only able to meet the rent because of the extra income provided by the children, with the income of the father being barely adequate to pay the rent.[22] That was the extent of its attempts to engage (at a distance) with the tenants in order to assess their needs.

Voluntary-sector surveys were far more extensive and offered a real sense of richness and depth, giving greater moral weight to their demands for reform. The surveys did not necessarily say anything new, but they were valuable because they kept the issue firmly in the public sphere and provided a precise and intimate sense of place. Vague generalisations were avoided because they were focusing on New Cross or Chorlton. Locality was important in revealing the depth and nature of the problem. The surveys also put 'people' firmly in the picture. Constructs, carried forward from the nineteenth century, still characterised slum dwellers as being part of an underclass, responsible for their own life of grime. Simon cited critics who argued that the slums could never be entirely cleared because "it is the slum dwellers that make the slum ... that quite a considerable proportion of those who now live under bad and dirty conditions in the slums are under no circumstances capable of bringing up their families decently". Simon, however, refuted the stereotypes, claiming that "the proportion of those who do not respond to environment is small", and that in his experience some of the poorest homes were "scrupulously clean, and reflected great credit on the housewife".[23]

Nevertheless, typecasts were embedded in cultural perceptions of the 'poor'. The surveys offered a challenge to the negative images.[24] The Chorlton report described a slum area consisting not of the unskilled or unemployed but of printers, wholesale clothiers, packing-case makers, finishers, pattern-card makers, yarn merchants, rubber-stamp makers, shippers, joiners, engineers, box makers and motor mechanics.[25] Many were extremely poor, but the investigators noted that "no one asked us for financial help, though it is quite obvious that many are only just on this side of starvation".[26] The concept of the dangerous slum dweller (not entirely imagined) was counter-balanced by these more detailed accounts.[27] Residents were described as "friendly and communicative". Accounts also challenged the idea that they were all dirty. The survey remarked on how, despite the vermin-ridden conditions in which they were forced to live, it was still "very wonderful that so many of the families in this district look healthy and are able to keep themselves and their houses clean".

One of the underlying problems facing residents was the lack of privacy. Established urban patterns, flats and tenements could not offer tenants the most basic amount of individual space.[28] This was one of the biggest problems of overcrowding. Lack of personal space impacted on individual health, cleanliness and moral environment. Reports claimed that conditions made it "very difficult and well-nigh impossible for these poor families to keep even moderately healthy, clean and decent", and that it was all the more remarkable that "so many do grow up to be good, healthy citizens, with infinite patience and perseverance keeping up a constant warfare against their disgusting conditions".[29] They argued that it was the lack of privacy, the way many of them had to live together in a single stifling room, which meant that decency was difficult "and premature acquaintance with conjugal relations all but unavoidable".[30] Added to this was the "ceaseless friction and recurrent irritation" which came with so many people living in overcrowded conditions, a problem which meant that "anger, worry and sexual instincts are always near the surface".[31] The lack of privacy affected living conditions outside as well as inside the home. At the back of one house, for example, a tenant described how the passage was "used for immoral purposes by men and women coming from the adjoining beer-house and from the adjacent well-lighted streets".[32]

Families lived in the face of innumerable interrelated problems, directly or indirectly a result of living conditions. The surveys showed that tenants were not inherently immoral, but the conditions created an intolerable situation. Reformers were reinstating the lives of ordinary people back into the housing debate. Views were actively solicited. The University Settlement's survey assessed tenant attitudes before and after their move to new estates. They found that most had a genuine sense of community and were not a constantly drifting mass of itinerants. People were rooted in the slum area, an area which their parents and even grandparents had regarded as a respectable neighbourhood and which was described by one investigator as having a village feeling. They were not dangerous social outcasts but were long-established in an area in which they felt a great deal of local pride. Nearly half of the families had lived there for over twenty years, while 259 of the 476 families had relatives in the area.[33] Investigators avoided the negative connotations of the term 'slum dweller' and pointed out that most of the families visited "were certainly not slum-minded". People waged a daily war to keep their dilapidated homes as clean and respectable as was humanly possible by painting the decaying woodwork, papering over the crumbling plaster on the walls, and donkey stoning the window-sills and doorsteps.

While the same conditions, and attitudes, may have existed in other parts of the city, and the country, this was still very much about the people of Ancoats. Broad similarities existed, but the surveys did not generalise. Their impact would have been diluted amidst the vagaries of the bigger picture. The investigators noted, for example, that most of the women chose bright-coloured casement cloth for their curtains. They were happy to point out that ragged lace curtains, "such as would be seen in a slum district in London", were not to be found in Ancoats. Here, tenants took pride in their homes, even though it was an uphill struggle. This was a "settled community with their pride as well as their roots in Ancoats". Poverty, poor housing and high unemployment levels may have characterised other districts, but tenants did not conform to a stereotype or to sweeping generalisations.

Specific details brought a greater intimacy and sympathy both from the investigators and the readers. Far from them being a singularly dangerous group, many tenants were portrayed as decent people who, all too often, were oppressed by their living conditions. Added to this was the exploitative landlord. A number of tenants were living in a climate of fear and intimidation. Dread of landlord reprisals meant they were reluctant to complain. Some tenants were told not to press for repairs because the landlord would close the property and evict them. In many cases, tenants were too frightened to complain.[34] They had no means of redress and, although they might protest and demand that repairs be carried out, they were worried that the landlord could serve them with a week's notice to quit. In one case, a lodger had been refused permission to take any of his own furniture to the house because it would make it more difficult to evict him.[35] Even while the reformers were carrying out their investigations they found themselves being followed around by landladies who were monitoring tenant comments. The Red Bank investigators claimed that their visiting was cut short on four occasions because of interference from a hostile landlady. Tenants were too afraid to provide information. On one occasion, they were talking to a woman who was then called outside by the landlady and asked if she wanted to move. In another instance, when they asked a woman about the amount of rent she was paying the woman replied, "I daren't say ... you must ask the land-lady".[36]

The council and the cottage

Bad conditions, exploitation, lack of privacy and low wages became part of the reformist discourse which demanded sweeping changes. It was part of a consensus in which tenants, reformers and the local authority were generally agreed that the council was the best vehicle for reform. Faced with private landlords, gross overcrowding, absence of individual space and vermin-infested conditions, only the local authority was capable of resolving the problem. The council was not motivated by profit, but by a desire to build a better society for everyone. Tenants trusted the local authority and reformers believed that it was the only institution with the resources and the political will to carry out large-scale changes. Only from the late 1960s would this trust begin to diminish and eventually collapse. In the 1930s, people were tired of private landlords and poor conditions. One tenant was quoted as saying he would "much prefer a dwelling under the Corporation to a house at the same rent under a private landlord, simply to be relieved of the fear of being bullied or turned out".[37]

Trust was important. It meant that the council was in a strong position when it came to clearing the slums, planning and building new houses. Policy decisions continued to be made from within the Town Hall, with reference to government and social reformers, but not the tenant. Civic culture provided the points of reference, the norms and signals influencing policy choices. This still included a strong belief in building cottage-style houses. In the 1930s, local social reformers again stressed that suburban cottage houses provided the ideal environment for nurturing a family and that the council's letting policy should encourage tenants with families to move away from the city and onto new estates in green areas.[38] The council agreed. Housing Director Leonard Heywood claimed that the general opinion of the Housing Committee was that flat development was a poor second-best.[39] This was a central part of Manchester's civic culture. Heywood stressed that there was a definite "preference shown in Manchester for the cottage type of accommodation with its small garden and its increased privacy". Heywood believed that "the cottage type of accommodation is generally accepted as the ideal form of dwelling", and that "the city has concentrated its activities (on building houses) since the war".[40]

Preference for housing was an ideal shared by the council, social reformers and tenants alike. In 1932, under the supervision of Avice Trench, the University Settlement conducted research into the city's tenement blocks. It drew comparisons with pre-war blocks and developments in London, Liverpool and Vienna. The survey solicited the views of architects, theorists and the tenant, "those who are actually living either in pre-war or modern block dwellings".[41] Municipal schemes were seen as dour, ugly and featureless, and privately owned schemes were even worse. One block in Ancoats was described as being of "unparalleled hideousness". Life for the tenants was "reduced to a dull dead level from which much of the spring and interest in life has gone", a life "without a vestige of beauty, with little privacy and constant noise". Tenants felt enormous social stigma at having to live in the tenement blocks and were "oppressed by their grim aspect". One claimed that, "this place feels like a prison … every time I turn into it I feel ashamed; it looks such a dreadful-looking place … you've no heart for your work here". Many were afraid to let their employers know where they lived and felt shame at the prospect of showing their home to relatives and friends.[42] Tenants complained about the complete lack of privacy and sense of embarrassment when they were visited by a Public Assistance inspector because it was certain to become public knowledge. Again, the lack of personal space was a primary concern. There was bitterness that two to three families had to share a lobby, toilet and sink. One moaned "you get tired of being in with so many; it's almost like being in lodgings", while another complained, "you're mixed up with everyone here; I'd rather have a home of my own".[43] Added to this was the perpetual noise, the lack of open space, the absence of recreational facilities and the way the central courtyard and balconies were a "lure to young hooligans". One poor tenant grumbled, "it's awful when you're lying in bed ill … I was thankful when they took me to the hospital. The noise nearly drives you mad." Added to this were the same moral problems identified in other slum areas. There was a real concern that the girls "see too much" and that "living here doesn't give the children a chance … you can't keep them right".[44] Mothers expressed concern that if they let their children play out they would be "much changed for the worst", and that it was difficult to stop them from "from getting rough".[45] The flats were overcrowded, with families of five to seven people occupying one-bedroom units. In some instances, adult sons and daughters had to share a room with their parents, while four people out of a family of five living in a one-bedroom flat had tuberculosis.[46]

Investigators were left in no doubt that tenants wanted to live in cottages. The survey concluded that "the great majority declared their strong preference for a cottage house".[47] A local discourse developed along a broad consensus. This was one area of policy where council, reformers and tenants came together. In this sense, the council appeared to know best, to be aware of the aims and ambitions of people and professionals. However, it proved impossible completely to ignore flats. Civic culture drove them to build quality cottages in clean areas, but physical barriers meant that what might be desired was not always achievable. The land shortage, density levels, land values and the pressing urgency of the slum problem forced a partial rethink. Yet even when the council reluctantly acknowledged that it might have to build tenements to ease overcrowding, it limited the size of developments. In June 1932, for example, Fred Platt presented a report on flats for rehousing slum dwellers. The report, generally negative, was based on evidence from Glasgow. The Housing Committee agreed that Manchester should never build tenements of more than three or four storeys in height.[48] In addition, any development should be of a high standard. This filtered through into policy. In the 1930s, the council built its flagship developments in Kirkmanshulme Lane and Smedley Point, using only five, four and two-storey blocks. The Kennet House flats at Smedley Point were developed by the Housing Deputy R. A. H. Levitt, who became a leading figure in housing. These, and other developments in Manchester, offered quality homes, with playgrounds and grassed areas for children, welfare centres, wash houses and drying areas. It wanted to incorporate modern designs which avoided a monotonous look.[49] The flats symbolised civic pride. They were named after and opened by the likes of the Minister of Health Sir Kingsley Wood (Smedley Point flats), Arthur Greenwood (Kirkmanshulme Lane) and Mrs Neville Chamberlain (Wythenshawe).[50] Other small developments were built on cleared sites around the city, including 244 flats on the Miles Platting clearance area, 32 flats on the Temple Estate, 244 flats at Ardwick and 221 at Gorton Lane.[51]

The voluntary impulse, the council and the tenant

Civic culture, based on a sense of prodigiousness, pride and dislike of flats, continued to underpin the creation and implementation of policy. There was always an underlying assumption amongst reformers and council officials that the tenants would learn to appreciate their new environment. To an extent, they were right. After a period of readjustment, large numbers of tenants did eventually enjoy life in their new homes.[52] In Wythenshawe, the Better Housing council found that 90 per cent of tenants were generally satisfied with their houses.[53] Many felt there had been a marked improvement in health, and enthusiasm was expressed for the houses, gardens, fresh air, and the country surroundings of the estate.[54] Tenants were happy with the rural atmosphere of the estate, the park, the grass and trees, and the general atmosphere of peace and quiet. One resident told the investigators, "do you know what I like about being here better than all? My bath and my garden – and especially my bath!".[55] The local headmistress claimed that many parents had moved out to the estate for the health of their children and were pleased at the general improvement they had witnessed. Most of the estate's problems were dismissed as a consequence of it being a new estate.

As part of the process of readjustment, reformers believed their professional guiding hand was needed to direct tenant behaviour. Elements in both the council and the voluntary sector believed that tenants, although victims of their environment, needed assistance in managing their homes (if not their lives). Some members of the council supported attempts by voluntary groups to establish social workers and community centres to encourage good habits. In 1928, the University Settlement carried out a social work experiment on the new Wilbraham Estate. Volunteers rented a house from the council and started a New Estates Community Centre, which, they claimed, was the prototype for others across the country.[56] They eventually built a new hall and extended their operations into a number of areas. The possible benefits of the new centres, especially with the onset of the Depression, were eventually recognised by the National Council of Voluntary Social Service (NCVSS) as well as the local authority.[57] By the mid-1930s, the council was helping to finance some of the new centres.[58] Other organisations campaigned for community centres on all new estates, including the New Estates Federation of Manchester and Salford, which counted amongst its member's prominent local academics such as Professor J. L. Stocks and Mabel Tylecote.[59]

Not everyone on the council was receptive to the creation of the new centres, or to the 'interference' of the social workers. In 1935, Labour councillors launched a bitter attack on a proposal to provide a three-roomed flat at Kennet House for a University Settlement worker to establish a community centre. Alderman Titt led the critics, claiming that the flats should be devoted entirely for slum-clearance families.[60] Titt pleaded with the council "for God's sake" not to give room to "these self-appointed social investigators who went about dissecting and vivisecting the life of the working classes".[61] He was supported by other Labour councillors. However, a majority on the council shared the objectives of the Settlement and the opposition was defeated.

Some Labour members viewed interference as an attempt to control the city's working classes. Not only did the University Settlement, along with the NCVSS, want to establish residential social workers in the heart of the new developments, but at least one local church saw this as an opportunity to promote the virtues of sobriety. In 1930, J. T. Martin wrote to the Housing Committee on behalf of the Primitive Methodist Church asking them to follow Liverpool's sterling example and "prevent the sale and manufacture of intoxicating liquors on the new housing estates".[62] It was part of the Victorian philanthropic impulse to control the habits of the working classes and although the council politely ignored the request, the fact remained that few pubs were built and many sympathised with the work of the Settlement and the NCVSS. This again reflected the influence of the voluntary sector in shaping council attitudes, a philanthropic impulse to influence and direct habits and behaviour. Anybody who lived in such filth had to be 're-educated'.

Council attitudes were manifested in the new tenant selection process. Houses built in the 1920s (and to an extent in the early 1930s) were not for slum dwellers. They were designed for the more respectable working classes. The Better Housing Council's report into Angel Meadow claimed that families who wanted to move usually had no chance of a council house because they failed to satisfy the requirements about income, furniture or, in some cases, "general satis-factoriness".[63] Many displaced slum dwellers were seen as unsuitable tenants for new Corporation houses. The Regional Survey in Chorlton claimed that although people remained anxious for council houses, many had become disil-lusioned and did not bother even to register because, they asked, "what's the use? We should never get one".[64] The council had erected a series of barriers that made it difficult for any slum dweller to move to the new houses. The University Settlement criticised the local authority for having three 'insurmountable obstacles'. They claimed that the council would not even consider an applicant unless they had an income exceeding 50 shillings, had suitable furniture and was clean and of a "satisfactory character".[65] Tenants had to be selected and properly managed. The Housing Committee was presented with a summary of procedures and methods for selecting tenants. The ability to pay was the most essential factor in determining eligibility, but this was followed by the issue of "general suitability", which included family circumstance, character and cleanliness. It did have a classification table that placed tenants in overcrowded conditions and larger families at the top, but if you failed to meet the other criteria then this alone would not guarantee favourable treatment.[66]

Even if tenants were fortunate enough to be given a new council house, they were still subjected to a series of rules and controls. In March 1932, the Town Clerk wrote to the Housing Director, Fred Platt, suggesting that the conditions of tenancy be altered for new tenants on Wythenshawe, making them responsible for taking care of grass verges and trees, making proper use of open spaces, preserving the parkway hedges and plants and prohibiting drying clothes outside at weekends.[67] These supplemented the seventeen basic rules and conditions of tenancy. In municipal flats, tenants' children were not allowed to play on the stairs, in the passages, balconies or in the laundries.[68] All tenants were ordered to sweep the passage floors, closets, sinks, entrance lobbies and balconies every day before 10.00 am.[69] These also had to be washed by them every Saturday before 6.00pm. If a flat was empty, or if tenants were classified by the Superintendent as unfit to carry out their cleaning duties, then the neighbours had to share the burden. All tenants were responsible for cracked or broken glass panes and any tenant who was judged to be an unfit lodger could be evicted within forty-eight hours.

Council, tenants and slum clearance

Although the council's attitude was to create problems in its relationship with tenants later in the century, there were signs of tension in the 1930s. Council policies were a top-down, Fordist reaction. It offered modern, large-scale solutions to deep-rooted problems. Although councillors were a part of the community, drawn from its ranks, living in the area and, very often, born in the city, once they became members of the council they also became detached from the community. They entered a world with its own structures, systems and culture, its own way of creating and implementing policy that did not necessarily refer directly to the people who had to live with those decisions. Civic culture was a guiding principle just as much as liberal idealism or municipal socialism. As was seen, from the end of the nineteenth century, reformers had stressed the need to develop large new estates, building quality cottages and creating open spaces. They wanted everyone to enjoy the benefits of a suburban life. It was an issue of both idealism and civic pride. By the 1930s, this had become a prominent feature of Manchester's civic culture. It continued to have a profound impact on policy throughout the twentieth century. Councillors wanted to do things on a big scale and to build quality developments. Leonard Heywood claimed that the Housing Committee had fought hard to maintain the high standards and ideals of the inter-war period.[70] Civic pride bristled beneath the surface as he boasted that while "other authorities have taken the line of least resistance and reduced standard and quality", Manchester had continued to build "in advance of the present accepted minimums".[71]

While there can be no doubt that this is what most tenants desperately wanted, the prospect of leaving their communities remained a major cause for concern. Many were anxious at the prospect of moving. The Angel Meadow survey revealed that while 60 per cent of participants were willing to leave the area, a further 40 per cent were adamant that they wanted to remain, despite the dire conditions, and only 10 per cent were willing to go as far as Wythenshawe. Tenants were unwilling to move because of work, low income, lack of furniture and the closeness to facilities. Local Jews, for example, were near the Hebrew school for boys and the Jewish shops. Others believed that municipal houses were jerry-built or they were afraid of the "snobbery of the new estates".[72] The main problem was the cost of the new council houses. Simon estimated that 70 per cent of slum tenants were unable or unwilling to pay the extra rents.[73] Coupled to this were the extra travel costs. But it was not just about money. While everyone desired better houses, many wanted to stay living in areas close to friends, relatives and familiar facilities. Several expressed a "prevailing feeling … of dismay" at what might happen if they were forced to leave. Tenants were worried about the prospect of moving far away, adding extra costs to their stretched budgets, and about the loss of the community network. They dreaded the thought of weary and costly daily journeys, and housewives were worried that higher rents would mean less money for food. When Marion Fitzgerald inquired into the reasons why some had returned from the new estates to Hulme, she found that increased rent and tram fares and the actual time spent in travelling were cited as the main reasons, while some simply returned through personal preference. People worked close to home and this allowed them to "pop home and see to the children's dinner and the shopping".[74] They knew the local shops, an important factor for families living on a hand-to-mouth existence. Knowledge of the local shops, of which was cheapest and which would give them credit, allowed them to budget carefully. They knew that the corner shop was "kind and purchases might be entered in the back of the book for a few days if money was short". Women relied on a network of family and friends who could "mind the children, come in for a game of cards, look after invalids, share the news". The University Settlement's survey into the New Cross area of Ancoats again found that despite the conditions, in which the average infant mortality rate was 125 per thousand as opposed to the national average of 65 per thousand, many were still unwilling to move.[75] From 393 who were asked if they were prepared to go, 49 per cent said they were willing but 51 per cent were unwilling. Once again the main reasons for staying were the costs and need to stay near work, though one man said that he "would not move for the Town Hall clock", one woman wanted "to be buried where they are all buried" and one man explained that there were no public houses on the new estates.[76] Compulsory clearance would inevitably lead to a break up of the intricate economic and social pattern of their lives.[77] Ultimately, the authorities would leave them with little choice. The "decree had gone forth", and the people had to move.

Despite their reservations, most tenants still generally trusted the council to help them out of the slums. However, trust was not universal and policies were not without occasional opposition. If trust was eroded, if tenants became disillusioned, then some were capable of articulating their views through organised protests. Tenant reactions to the Hulme slum–clearance programme showed that not all were prepared to accept whatever was presented. Some were ready to stand up against the municipal machine. In 1931, a Joint Sub-Committee was established between the Housing Committee and the Public Health Committee to consider slum–clearance issues.[78] It was a process undertaken without reference to the community. In June 1931, the Joint Committee reported to the council , recommending that a large section of Hulme should be the first district to be designated for slum clearance. Hulme was to be a symbol of council policy across much of the twentieth century. During the inter-war period, it reflected the way the local authority was prepared to implement its own policy with little or no reference to the tenants. In the 1960s, it highlighted how it mistakenly used system-built programmes to ease the continuing slum problems, again with no meaningful consultation with the tenants. Finally, in the early 1990s it reflected a new approach that embraced the idea of partnership and consultation. The tenant finally became recognised as a consumer with opinions, hopes and ambitions.[79]

During the inter-war period, this was an unthinkable concept. People wanted to move, were less likely to form organised protests and were confident in the ability of the council to deliver. But the tenant groups that emerged from the late 1960s were not without precedent. Reactions to slum-clearance plans in Hulme were an early indication of tenant capabilities when faced with unpopular policies. As early as 1914, a petition had been presented to the council by local ratepayers asking for improvements to the district, including open spaces and public amenities. It was ignored. In 1920, the Medical Officer of Health called for improvements or demolition of 1,065 houses, but the council improvements affected only 199 homes.[80] These were finally demolished by 1925. The area was one of the unhealthiest in the entire city. During 1930–32, the mortality rate for Hulme was 18.9 which contrasted sharply with the 13.3 for the city as a whole, while the infant mortality rate was 125 for Hulme and 83 for the city. In 1930, the Housing Committee decided that another large part of Hulme would be designated for slum clearance. The council was backed by the Medical Officer of Health, Veitch Clark. In his report on the Hulme Area proposals, Clark called for demolition of all buildings in the area.[81] He claimed that deaths from measles were three times greater than in the rest of the city, consumption levels were double and "either just under two or two and a half times as great were nervous diseases, diseases of the heart and blood vessels, bronchitis, and pneumonia".[82] Crucially, he also pointed out that it had not been possible to obtain any suitable sites near to the Hulme Clearance Area within a radius of two miles for possible rehousing. Displaced tenants would have to move.

Given the sheer scale of the problem, it was no wonder that the council believed it had to take sweeping action. There was no time to consult the tenant and, in many respects, no point. It was simple – the area would be cleared, whether the slum dwellers agreed or not. There was strong local public and central pressure to do something. The voluntary reports showed that houses were beyond redemption. The Housing Committee were told to use Compulsory Purchase Orders under the 1930 Act. Although it would build self-contained houses to replace the slums, it also considered a few tenement buildings, though, again, none of these were to be erected at a greater height than four storeys. Density levels gave them little choice. Whilst it failed to identify where it proposed to house the displaced tenants, it did point out that it would be necessary to transfer all dispossessed families to existing estates.[83] After two months, the council accepted the recommendations and decided on wholesale clearance and rehousing on estates around the city and in Wythenshawe. Hulme residents would have to move. The council felt it had little choice. It was coming under increasing pressure to ease the city's chronic slum problem. In June 1933, the results of a survey by Philip Massey into the slums in Manchester, Leeds, Birmingham, Liverpool, Glasgow and Sheffield were published in the *Architects'*

Journal. Massey claimed that although Manchester was acutely aware of its slum problem, the council was doing "very, very little" to solve it, especially when compared with Liverpool, Sheffield and Bristol.[84] He claimed that while it had plans that should have led to the demolition of 2,500 houses, the fact was that it had failed to clear a single slum house. The council had stalled because it had a chronic shortage of new houses and sites. Nevertheless, by the summer of 1933 it was ready to press ahead with its slum-clearance plans for Hulme.[85]

In July 1933, a public inquiry was held into the proposals. Despite the deep-seated problems and damning figures, a number of residents in Hulme remained opposed to any large-scale clearance programme. Many wanted improvement or gradual redevelopment which would enable them to stay in the community. At the public inquiry, the Property Owners' Association questioned both Clark's findings and the council's entire slum-clearance plans.[86] It was joined by the Hulme Housing Association, a tenant support group formed in 1931 to defend the rights of the tenants. Members included Rev. Chevassut, Rector of Hulme, James Murray, the Rector of St Wilfred's, and P. T. Barnes, the councillor for Medlock. Although they agreed that housing conditions were extremely bad and that overcrowding was a serious problem, their main contention was that a considerable measure of rehousing should take place in Hulme itself. They acknowledged that the problem was a "gigantic one" which would require the rehousing of between 35,000–50,000 people, but they also claimed that the majority of inhabitants were "decent folk" who wanted to stay in the area.[87]

On the night before the inquiry the group held a large public meeting attended by over 1,000 residents at George Street Chapel. Most of the audience consisted of women.[88] They condemned the plan to rehouse Hulme tenants in Wythenshawe and other surrounding estates, and demanded that new homes should be built in Hulme for everyone who wanted to stay.[89] Chevassut stated that people were entitled to have a say in where they lived, and that the tenants association was "fighting for something more than housing – it was fighting for liberty".[90] He was joined by the local MP, Sir Joseph Nall, who claimed that while some residents were in favour of the scheme, their survey had found "they were not numerous", and that "the overwhelming majority, so far as could be ascertained, were opposed to it as it stood".[91] He pointed out that the council did not have any plans for the area after demolition and, in a tirade which was to echo across the twentieth century, he condemned the council, stating "the Corporation had left the Newcastle Street site, which had been cleared, as a nuisance to those living near; it was a monument to the inefficiency and gross inability of the Corporation".[92] Nall criticised them for being incompetent and for attempting to "boss" the people.[93] The council was openly attacked for not listening to tenants and for forcing its own vision, its own views, on the people, whether they agreed or not. The criticism continued throughout the inquiry. Chevassut defiantly claimed that the Hulme tenants would prefer their children to live in overcrowded conditions rather than have them left with "empty stomachs because they could not afford to live on new estates away from their jobs", and ended by stating that tenants would "fight to the limit, being convinced that without rehousing on the site there would only be increased misery".[94] He begged the council to spend nothing unless it genuinely met the needs of Hulme people. Although the programme was forced through, Chevassut's prophecy was partially realised when it was revealed that from 200 families dispossessed by the programme, only 140 agreed to move two miles to Fallowfield, while a further sixty refused the offer. Within three years, only sixty-two families had remained in their new homes.[95]

Entire communities were to be broken up and people moved, many against their own wishes. Yet they also wanted new homes. The council was being asked to put square pegs in round holes. There were no realistic alternatives. The scale of the problem, the number of houses beyond redemption and the high density levels, was too great. Many wanted to stay in their existing community where they could afford to live and where they enjoyed familiarity with neighbours and facilities. Their anxiety was understandable. Fear of the unfamiliar and higher costs were reasonable, although, in practice, houses built under the 1930 Act were usually cheaper to rent than under previous legislation and anxiety for most people passed with time as communities reformed.[96] However, this masks the underlying problem in the relationship and attitudes of the council towards the tenants. Fears may have been more perceived than real, but they were still ignored. The council may have had no choice but to pursue its policy direction, but it was sowing the seeds for tenant discontent which were to grow and develop later in the century. Tenants would do as they were told. It was an attitude which could be understood in the context of the period, but it became so embedded in civic culture that it turned out to be difficult to adapt to the changes of society in the post-1960s period.

In mid-September it unveiled its five-year plan for extending slum clearance to four other districts, Red Bank, Collyhurst, St Clement's, and West Gorton. This was in response to a Ministry of Health circular demanding that the pace of slum-clearance programmes be increased. A total of 3,602 houses were to be demolished over the following three years, with 15,303 residents being displaced.[97] For the council, these figures were the core issue. It was faced with massive problems. It was being told by central government to take sweeping action, and it was undoubtedly keen to clear away huge areas of inner-city slums, but it found the number of suitable sites for replacement building in the city disappearing. Compounding its problems was the cessation of resources for general-needs building. In 1933, Sir Hilton Young decided to concentrate resources on slum clearance and replacement.[98] The government was looking at alternatives. Lord Moyne's committee proposed a shift in emphasis to public utility societies. Letters were sent to all the major cities asking for their opinions.[99] Alderman Jackson, Chair of Manchester's sub-committee appointed to respond to the letter, condemned the move. It constituted an assault on local authority power. He claimed that public utility societies had no advantage over the local authorities in the management or the reconstruction of houses, and that local authorities now had the staff and experience better fitted for the job.[100]

Pressure was mounting on the council. Time, money and the size of the task were forcing it into action. Nevertheless, Chevassut was adamant that its failure to include tenant hopes in any plans was the "upper limit of cynical brutality", and he wondered if its aim was to cause the greatest possible inconvenience and misery. It was proposing to break up long-established communities, moving people from one area where they lived and worked for many years, to another area, and then replacing them with other displaced slum dwellers who would also have to move from their community and work. He declared that if the people of Hulme were Ukrainians in Poland then the League of Nations would be forced to appoint a Commission about their grievances, that if they were Austrians in Italian territory then the *Manchester Guardian* would take up their cause and that if they were Jews in Germany then "all England would hold indignation meetings".[101] Hulme residents were not alone in voicing concerns over the council's five-year plans. Tenants in Collyhurst were panicked at the very sight of local authority inspectors. Local councillor, W. Johnston, was alarmed at the council's plans and he urged it to purchase the land and rebuild on the same site because "the people of Collyhurst would suffer considerably if they were not re-housed in the district".[102] Later, Leonard Heywood admitted that in most cases there was antagonism to compulsory removal.[103] He acknowledged that families were being forced against their will to leave areas "where they and their ancestors have lived for generations, where ties of friendship and social intercourse mean much in the lives of the inhabitants and when a removal means the breaking of lifelong associations".[104] The council did little to allay people's fears or smooth the process of transition. Its high-handed approach did them few favours. The logic of its policy was reasonable, but its attitudes to the tenants remained dismissive. Only in the 1980s did it really begin to change.

By early October, the council finalised its plans.[105] The local election campaign, held in the same month, was dominated by the issue. Opposition came from across the community. Catholics, led by the Bishop of Salford, Dr T. Henshawe, were concerned that rehousing would mean families moving to areas without any religious infrastructure and, consequently, children attending non-Catholic schools. The Church had spent an estimated £300,000 on building and refurbishing schools over the previous eight years and there was a fear that this would be wasted as people were moved out.[106] Richard Murray, director of the Manchester Housing Company Limited, called for reconstruction and refurbishment. He claimed that this would allow tenants to "live where they desire".[107] During the election campaign, Conservatives gave their support to rehousing on the same site. The *Manchester Evening Chronicle* claimed that Conservatives recognised that there was a "growing volume of support for the policy of rehousing on the same sites at rentals within the reach of the working man".[108] Despite the criticisms, Labour and Liberal members held firm to their commitment to mass clearance programmes. They were supported by the *Manchester Evening News* which claimed that "in some places there are houses still inhabited which were condemned nearly forty years ago". In frustration, its headline cried "DICTATORS WANTED", and it called on all political parties to stop making slum clearance a political football and to take immediate action, to "GET IT DONE".[109]

Eventually, the council did 'get it done', but the fractious nature of the process meant that some distrusted the council. Other tenants were also angered by what they perceived to be unjust policies. In July 1933, for instance, a group of Blackley tenants embarked on a rent strike. The strikers lived in houses built under the Addison Act, but while others in the city were paying only 11s 5d because their homes were built under the Wheatley Act, they were paying 15s 10d. The council made it clear that, while it had every sympathy with the tenants (and it did ask the government to lower the rents), it would not allow them to live rent free and if they failed to pay up they would be evicted.[110] Their anger was understandable, but it also anticipated a fundamental change in the council-tenant relationship. Rather than behaving as recipients of municipal benevolence, tenants were acting as paying customers. They were buying a product, but the customers down the road were paying nearly 40 per cent less. This was not the council's fault but was an unfortunate result of government legislation. However, crucially, it was perceived to be the council's responsibility. After all, it was the one who implemented and managed the policy, and it was the council's name on the rent book. In the following year another group of tenants at Wythenshawe organised a series of protests against rent rises. At one meeting (attended and supported by three local councillors), it was claimed that they had been "shang-haied" by the council who it accused of a gross breach of faith.[111] The meeting convenor, Mr S. E. Wharton, accused the local authority of taking them to the estate under false pretences and that it now intended to use them "as they think fit".[112] The Wythenshawe Residents Association also held a mass meeting to protest about the poor public transport service and high fares.[113] They were angry customers of a service, not recipients of charity. The council now had a virtual monopoly stranglehold on them – they could stay or go private which, in effect, would mean a return to the slums. Before the 1960s, such anger and frustration at council policies was rare, but it did show that, although many tenants might be grateful for their new homes, they were not going to accept everything that was thrown at them. This did not herald the beginnings of the type of consumer protests that emerged later, but it did indicate how relations would diminish once trust in the council deteriorated. The rent strikes, and the protests over Hulme slum clearance, showed a willingness and ability by some tenants to organise and fight if they were pushed too far.

Although the council was able to produce grand plans and show real vision and drive in its determination to resolve the city's housing problems, it also displayed an inability at least to respond to tenant concerns. The period was not one which was ever likely to embrace notions of consultation or participation. But the council showed an attitude to tenants which was a part of civic culture and which was to have an impact on government and governance later in the century. Its attitude was reflected in its management of cleared sites. Although many residents had expressed a desire to stay in the slum areas, the cleared sites were not redeveloped for housing. council plans for redeveloping slum-clearance areas were openly criticised. Early in 1937, Lieutenant Colonel George Westcott, city Alderman and President of the Manchester Society of Architects, claimed, "we in this city are missing our way in the re-planning of cleared areas".[114] Some of the sites in Hulme and Collyhurst were being used for small factories and workshops rather than new housing. He maintained that there had been no system of replanning and felt that "the corporation should plan the clearance areas properly so that those who follow us may not be ashamed".[115] Some councillors shared the growing sense of frustration. Councillor Barnes tried to force the issue of redevelopment on cleared sites in Hulme by demanding that the Ministry of Health, the Housing Department and the City Surveyor report on the progress of plans to redevelop cleared areas within two months.[116] A Joint Committee report claimed that while some of the land was being used for small businesses, much of the remaining land was simply too expensive for housing. No other land was available, so proposals struggled. The council decided to enter negotiations to buy eight acres to build flats, but these also faltered.[117] The row rumbled on. Councillor Bentley urged the council to rezone the area for planning and housing purposes, but it was unable effectively to manage the situation and provide Hulme residents with the opportunity of returning to their community.

Slum clearance continued to be its primary objective. New clearance sites were announced for Newton Heath, Bradford and the St Michaels Ward area, raising the total number of houses under clearance schemes to 6,228.[118] Later in 1936, this increased to 10,475, but new housing schemes in the city only totalled 8,053. New developments were needed to bridge the gap, and although the council unveiled plans to build small estates at West Didsbury, Blackley and Openshaw, these were not sufficient to keep pace with the number of demolitions.[119] By late 1937, the number of houses under clearance schemes totalled 12,136, but still only 9,435 new ones were being built.[120] Problems were mounting for the council which were beyond its control. The rearmament programme was having a negative impact on progress, both in terms of rising costs and skilled labour shortages.

Despite these obstacles and constant frustrations, many on the council had not lost their zeal for reform. The slum-clearance programme continued in 1938 with proposals to sweep away 1,855 houses in New Cross. The public inquiry was one of the biggest held in the city. Resistance was intense. However, not all were campaigning for the rights of the poor. There were thirteen barristers and a host of solicitors sitting in opposition to the plans, one of which represented the Mayor, Alderman Grime, who had four properties under threat. Leading the defence was the indomitable Alderman Jackson. Jackson was on a crusade and nothing would stop him. He likened opponents to the resistance offered by property owners to the closure of cellar dwellings in the nineteenth century. When asked by counsel if he was trying to rearrange the whole of Manchester, he defiantly exclaimed, "that is a quite laudable object".[121] Jackson was only stopped by the outbreak of war, but he lost none of his drive, vision or ambition. By the end of the war he was ready to recommence battle.

Progressives like Jackson had continued to drive the reformist agenda in the 1930s. The council had been faced with an array of complex and conflicting problems and attitudes. In addition, the scale of the housing problem remained daunting. This was evident in the slum-clearance programmes. Entire communities, often close-knit, would have to be swept away. Large sections of the city had to be demolished, huge areas laid waste. The council was as bold and ambitious as ever. Yet the values emanating from civic culture, the hopes and ambitions evident in local discourse, could not always overcome local problems. The pressure was increasing from all sides. It was faced with a large number of issues – what to do with the tenants, how to manage them and where to put them. Again, the result was a limited policy, further curtailed by economic and physical barriers.

Faced with such problems, tenant aspirations, above and beyond living in a new home, were never considered. The council's attitude to tenants continued to be characterised by a top-down, philanthropic outlook. While it was generally accepted that they were victims of their environment, there remained a sense that tenants needed to be controlled through a series of rules (and superintendents for the flats). The council's approach was never seriously questioned. Society remained largely paternalistic and trust between the council and the tenant was undiminished. However, the limited tenant protests that occasionally emerged anticipated a different attitude. They were capable of developing their own discourse, even though it was largely ignored. If tenant confidence in the council faded, and if tenants felt injustices were being perpetrated, then some were prepared to make a stand. It was a lesson that was to be lost for several decades.

Notes

1   E. D. Simon, *How to Abolish the Slums* (London, 1929), p. 1.
2   I would like to thank Professor Pat Garside for generously providing much of the material that follows.
3   E. White, *A History of the Manchester and Salford Council of Social Service 1919–1969* (Manchester, 1969).
4   M. Fitzgerald, 'Manchester and Salford Better Housing Council', *Social Welfare*, January (1931), 91–2.

5 The government attempted to carry out its own national survey during 1935–36 to determine the extent of overcrowding across the country. See J. White, 'When every room was measured: the overcrowding survey of 1935–36 and its aftermath', *History Workshop Journal*, 4 (1977), 86–94.

6 M. Fitzgerald, 'The Manchester and Salford Council of Social Services', *Social Welfare*, October (1931).

7 Fitzgerald, 'Manchester and Salford Better Housing Council'.

8 *Some Housing Conditions in Chorlton-on-Medlock*, Manchester and District Regional Survey Society, No. 12 (Manchester, 1931).

9 Ibid.

10 Ibid.

11 Women were again prominent amongst the serving officers, with D. L. Pilkington acting as Honorary Treasurer and A. Trench as the Honorary Secretary.

12 *Report of a Survey Undertaken in Part of St. Michael's and Collegiate Wards of the City of Manchester, 1931*, Manchester and Salford Better Housing Council, the Red Bank Survey Group (Manchester, 1931).

13 Ibid.

14 *Under the Arches (Behind London Road Station), Report of a Survey Undertaken for Manchester and Salford Better Housing Council in St. Clements Ward in the City of Manchester*, Manchester and Salford Better Housing Council, the Red Bank Survey Group (Manchester, 1931). Also, Spurrier wrote a graphic description of the area published in the *Illustrated London News* (25 November 1933).

15 *Report of a Survey Undertaken in Part of St. Michael's and Collegiate Wards*.

16 *Ancoats: A Study of a Clearance Area, Report of a Survey Made in 1937–1938*, Manchester University Settlement (Manchester, 1945).

17 Ibid.

18 The actual figure was 26.5 per cent. *Ancoats: A Study of a Clearance Area*.

19 Ibid.

20 J. Inman, *Poverty and Housing Conditions in a Manchester Ward* (Manchester, 1934).

21 *Manchester Guardian* (28 March 1934).

22 Housing Committee minutes, 14 March 1932.

23 Simon, *How to Abolish the Slums*, pp. 99–101.

24 Again, see A. Mayne, *The Imagined Slum: Newspaper Representations in Three Cities, 1870–1914* (Leicester, 1993).

25 *Some Housing Conditions in Chorlton-on-Medlock*.

26 Ibid.

27 This is not to romanticise slum dwellers or to claim that 'dangerous' elements did not exist. The reality is complex. While there were respectable and misrepresented residents in working-class communities, evident in these reports, there were also rougher elements. See, for example, R. McKibbin, *Classes and Cultures, England 1918–1952* (Oxford, 2000).

28 *Some Housing Conditions in Chorlton-on-Medlock*.

29 Ibid.

30 Ibid.

31 Ibid.

32 Ibid.

33 *Ancoats: A Study of a Clearance Area*.

34 *Report of a Survey Undertaken in Part of St. Michael's and Collegiate Wards*.

35 Ibid.

36 Ibid.

37 *Some Social Aspects of Pre-War Tenements and of Post-War Flats*, Manchester and District Regional Survey Society, No. 12 (Manchester, 1932).
38 Ibid.
39 L. Heywood, '50,000 Houses below a reasonable standard of habitation', Manchester Central Reference Library cuttings, 1934.
40 Ibid.
41 *Some Social Aspects of Pre-War Tenements and of Post-War Flats*.
42 Ibid.
43 Ibid.
44 Ibid.
45 Ibid.
46 Ibid.
47 Ibid.
48 Manchester Housing Committee minutes, 13 June 1932.
49 Ibid., 14 May 1934.
50 Ibid., 8 July 1935, 15 June 1936.
51 Ibid., 20 May 1936, 14 June 1937, 20 December 1937.
52 See, for example, M. Clapson, 'Working-class women's experiences of moving to new housing estates in England since 1919', *Twentieth Century British History*, 10:3 (1999), 345–65.
53 There may be a direct correlation between satisfaction levels and the level of slum conditions from which people were being rehoused. In some areas, the worse the conditions the greater the desire to leave. See Clapson, 'Working-class women's experiences'.
54 *Wythenshawe, Report of an Investigation* (Manchester and Salford Better Housing Council, 1935).
55 Ibid.
56 *Manchester University Settlement Diamond Jubilee – Souvenir Brochure*; H. Cashmore, 'An interesting co-operative venture', *The Woman Citizen* (20 July 1929).
57 S. Adderley, 'Bureaucratic conceptions of citizenship in the voluntary sector, 1919–1939' (PhD dissertation, University of Wales, Bangor, 2001).
58 M. Tylecote, 'Community Associations on new estates', *The Woman Citizen*, March (1937).
59 Manchester Housing Committee minutes, 8 April 1935.
60 *Manchester Guardian* (3 October 1935).
61 Ibid.
62 Manchester Housing Committee minutes, 8 December 1930.
63 *Report of a Survey Undertaken in Part of St. Michael's and Collegiate Wards*.
64 *Some Housing Conditions in Chorlton-on-Medlock*.
65 *Social Studies of a Manchester City Ward*, Manchester University Settlement (Manchester, 1931).
66 Manchester Housing Committee minutes, 9 March 1931.
67 Ibid., 11 April 1932.
68 Rent Book for 1932, Manchester Central Reference Library.
69 Ibid.
70 Heywood, '50,000 Houses below a reasonable standard of habitation'.
71 Ibid.
72 *Report of a Survey Undertaken in part of St. Michael's and Collegiate Wards*.
73 Simon, *How to Abolish the Slums*, pp. 34–48.
74 *Ancoats: A Study of a Clearance Area*.
75 Ibid.

76 Ibid.
77 Ibid.
78 Manchester Housing Committee minutes, 18 April 1931.
79 See below Chapter 7.
80 *Manchester Evening News* (26 July 1933).
81 Manchester Housing Committee minutes, 3 July 1933.
82 *Manchester Evening News* (26 July 1933).
83 Manchester Housing Committee minutes, 3 July 1933.
84 *Manchester Evening News* (21 June 1933).
85 Manchester Housing Committee minutes, 29 March 1933.
86 Hulme Housing Association, Survey Section Report, 15 March 1931.
87 Hulme Housing Association, Preliminary Report, 15 May 1932.
88 The involvement of women is a characteristic of tenant action and organised groups throughout the century.
89 *Manchester Guardian* (22 July 1933).
90 Ibid.
91 Ibid.
92 Ibid.
93 *Daily Dispatch* (22 July 1933).
94 Ibid. (7 August 1933).
95 M. Fitzgerald, 'Report on the Tenants concerned in the Hulme slum clearance scheme', cited in Simon, *How to Abolish the Slums*, p. 45.
96 See Clapson, 'Working-class women's experiences'.
97 *Manchester Evening Chronicle* (12 September 1933).
98 *Daily Express* (11 November 1933).
99 Manchester Housing Committee minutes, 10 April 1933.
100 *Manchester Guardian* (4 August 1933).
101 *Manchester Evening Chronicle* (15 September 1933).
102 *Manchester Evening News* (13 September 1933).
103 L. Heywood, '50,000 Houses below a reasonable standard of habitation'.
104 Ibid.
105 Manchester Housing Committee minutes, 9 October 1933.
106 *Manchester Guardian* (1 November 1933).
107 *Manchester Evening News* (27 October 1933).
108 *Manchester Evening Chronicle* (30 October 1933).
109 *Manchester Evening News* (17 November 1933).
110 *Manchester Guardian* (15 July 1933); Manchester Housing Committee minutes, 9 August 1933.
111 *Daily Dispatch* (11 April 1934).
112 Ibid.
113 Manchester Housing Committee minutes, 8 July 1935.
114 *Manchester Guardian* (11 February 1937).
115 Ibid.
116 Manchester Housing Committee minutes, 8 March 1937.
117 Ibid., 10 May 1937, 14 June 1937.
118 Ibid., 15 June 1936.
119 Ibid., 12 October 1936, 31 March 1937, 15 November 1937.
120 Ibid., 15 November 1937.
121 *Manchester Guardian* (29 April 1937).

5 The post-war housing problem and the great overspill drive[1]

After the Second World War, Manchester council's housing reformers were determined to force the pace of change. Although it had accomplished much in the inter-war period, the council was still a long way from achieving its aims. It had a clear vision – build a New Jerusalem of 40,000 homes for inner-city slum dwellers in a series of estates in towns outside the borders of the Manchester conurbation.[2] Overspill estates would allow them to build high-quality homes in leafy areas like north Cheshire. Civic culture again provided the framework of reference. Cottage-style homes built in clean green areas were supposed to provide an idyllic environment for the working classes. Wythenshawe had provided the benchmark. With the onset of war came a fresh determination to sweep away the slums and create a brave new world. After 1945, it was decided that over half of Manchester's housing needs had to be met with overspill estates. Yet Manchester still had to overcome its old problem of lack of available land. The lofty aims of the local discourse needed to overcome an on-going and all-too-real problem. Land could only be secured at the expense of other local authorities.

Unsurprisingly, many of these resisted plans to decant thousands of slum dwellers, still under the jurisdiction of Manchester city council, into their neighbourhoods. Securing the land at Wythenshawe had been problematic, but further large-scale expansion was to involve a series of lengthy and often bitter disputes. These quarrels between local authorities played a key role in shaping housing strategies. Council-wars broke out, seriously affecting the ability of Manchester to fulfil its utopian dreams. The grand narrative stumbled on a fundamental local problem. There remained an intense dislike of high-rise flats, lack of suitable land and thousands of houses were in a serious state of decay. Ultimately, the overspill struggles curtailed the council's plans. Only half of its original targets were completed, leaving a trail of recriminations along the way.

The post-war vision

Manchester's immediate concern after the war was general needs provision. The acute housing shortages had increased because of bomb damage, the rising number of private families and the suspension of building. In November 1944, the Housing Committee agreed to build 3,000 temporary homes.[3] This was a provisional measure designed to meet the immediate housing crisis. Slum clearance was pushed further down the agenda. At this stage, any house, even a slum, was better than no house.

However, there remained a keen awareness of the underlying long-term problems. The 1942 Housing Committee Report laid bare the stark reality facing the city. It estimated that 68,837 houses were needed to replace homes described as unfit for human habitation, while a total of 76,272 houses were needed in the long-term to meet increasing demand and 11,524 houses needed to meet immediate priorities.[4] Alderman Jackson again led the agenda for reform. As Mayor, he was partly responsible for the council's *1945 Redevelopment Plan*. In the plan the City Surveyor, R. Nicholas, claimed that, "in many respects the Manchester citizen of 1650 was in a better position to enjoy a healthy life".[5] He painted a grim picture in which people were condemned to live under a cloud of "perpetual smoke ... which enfeebles the health-giving property of the sun's rays and lowers our general vitality and to resist infection". The whole environment was decrepit. Structural defects and overcrowding were a constant source of misery for hundreds of thousands across the city. Although there had been some progress, the bulk of the problem had changed little since the damning reports of the 1930s. People continued to be huddled in houses that lacked individual space and even the most basic modern amenities. The problems were underlined by the former leader of the council, Councillor William Egerton. He described the "mass of multi-occupational dwellings which were all unfit ... outside toilets, no hot water, some hadn't even got electric". He remembered that his auntie "did not even have electric until she was moved up to Hattersley ... she did not know what it was to have electric, or hot water ... she only had a cold tap".[6]

The pressure to build quickly, and in large numbers, came from the local political desire to act. Egerton claimed that the waiting lists rather than central government drove them. He declared, "you were being pressurised by people who were living in crummy conditions, in houses they wanted to get out of ... pressure [came] from the housing waiting list". Added urgency came from central government, but "pressure came from tenants, the pressure of the housing list". The human need was desperate and pressing. But plans were still framed by the ideals of its civic culture. In the *1945 Manchester Redevelopment Plan*, Nicholas posed the question, "is Manchester prepared once again to give the country a bold lead by adopting standards of reconstruction that will secure to every citizen the enjoyment of fresh air, of a reasonable ration of daylight, and of some relief from the barren bleakness of bricks and mortar?"[7] By taking a "bold lead" Manchester would again be a city of firsts. Housing was to be an extension of the city's heritage, its structure of feeling.

General needs provision, it was hoped, would be met by a series of new towns and overspill estates. These were an extension of the out-county estates of the inter-war period. The idea of developing new towns was developed by the Garden Cities and Town Planning Association and, from 1936, by its campaigning secretary F. J. Osborn. Osborn wanted a hundred new towns to help rehouse millions of inner-city slum dwellers in clean, green areas. These would be carefully planned, with, again, the working man's cottage as the housing template. The dispersal of a huge section of the population became central to immediate post-war thinking. It was evident in the Barlow Commission Report, which set the standards after the war, and in the 1946 New Towns Act, which led to the creation of a series of planned and self-contained towns away from inner-city misery. The council's thinking was also in step with the Dudley Report of 1944. In many respects, this was 1918 revisited. Like the Tudor Walters Report, it recommended building quality cottage homes with indoor bathrooms and toilets.[8] The Housing Committee fully supported the proposals.[9] Tower blocks were rejected in favour of working-class suburban overspill estates. The *1945 Redevelopment Plan* included a survey which concluded that "the majority of people with young families wish to move into dwelling houses". Nicholas stated that while some believed that redevelopment should embrace "large blocks of flats, with trees, lawns, playgrounds and flower-gardens in between", he thought "it would be a profound sociological mistake to force upon the British public, in defiance of its own widely expressed preference for separate houses with private gardens, a way of life that is fundamentally out of keeping with its traditions, instincts and opportunities".[10] Tower blocks were fine for people "on the continent", but not for the British workers.[11]

The press again provided an important platform for the promotion of its vision. In 1954, the *Manchester Guardian* argued that building upwards was "no solution for Manchester". Tall blocks of flats were seen as unsuitable for families with young children, cost twice as much and would prove so unpopular that they would be a "dead loss" once the housing shortage was over.[12] The message went to the top of government circles. Evelyn Sharp, the Permanent Secretary of the Ministry of Housing and Local Government, recognised that Manchester always "disliked flats", because it believed that they "produce a bad social result and increase your building costs".[13]

The influence of Manchester's civic culture was given fresh impetus by a new and more determined council. Post-war Manchester city council was dominated by Labour. With the brief exception of 1967–71, Labour has since had a complete monopoly of power.[14] Post-war Manchester, therefore, has effectively been a one-party state. Like cities across the country, Labour members in Manchester dreamed of building a New Jerusalem. The desire to secure the best possible housing, whilst also improving the status and profile of the city, were not mutually exclusive objectives. Even though overspill would form the central feature of future plans, Nicholls had been keen to stress that there would be "plenty of scope for taste and imagination and vision", and that "the ultimate achievement of the city beautiful should be our constant purpose".[15] The council's ambition to do things big was also a feature of its post-war plans. Large-scale redevelopment, however, could not be achieved within the existing city boundaries. The land trap continued to be a thorn in the council's side. It was desperate to secure land outside of the city's boundaries. Expansion into other areas would provide it with the opportunity to maintain control and influence over its population, whilst also freeing up space for inner-city development. Councillor Ottiwell Lodge, Chairman of the Town Planning and Buildings Committee, claimed in the *1945 Redevelopment Plan* that the biggest problem of all would be moving 120,000 people to a new town or to existing towns outside the city. In 1945, the Housing Committee stressed that the most urgent question facing it was how to secure enough land for a series of large developments.[16] Its ambition depended on overspill. If it was to meet the standards it had set itself then it was vital that immediate and decisive action be taken to acquire lands beyond the existing boundaries, to "provide houses for the overspill".[17]

Overspill – the great estates

Manchester came to embrace the policy of overspill more than any other city. Its open hostility to tower blocks marked it out. It was the only city which embraced it as official municipal policy.[18] The strong local tradition of building cottages led the council in 1944 to ban building flats higher than four storeys.[19] Horsfall, Marr and Simon's enduring influence, and its unswerving belief in suburban cottages, influenced the council's decision to look towards developments outside the conurbation.[20] Like the creation of Wythenshawe, it was supported by Lady Simon, the *Manchester Guardian* and the City Surveyor.[21] The case for expansion was underlined by Maurice Fizgerald KC, who told a House of Lords Committee that Manchester must "expand or die".[22] He pointed out that, with the exception of London, Manchester was unique in the way it was enclosed by the surrounding conurbation.[23] Neighbouring Salford MP, Frank Allaun, publicly argued that Manchester had to build 43,000 new homes outside the existing city boundaries. The council hoped to build 51,500 houses during 1951–71 at a rate of 2,400 per year.[24] It was a huge target and even Evelyn Sharp recognised that it could not possibly carry through the programme within the city limits.[25]

The desire for large-scale overspill was constantly reiterated throughout the 1950s and much of the 1960s. Even in 1965 when, as will be seen, the council had been scarred by years of dispute with other local authorities, it was still making the case for new schemes. It was impossible to build at the same density levels on inner-city sites. Even building flats would not have provided a solution. Edgar Rose, the Deputy Planning Officer, commented that "the same situation arose in every other residential redevelopment area, and this is why the city needs overspill areas".[26] Rose added that, with a slum clearance rate of 5,000 houses a year, the city had to find new areas. It had used almost every metre of available building land within its boundaries and now had no choice but to build outside the city. Developing new towns and extensive overspill estates were absolutely vital.[27]

Estates were built in several surrounding areas. They included the largest at Langley near Middleton, which was started in 1953 and which eventually had 4,500 new homes. Initially, the council had bought land on the Bowlee Estate in 1937.[28] Its original plan was to build 8,000 houses on the 550-acre site, but building was delayed until after the war. The Manchester Corporation Bill finally went before the Lords in 1950, and, following the first batch of 696 homes, plans to build 1,000 new homes were unveiled in 1952.[29] Although, like many schemes, responsibility was divided between the local Middleton Corporation, the county council (in this case Lancashire) and Manchester Corporation, the city remained the principle landowner and developer. It built the houses, shops and roads and was responsible for public transport. Middleton was only in control of the basic maintenance of amenities such playgrounds and street cleaning, while the county managed the schools. It was also hoped to build a full range of social facilities and to attract new industry into the area. The population rose from 32,607 in 1951 to 42,367 in 1955, and was estimated to continue rising to 56,000 by 1971.[30]

Broadly, this was the pattern that Manchester city council wanted to replicate across the region. It had a clear vision that extended the work and ideas of the Simons and other progressives from the inter-war period. This included expanding south into the clean air of Cheshire. Manchester would own and maintain the properties with its own Direct Works Department. This secured both jobs and finance. The council did not want to dilute its own power base. Bill Egerton stated that "overspills were Manchester houses and we retain ownership". He admitted that "basically, it was a bit of intransigence on our part" and that it was "trying to retain Manchester stock for Manchester people".[31] There were only three problems with the grand plan. First, it did not always have the support of neighbouring local authorities on whose land it was planning to build. The tension between town and country had emerged throughout the inter-war period, with the likes of J. B. Priestley and H. J. Massingham passionately promoting the defence of the rural idyll in the face of expanding urbanisation.[32] Second, it was perceived as a city trying to expand its own political power base. Third, it never consulted tenants.

Manchester's problems were illustrated with its ambitious plans to build large estates at Mobberley, Knutsford and Hattersley (all in Cheshire), and Westhoughton in Lancashire. Mobberley was proposed as the first area for expansion. In March 1946, the government raised the possibility of building a new town in Mobberley for between 50,000-60,000 people. In November 1949, Manchester city council sought powers to acquire 2,650 acres of land at Mobberley for housing. Lymm soon followed. It was estimated that this could lead to a population dispersal of 80,000 tenants. Victory appeared to be in sight when the city obtained permission to purchase land. It had the backing of Town and Country Planning Minister Lewis Silkin, but a town meeting and a poll of electors both rejected the scheme. Battle had commenced.

Opposition grew in ferocity as the years passed. Wartime unity, together with the dreams and promises of a brave new world for everyone, drifted away as neighbouring local authorities realised that Manchester's vision could only be realised at their expense. There were many issues at stake, including land values, preserving agricultural pastures and the more basic issue of power and authority. Although never stated, there is also a suspicion that residents in affluent areas around Cheshire did not relish the prospect of thousands of inner-city slum dwellers moving into their towns and villages. The impact would have been immense. Resistance emerged as early as 1946 when the *Manchester Evening News* pointed out that "county councils dislike outside authorities having greater power in their counties".[33] In 1950, Councillor Tom Nally, Chairman of the Planning Committee, claimed that the council had lost three years in developing new estates and clearing slums because it was being continually frustrated in its attempts to build outside the city boundaries due to the "jealousy and competition between districts around Manchester".[34] But this was not simply an issue of 'jealousy', or of Tory middle-class Cheshire waging a class war with Labour working-class Manchester. There was much more at stake.

Cheshire county council began its resistance by refusing to co-operate over the proposal to build new houses in Lymm. A co-ordinated resistance campaign emerged across a broad front as opposition came from across Cheshire. The main argument centred on the preservation of quality agricultural land. In 1949, the Bishop of Chester expressed his fears at a diocesan conference. Dr D. H. Crick said that, "if there was any county in England where agricultural land should be carefully safeguarded, that county was Cheshire, with its long history of skilled and productive husbandry".[35] Like many others in the county, Crick felt that it was disturbing to hear that some of the nation's most fertile acres should be appropriated for new housing estates. *Cheshire Life* lamented that it was no good giving people homes if they could not have food, and that new towns of 40,000 people living in areas "properly belonging to cows and corn" was a desperately serious matter.[36] In 1953, the Cheshire branch of the National Farmers' Union decided to set up a fighting fund of £5,000 to cover its costs in opposing the scheme.[37] It took its battle to the public inquiry, which began in October 1953. Joining them was an amalgamation of interest groups including the county council, other local authorities and the Cheshire County Landowners' Association. Leading figures in planning and land utilisation were brought in to

strengthen their case, including Sir Patrick Abercrombie, who, somewhat ironically, had given his support to the development of Wythenshawe in the 1930s,
and Professor Dudley Stamp. Both supported the case for preserving the land in
the interests of farming and green belt protection.[38] They enjoyed the sympathies
of the Tory government which, throughout much of the 1950s, supported their
fellow Conservatives.[39] In October 1954, Harold Macmillan, Minister of
Housing and Local Government, refused to allow Manchester permission to
carry out the proposed developments at Mobberley and Lymm. Agricultural land
values were again stressed in a letter sent by the Ministry to the council. The
Ministry pointed out that in view of the agricultural quality of the land in both
Mobberley and Lymm the "Minister is clear that it would be wrong to allow
development in either place if that can be avoided".[40]

The council refused to roll over. It continued to make objections and
campaign for a reversal of the decision. In 1957, it tried to step up its campaign.
The city's MPs gathered to form a plan to fight on all fronts in order to rouse
public opinion and force the government to change its mind. They believed that
the new Minister, Henry Brooke, had to be "worked on" unrelentingly.[41] MPs
met the council over Easter to produce a combined plan of action. They aimed
to increase pressure on the government through a series of public protest
meetings and a three-hour parliamentary debate.[42] Verbal blows between the two
sides were exchanged later in the month. At a local town and country planning
conference, attended by eighty local authorities held in the city, the council
warned that it would "never give-up" in its determination to acquire the green
acres of Cheshire for its slum-suffering families.[43] Alderman R. E. Thomas, Chair
of Manchester's General and Parliamentary Committee, warned the Cheshire
delegates that the city could not relinquish its claims on Mobberley and Lymm
even if its application was rejected. Councillor Biggins added that if the Minister
refused it would have to "apply to the next minister and the minister after him
if need be".[44] Cheshire's politicians were unmoved. Alderman Howard Robinson
replied that Manchester was not fully developing land already available in the city
and that it should fill in these sites before attempting to take over good-quality
agricultural land.[45] Equally unmoved, the city officials denounced Cheshire's lack
of co-operation, claiming it was time the county did something for the benefit
of humanity in large and not just for Cheshire.[46] Alderman Thomas added that
only "one and a half per cent of the total arable land of the county was needed
for housing development", and that such a loss could be met by increasing
efficiency.[47]

The issue of agricultural land was also raised when Manchester unveiled its
proposals for a large overspill development of 4,500 new homes for over 20,000
tenants in Hattersley, near Hyde, in north-east Cheshire. In 1955, when the
proposals for the estate won a narrow victory in the local council, one of the
objectors claimed that Hyde would lose its farmlands and become one vast built-
up area as the "folds we have referred to with affection will go".[48] However, on

this occasion, Tory-dominated Cheshire county council was prepared to sacrifice an area on its north-east outskirts, bordering on the damp Pennines, and, most importantly, controlled by Labour. Hyde was an established Labour area with a large working-class population. Cheshire county council was prepared to make the sacrifice.

In contrast, it remained steadfast on the issue of overspill in the affluent middle-class districts of Mobberley and Lymm. Cheshire county council produced proposals to create a green belt designed, in the opinion of the city, to prevent Manchester from obtaining land at Mobberley and Lymm.[49] The Tories had built a brick wall against which the Labour council failed to make any impression. Tory unity on the defence of Cheshire was never stated in public, but as early as October 1954, following the initial refusal by Macmillan to allow building at Lymm and Mobberley, Duncan Sandys, the Minister for Housing, received a brief private note from someone inside government, signed Sir Robert, exclaiming "all my congratulations: and you have done it alone!"[50] He described the struggle as the "dark days of (a) war", fought between Labour-controlled Manchester and Tory Cheshire. The following day Sir Robert again wrote to Sandys expressing his fears that Manchester would continue with what he repeatedly described as its "war of nerves" against Cheshire.[51] Evelyn Sharp had actually agreed that Manchester should be allowed one of the two big sites, preferably at Lymm, but Macmillan had refused.[52] With the Tories in power, Manchester faced an uphill struggle. In July 1958, the Ministry turned down yet another application. The inquiry, carried out by Ramsay Willis QC, reiterated the case made by Cheshire's agricultural lobby.[53] In a draft minute to the Prime Minister, Henry Brooke admitted that "to be candid, I do not think that Mr. Willis' report is of the first quality", and that it was not as thorough and cogent a piece of reasoning as he would have liked.[54] Officials privately agreed that much of the Willis report was open to criticism.[55] Nevertheless, the Tory government supported the findings and, once again, rejected Manchester's application. Vested partisan interests were operating behind the scenes.

The council became understandably disgruntled. In 1959, Alderman Thomas told *The Times* that the city's patience was "wearing very thin with Whitehall". For a short time in 1959, it appeared that the government might relent. It was reported that Henry Brooke was to announce to the Commons that the government was satisfied that Manchester needed a large area for development of new town proportions.[56] Again, this proved to be a false dawn. When Labour returned to power and Crossman visited Manchester in January 1965, he was told that the city still wanted to build at Lymm, but when he met the President of the National Farmers Union it was made clear that Lymm "was the apple of the N.F.U.'s eye", and that it would fight for it "tooth and nail".[57]

Manchester had to concede defeat. Small-scale developments had been built around the outskirts of the city, but officials were insisting that it needed one or two larger developments.[58] Necessity, and an unswerving belief in the value of overspill estates, meant that attention now turned elsewhere. The attitude and reluctance to co-operate on the part of both the Tory government and Cheshire county council created frustration, bitterness and suspicion in the city council. As a result, its attitude hardened. When Macclesfield town council refused to discuss proposals for an estate in the town, Councillor Thomas made it clear that the city would not be able to get its own way through agreements but would have to pressure government into taking action over the heads of the local authority.[59] From its perspective, it was trying to create a new environment for its tenants, to give them a fresh and better start in life. It wanted to end the misery of the slums by decanting tenants to green areas with low density levels. This had been its objective since the creation of the Housing Committee in 1919. Civic culture revolved around a certainty in the moral value of this ideal. The alternatives were high-rise tower blocks which it had never felt suitable for families. From its perspective, the council was simply trying to improve the lives of ordinary people and transform the physical appearance of the city. But it was met with resistance and suspicion.

Manchester met opposition in a number of areas. There was a fundamental power issue at stake. Neighbouring authorities had a different interpretation of Manchester's motives. Relations between Manchester and Cheshire continued to deteriorate. When Evelyn Sharp considered arranging a conference between north-west authorities, she realised that it would be difficult as the antagonism between Manchester and Cheshire was as "bitter as anywhere".[60] Cheshire county council, however, was not the only one to consider Manchester's actions as politically suspicious. A number of local authorities felt that Manchester was ignoring them and that it was trying to expand its sphere of influence across the whole of south-east Lancashire and north-east Cheshire at their expense. The council seemed to be pushing through its own agenda without considering what other local authorities had planned. Middleton Corporation, for example, reacted angrily to proposals from the city to expand its estate in Langley to neighbouring Alkrington because it had earmarked the site for a development of its own.[61] Manchester was accused of being dismissive. Similarly, plans for a hundred-acre site near Altrincham were resisted by the local authority because it wanted the land for its own purposes.[62] Local councils became increasingly agitated at Manchester's seemingly relentless drive to purchase all available sites. The interests of the existing local authority were being ignored. When the council announced plans to build a small development in the affluent area of Bramhall, the local Councillor G. E. Wilson conceded that "there is no hope whatsoever that consideration will be given to our views by Manchester Corporation", and that, although it had taken every step possible to keep Manchester out of the area, the city council had made it clear it would proceed.[63] A number of local authorities began to interpret the city's action as evidence that Manchester was seeking to expand politically, to become a large imperial city. In 1963, Cheshire MP, Mrs E. Hill, wrote to the new Minister, Keith Joseph, urging him to look carefully at any scheme put forward by Manchester because the city was "looked upon as a great big octopus" intent on spreading its tentacles everywhere, building council houses and ruining surrounding areas.[64] A Cheshire county council memo of August 1965 pointed out that large-scale overspill would inevitably have a devastating effect on the county, not only in providing services to a large new population but also on the structure of government itself.[65] It was claimed that it would only be human nature that, if Manchester was permitted to take a large slice of north Cheshire, it should also become the local authority.[66]

This was a major issue as Manchester tried to expand into other areas, most obviously in Westhoughton near Bolton. There is little evidence to suggest that the council was planning a gradual takeover of the entire region. If any on the council did have imperialist ambitions they were not expressed. But Manchester did want to keep as much control over the process as possible, a fact underlined by Evelyn Sharp who recognised that the city was adamant that it should build all overspill houses.[67] However, from the council's perspective this was not the primary motivation or objective. Its consistent aim since the 1920s had been the development of new suburbs, quality houses in green areas. Manchester's councillors believed they were being exploited and that they were constantly being held to ransom by local authorities over issues such as who should pay for new services and infrastructure, not just for the estate but for the existing town.[68]

In 1962, the director of the Town and Country Planning Association, Wyndham Thomas, gave the city his full support in a fresh bid to win government approval for new overspill schemes.[69] Initial proposals for Westhoughton had been unveiled in 1958 and had been met with a cautionary welcome by some local councillors. After the frustration of Cheshire, the city decided to pursue its plans with vigour. Following his inquiry and recommendations about Lymm in 1958, J. Ramsay Willis QC told the government that Westhoughton might be the best area for Manchester overspill. Proposals were extremely ambitious, with Manchester hoping to build 12,300 new homes. If the plans were successful then the population of the small Lancashire town would increase from 15,000 to 57,000, with further private developments taking it to a massive 78,000 by 1981.[70] This would have provided a huge fillip for Manchester, but the reaction to its plans caused a bitter split inside the town. Objectors to the Westhoughton proposals made unsubstantiated accusations that Manchester was trying to expand its territory at their expense. Again, this was a misinterpretation of its ambitions. Nevertheless, the two sides locked horns in what became a long and angry struggle. Although many appreciated Manchester's need for land, opponents were convinced that Westhoughton was being asked to sacrifice too much.[71] These opponents became furious with the publication of the proposed town map, showing the extent of the development. Again, there was a perception that Manchester would swallow them up. The arguments about overspill were inevitably linked with debates about the future of local government, and opponents made it plain that Westhoughton would prefer to continue under the two-tier system of government than to be linked with a "new Manchester county".[72]

The controlling Labour group on the local authority desperately attempted to sell the idea to residents. One local councillor, Mary McIntyre, claimed that the new Westhoughton would be a thrilling place in which to live, work and play. In the local party news-sheet, she hit back at letters in the local press criticising the proposals, claiming she had not found a single constructive idea – just a lot of "windy criticism". She heralded the proposals as a bright new dawn for the town, with new shops, facilities and jobs. McIntyre claimed that the project was a vast one and that it was "too big, too visionary, too magnificent" for some to imagine. She felt it was all "too human, too glorious, an idea to be destroyed by men with no vision in their souls".[73] Some residents were also willing to put their heads over the parapet and express their support. In a letter to the local newspaper, D. H. Wright hoped that the locals would set aside their fears and criticisms and, with goodwill, make their new fellow citizens conscious of a "warm and friendly welcome".[74] He even suggested that people should stop using negative terms such as 'overspill', in favour of 'The Manchester Resettlement Scheme'.

Others were not as generous and understanding. The political backlash left blood on the carpet. Backed by the Chamber of Commerce and Ratepayers Association, some local residents and councillors formed the Anti-Overspill Association to campaign against the plans. Local elections led to the defeat of three Labour councillors in safe seats and loss of overall control for the first time in the history of the local authority. There was little doubt that the dominant factor in the result was the attitude of locals towards Manchester and the overspill proposal. The severity of the swing against Labour at the local level was highlighted by the national resurgence in support.

Attitudes between the two sides hardened. In July, the atmosphere started to turn ugly. The city council proclaimed it would continue with its plans, regardless of what was being said in Westhoughton. Alderman Quinney, leader of the council's special sub-committee, threatened that the city would "still go on if Westhoughton will not co-operate". Quinney's posturing intensified the belief in Westhoughton that it was being bullied. The leader of the opposition in Westhoughton, Councillor Davies, retorted that Quinney's comment left little to the imagination about the future of Westhoughton under "Manchester's dictatorship". He asked what it hoped to achieve by "these dictatorial methods", and stated that for Manchester to force its will on the people of Westhoughton did not reflect any credit on the city. He asked them "not to confuse might with right".[75] After the end of a meeting, at which Westhoughton council officially withdrew its support for the overspill project, the allegations of dictatorship levelled against the city council were reinforced when one anonymous member unveiled a black and white swastika which "fluttered gently in the breeze from the flagpole on top of the town hall".[76] Councillor Battersby argued that this was a reaction against a city that was employing steam-roller tactics. It was certainly a gesture to emphasise allegations of dictatorship being levelled against the city council, whose representatives at the meeting were accused of threatening to force through the overspill project on its own.[77] The same allegations against the council had been made over Lymm. The struggle between Cheshire and Manchester was described as nothing less than a cold-blooded bid for "political power and aggrandisement by one very large and very rich community at the expense of another much smaller community (the comparison with Nazi Germany and Belgium is inescapable)".[78]

The next major hurdle for the battle of Westhoughton was the public inquiry, held in October. When the date of the meeting was announced it was claimed that, with the possible exception of a day in 1812 when the town's first power-driven factory was destroyed, there had never been a date more important in the town's history. Opponents to the scheme formed a petition which attracted more than 9,000 names from a possible 12,000 electors, and a fighting fund with more than 2,000 donors. On the eve of the public inquiry a public demonstration was organised by the Anti-Overspill Association. The demonstration was held at Bolton Town Hall and free transport was provided by local coach companies. Feelings were running so deep that a local taxi driver, Jim Sharples, offered to give anyone a lift that was suffering from infirmity.[79]

By March 1965, the battle was all but lost for Manchester. The Labour Minister of Housing, Richard Crossman, announced at a press conference in Preston that he had ordered 850 out of 913 houses that Manchester had tried to purchase under a Compulsory Purchase Order (CPO) to be reprieved. He also greatly reduced the amount of land for future development. Crossman claimed that relations between the warring councils were so bad that it was impossible for Manchester to make any realistic progress. Besides, by the early 1960s both Conservative and Labour governments were promoting technological solutions to the slum problems and to what they saw as an inherently backward building industry.[80] The Westhoughton Anti-Overspill Association secretary, Frank Davies, thanked Crossman for his "humane understanding" of the position at Westhoughton, adding that the bitterness and anger displayed underlined how much the people of Westhoughton felt about the proposal.[81] City council officials met Crossman in April, telling him that the diluted plans meant the whole scheme was little more that another corporation estate. Crossman promised to reflect on the issue, but nothing more. Yet again it had lost. Frank Davies was unsympathetic. The enmity and personal hostility had left a deep impression. He accused the city of trampling on nearly every town in this part of the north-west with its compulsory purchase orders, and smugly added that it had been put in its place by Crossman.[82] Events came to a conclusion in October 1966. The Labour Housing Minister, Anthony Greenwood, finally withdrew government support, explaining that he was satisfied that no further progress was possible because of the differences of opinion.[83] Greenwood claimed that he did not wish to comment on the dispute, but that it appeared to him that the issue was a substantial one that went wider than the drafting of terms of reference for consultants. For him, the two sides were in a deadlock and, quite simply, there was no way out. For the city, it was the final nail in the coffin. Sir Richard Harper, Chair of the Manchester-Westhoughton Overspill Sub-Committee, described the Minister's statement as a "tragedy", while Councillor Winifred Smith, Chair of the city's Housing Committee, realised that the news was a "terrific blow".[84] Westhoughton believed that it was just rewards for a city that wielded a big stick to get its own way.[85]

Westhoughton was not the only local authority to accuse Manchester of behaving like a despot. When the council changed the design of 1,000 houses for the Gamesley estate near Glossop, members of Glossop town council claimed that "this is dictatorship".[86] Equally, when Manchester unveiled its plan for a large 1,900-home estate at Walshaw near Bury, the local authority wrote to Manchester accusing it of using a "big stick" and warning them it was not prepared to be "pushed around".[87] At the public inquiry, the counsel for Bury Corporation accused Manchester of harbouring territorial ambitions over the area and charged them with oppression.[88] Small districts objected to what they regarded as insensitive bullying tactics. The issue of political domination was raised at Hyde council's debate into the proposed Hattersley estate. Alderman W. Barton alleged that Manchester's objective was a Manchester county council.[89] Some, like the Mayor, felt that Hyde was being sold down the river, while others were convinced that if it was not careful then it would find itself being governed from Albert Square, Manchester, and not from Hyde Town Hall.[90] At the heart of the issue was control over the new houses and tenants. Manchester demanded full control. This meant that a colony of 10,000 Mancunians would be living only ten miles from Manchester Town Hall. Why was Manchester doing this if, ultimately, it did not intend to use it as a means of creating a Manchester County?[91]

Ultimately, the Hattersley estate was successfully completed. It was not the only one. As Table 5.1 shows, the council was triumphant in building a number of overspill estates across the whole region, totalling over 21,000. Some are still owned by Manchester, though most have, or will be transferred to receiving local authorities. Fears of a Manchester take-over were, in the end, a little exaggerated.

Overspill and tenants

The figures would be impressive were it not for the fact that the city had aimed to build twice as many houses. Manchester's failure highlighted one obvious problem with its overspill policy – it was not always shared by other local author-ities. Nor was it always shared by people in the receiving areas or even the tenants it was hoping to move from the slums. The council was desperate to move people into new suburbs. Its slum problems were vast and the land trap was

Table 5.1   Overspill estates (approx. figures)

Overspill estate	No. of properties	District	Current status
Partington	1800	Trafford	large-scale transfer 1996
Langley	4500	Rochdale	transfer imminent
Darnhill	1800	Rochdale	large-scale transfer 1999
Whitefield	1500	Bury	large-scale transfer 2000
Hattersley	3500	Tameside	still owned by Manchester
Haughton Green	1500	Tameside	still owned by Manchester
Sale	2000	Trafford	large-scale transfer 2000
Handforth	1000	Macclesfield	large-scale transfer 2001
Knutsford	600	Macclesfield	large-scale transfer 2001
Stockport	2000	Stockport	still owned by Manchester
Wilmslow	900	Macclesfield	large-scale transfer 1999
Carrbrook	100	Tameside	tenant management co-op
Total	21200		

(*Source*: Manchester city council Housing Department)

an insurmountable barrier for an authority that had been so determined to avoid building flats. Despite all the difficulties, this remained a part of its civic culture. But it was, in many ways, an idealistic vision which ignored practical problems, including prejudice. Although rarely stated in public, people in receiving areas dreaded the thought of having thousands of slum dwellers dumped on their doorsteps. There was an undercurrent of feeling against slum dwellers that had echoes of the pre-war perceptions of them as socially inferior and even a little dangerous. They were often described by protestors as 'immigrants'. *Cheshire Life* bemoaned the fact that in Partington, near Lymm, Manchester had "unloaded a large alien community on to a hostile countryside", leading to an increase in the crime rate.[92] Similarly, Cheshire resident Morton Forrest claimed that a projected "immigration of 80,000" would destroy the county's contribution to the nation's food supplies and would strike at the roots of "England's heritage, the land and its people".[93] When Manchester announced its plans for 3,500 houses at Church Coppenhall near Crewe, villagers protested that it would spoil their select village. Residents such as Mr Bostick moaned that the new tenants would "ruin the place", while another local, Geoffrey Dale, claimed it was nice and peaceful in the village and "I want it stay that way".[94] There was a similar response from residents in Marple. Over 2,500 signed a petition in protest against a scheme to build 400 houses. Members of the Petitioners Committee, such as Kathleen Moore, bluntly exclaimed that tenants should "go elsewhere", while G. E. Crossley was in no doubt that "the place would be ruined".[95]

Slum dwellers were associated with trouble, with lower standards and, if they were being honest, most people did not want them living in their backyards.

When the Hattersley plans were announced the Mayor, J. Walker, asked, "will this be slum clearance for Manchester?" Walker did not pull any punches. He claimed that "this large immigration" had been strongly resisted in other parts of Cheshire and that Hyde, being a likeable place, would be "altered by people who perhaps come from the slums of Manchester and Salford". He wanted to screen all applicants for the overspill houses, while the Housing Chairman, Alderman E. C. Byle, expressed fears that Hyde would not only lose its individuality but that crime and lawlessness would increase and that there was "many a thing that is big and rotten". While sympathy might be expressed for the plight of the slum dweller, many were fearful about the impact on existing communities. The Mayor Walker was so worried that he hoped to "make them into good citizens before they come to Hyde".[96] This fear about the moral habits of the prospective tenants was shared by other local authorities. Bury Corporation suggested that it should be able to choose the tenants from Manchester, a proposal that Manchester's Town Clerk, Sir Philip Dingle, claimed was worse in principle than discrimination against immigrants. In the south of the city, Councillor Frank Hatton reacted angrily when, after the completion of an estate in Sale, existing residents were given a large £10 reduction on the gross rateable value of their homes because it was felt they were so close to the overspill estate that their sale price had been significantly reduced. He claimed that this obviously suggested that the tenants were "inferior because they happen to live in a different type of house".[97] Alderman Elizabeth Yarwood added that this was a deplorable situation because it "stigmatised council tenants".[98]

Stigmatisation was a serious problem. Slum dwellers still carried connotations of crime and grime. These were embedded in depictions of slum life since the Victorian period. Residents in some of the reception districts were filled with anxiety at the influx of slum dwellers. A group of homeowners in Bredbury Green became separated from their overspill neighbours by building a six-foot 'iron curtain' between them and the council houses. They accused the overspill tenants of dumping rubbish on their grass verges and of vandalising new properties. Overspill residents believed the fence was simply a "symbol of snobbery".[99] When the plans for the Walshaw estate were announced, the local council chamber was filled to capacity and sixty people were locked out. Inside the meeting, Councillor Kenneth Whyman claimed that locals had reacted so badly that the situation had almost reached riot proportions.[100] The Elton Ward and Church Ward Residents' Associations asked residents across Bury to establish a 'shock force' in opposition to what they described as "the most important thing in Bury since the declaration of war".[101]

Generally, and publicly, neighbouring districts expressed sympathy with the slum dwellers and the city council, but in reality it was limited. The loss of valuable agricultural land was one issue, but it was linked to wider concerns about the preservation of the environment and the rural or semi-rural middle-class lifestyles enjoyed by existing residents. An influx from the city meant the

disruption if not destruction of a comfortable life. Coupled to this was the issue
of power and control. Initially at least, Manchester did not intend to give away
its population, rents, rates and jobs for its own Direct Works Department. Small
district councils felt they were being consumed by Big Brother. Not everyone
objected. Councillor H. Wilcox pointed out that Manchester overspill would
help with the rates, and that, although slum dwellers were tainted with negative
stereotypes, they were still "ordinary human beings, good citizens and we should
welcome them". However, the fact remained that many were not so generous
and understanding and remained fearful about the impact of slum dwellers.

As for the 'immigrants', 'slum dwellers' and those simply in need of lessons
in how to be a 'good citizen', they were not universally content with life on the
new estates. Many of the positive and negative experiences of moving outside
the city were expressed in the 1930s by tenants who had moved to Wythenshawe
and Belle Vue. As was seen above, in Wythenshawe the Better Housing Council
conducted a tenant satisfaction survey. It found that most were content and any
problems that existed were blamed on it being a new estate and, therefore,
incomplete. In 1942, the University Settlement carried out a similar survey in
Belle Vue. The research was conducted by Miss Remington, the Sub-Warden of
the Gorton Branch of the Settlement, who had previous experience as an inter-
viewer with the Bournville Village Trust Survey in Birmingham. She based her
study on a random sample of 150 homes in Belle Vue. Unlike Wythenshawe, most
of these tenants were former slum dwellers. Similar to Wythenshawe, the vast
majority liked their new houses, though a surprising 20 per cent actually
preferred their old homes. Those who were happy with the move felt their health
had improved, were pleased that most shops were within a ten-minute walk of
home and were satisfied with the condition of the houses. In the post-war
estates, initially, the signs were also positive. At the Town Planning Association's
regional conference on Dispersal in the Manchester Region in 1957, the
Middleton councillor, L. Biggins, pointed out that a survey of tenants on the
Langley estate (in Middleton) revealed that over 90 per cent expressed satisfaction with their new homes.[102] Despite the demolition of inner-city communities, the removal to strange surroundings and the costs of travelling, many tenants
clearly appreciated their new homes. They were a world away from the
overcrowded slums. One Hattersley tenant, Margaret Bromley, claimed that
although she had initially hated the estate she had gradually changed her opinion
because it was a "nice clean area" for the children.[103] Similarly, at Langley, local
resident Jack Whitworth admitted that while he would probably be dead before
the council provided the necessary facilities on the estate, he enjoyed his nice
three-bedroom semi-detached house and would never return to the city.[104] For
both of these tenants, life on the estate for a young family was preferable to the
old slums.

However, despite the many positive reactions, a number of residents
struggled to settle. Council management of the estates was deficient. It failed to

provide the necessary amenities. Tenants criticised the poor facilities and the extra costs involved in travelling to work. In the early developments at Wythenshawe and Belle Vue, tenants had made a number of complaints that had parallels with the later estates. A minority, it was claimed, missed the greater sociability and the life of the streets and shops in the heart of Manchester. More serious were the complaints at the lack of amenities. These included the need for welfare centres, a Post Office, more shops, bus shelters, fire alarms and telephone boxes, a library and an employment exchange. Shops were thought to be more expensive and there was an absence of recreational facilities. The Better Housing Council survey pointed out that residents complained that life on the estates was dull, that there was little to do in their spare time and that they found it difficult to make friends.[105] There was a shortage of outdoor facilities, including playing fields, tennis courts, bowling greens or a swimming bath. Tenants also complained about the need for a cinema and a meeting hall for community groups. People felt isolated from friends and family. Many disliked the journey to work that was seen as time-consuming and expensive. It forced a number of workers to cycle, something which, ironically, the survey felt that for many "on grounds of health it would be advisable that they should not do". They needed more jobs in the area and a cheaper transport service. Some of the Belle Vue tenants still complained about higher rents and, even though it was only a few miles from the city centre, others grumbled at having to travel greater distances to work. Of those 20 per cent who wanted to return home, most were elderly. They missed their old friends and haunts, liked to be closer to their neighbours, preferred the old houses of their childhood days (but not the slums) and believed the new estate was colder in winter. They wanted a community centre and felt the estate was too monotonous and bleak. It was claimed that everyone wanted more flowers and greenery, open spaces and trees. Tenants also complained about the absence of a children's playground and washhouses, and despite the fact that Belle Vue was much closer to Ancoats, many tenants still complained of a feeling of isolation, which was not apparent in the closely settled neighbourhoods from which most of them came.

Despite such complaints, satisfaction levels did remain high. Trust between council and tenant was largely intact. It was perceived to be doing its best in what was still a largely new venture. People became more settled over time.[106] However, the council never learnt from these problems and grievances. There was no attempt to listen and learn for the future, no thought about improvement. In the post-war period, its attitude and approach to tenant relations was storing problems as aspirations and expectations began to rise with the creation of the welfare state. Tenants in the overspill estates expressed very similar complaints, suggesting that the council failed to act on earlier experiences. Its approach continued to be focused around the grand vision, around getting the big job done. Whilst it produced homes of far greater quality than most tenants had ever dreamt of, the council failed to provide a complete service to support the quality of life on the estates. Tenants were still perceived as the fortunate recipients of municipal policy, not the consumers of a welfare service. But tenants had started to change. Society was moving on. When a public meeting was held at a local school in Hattersley, tenants gathered to moan about the lack of bus services, bus shelters, medical and dental services, shopping facilities (especially a chemist in the first shops), educational and library services and the urgent need to retain the railway link with Manchester.[107] It was claimed that there were no amenities or social facilities for the estate's youth, no playgrounds or cinemas. When a survey was carried out on the estate, it was estimated that 90 per cent of the people living at Hattersley were said to be unhappy and wanted to return to their old districts.[108] This was a stark contrast to the inter-war satisfaction surveys. Some local cynics described the estate as the 'Isle of Nothing' and 'The Prison'.[109] Tenants complained that they had been disowned by Manchester and that they were treated as untouchables.[110] The Mayor of Hyde added "this is a very sore point with some of us – a lot of us … we have done our best to receive the people … whether they will be integrated completely into our borough we have to wait and see".[111]

The council was so focused on building its large estates that it failed to provide the type of social amenities that people needed to maintain a reasonable quality of life. It was insensitive to tenant demands. This was underlined at Langley. Parents complained about the lack of fences around gardens and the absence of garden gates. This was not just about aesthetics but a basic safety issue. Their complaints were supported by the police who commented on the high accident rate caused by children playing in the streets. The problem was compounded by the lack of playing fields.[112] Given that part of the reason behind the estates was to provide more open spaces for families, this seemed an obvious omission. Other criticisms included the lack of nursery schools, public telephones, a cinema, youth clubs, library, post office, post boxes, a social club, a community centre, a pub and a bowling green.[113] Even medical provision lacked behind demand. As a short-term problem, this was understandable and excusable. The council was desperate to build houses as quickly as possible. However, nine years later residents were still complaining that there were no pubs, playing fields, sports grounds, cinema or permanent library.[114] They did have a social club, but it had 1,000 members and, after only four months, a waiting list of over 200. At Hattersley, the feeling of isolation amongst the older tenants was so bad that the local vicar, Noel Pryatt, and the estate's sole doctor, Ian MacPherson, established an SOS service to exchange the names and addresses of people who needed help.[115] The elderly were not the only ones to suffer. Rev. MacPherson claimed that many housewives suffered severe bouts of depression of up to six months after moving on to the estate due to loneliness.[116]

For many residents, overspill proved unpopular. Its reputation became so bad that some of those who remained in the slums were worried that the council would force them to move to the new estates. In 1970, tenants who wanted to leave their slum houses for health reasons were told by the Housing Department that the nearest available places were in the overspill estates. In response, one group from Ancoats approached their local councillor, Ernest Crank, in an attempt to reverse the decision. Crank claimed that although the people were desperate to move because of overcrowding or for medical reasons, they were only being offered flats or houses on overspill estates which they "definitely do not want". He added that "in other words they are being told: Get out of the city or stay where you are! They are being made prisoners in their own homes".[117] During the protracted dispute between the city and Westhoughton, one Manchester resident wrote to the local press asking "who wants to go to Westhoughton anyway? Most of us in the slums are already paying 7d each way in fares to and from work so what is the Housing Committee thinking about?" He added that "Westhoughton is a dump. I wouldn't be found dead there. What is there in these one-eyed places that the working-class snobs rave about?"[118] One social worker based at Winsford, Ken Jardine, claimed that many overspill tenants from Manchester and Liverpool simply "couldn't stick it".[119] The issue of increased travel costs even caused Sir Walter Bromley Davenport, MP for Knutsford, to allege that Manchester's overspill policy had caused wage inflation.[120] Once the cleared areas of Miles Platting and Ancoats had been redeveloped, a number of families asked the council to provide them with exchanges back from the Langley and Partington estates. Once again, tenants were annoyed about the extra travelling expenses, lack of social amenities and the feeling of isolation and loneliness.[121] They had only moved five or ten miles away, but this was irrelevant. For many, it might as well have been another country. Yet the council never appreciated these feelings. One tenant, Ethel Yates, claimed that even after three years she had failed to settle on the estate which she believed was like the "back of beyond". Ethel eventually returned to the city because she missed the "activity and good neighbours".[122] Some housewives in Miles Platting admitted they had returned to sub-standard homes because they were preferable to living in Heywood and Langley, while one pointed out that "new houses aren't everything".[123] This sentiment was alien to Manchester's civic culture. Local discourse did not play out effectively with people who had to live with the impact of housing policy.

The story of overspill is important in what it tells us about the Labour council, its relations and attitude to neighbouring local authorities and how it regarded (or disregarded) its own tenants. Manchester's battles with neighbouring councils had serious implications for future housing policy. Its inability to meet its ambitious targets led to even greater pressure amidst the demand for slum clearance and new homes. This strain came from tenants and successive govern-ments, forcing Manchester to look at alternatives, including modern system-built designs. The council had to clear its inner-city slums and build quickly and economically, but the overspill wars had increased its difficulties. All the council had wanted was to provide the best environment for its inner-city slum dwellers.

This meant good cottage-style homes in decent leafy towns around the outside of the conurbation. Why should inner-city slum dwellers be denied the type of environment enjoyed by the affluent middle classes? Besides, the city was caught in a serious land trap. There were no suitable sites available for development inside its boundaries. This, coupled with its aversion to flats, led them to look outside the city.

Frustrating though it was, its Manchester-centred vision had not taken into account any other views. Neighbouring districts were generally sympathetic, but only to a limited extent. Overspill was fraught with problems. Ultimately, nobody was entirely happy. Locals in the receiving areas complained. They wanted environmental and agricultural preservation and did not relish the great imperial city expanding into their territory. Neither did they appreciate an invasion of former slum-dwelling council tenants who still carried connotations of dirt and crime. Manchester's utopian vision was not even necessarily shared by many of its own tenants, who wanted to be close to family and friends and who enjoyed city life. Some preferred living in their old inner-city slums than moving up to twenty miles away. But they were given little choice. Tenants would conform or find their own way in the world. This was to prove difficult in the following years, as tenants increasingly demanded a greater say in housing policy and management issues.

Notes

1 For the period 1945–79 see also P. Shapely, D. Tanner and A. Walling, 'Civic culture and housing policy in Manchester, 1945–79', *Twentieth Century British History*, 15:4 (2004).

2 There are few recent historical studies of overspill. See, for example, M. Glendinning and S. Muthesius, *Tower Block: Modern Public housing in England, Scotland, Wales, and Northern Ireland* (New Haven, 1994), pp. 158–61. Other research is limited to contemporary social and political studies, including E. Farmer and R. Smith, 'Overspill theory: a Metropolitan case study', *Urban Studies*, 12 (1975); P. Hall, *The Containment of Urban England* (London, 1973); J. B. Cullingworth, *Housing Need and Planning Policy: Problems of Housing Need and Overspill in England and Wales* (London, 1960); N. Hayes, *Consensus and Controversy: City Politics in Nottingham, 1945–1966* (Liverpool, 1996).

3 See Glendinning and Muthesius, *Tower Block*, p. 158.

4 Manchester Housing Committee, report to City Council, 1942, p. 533.

5 *1945 Manchester Redevelopment Plan* (Manchester, 1945), p. 4.

6 Interview with Councillor William Egerton, 25 January 2002.

7 *1945 Manchester Redevelopment Plan*, p. 4

8 Minutes of the Housing Committee, 1944–45, vol. 26, p. 54.

9 Ibid.

10 *1945 Manchester Redevelopment Plan*, p. 4.

11 Scepticism towards new modern building trends continued long after the war. See N. Hayes, 'Making homes by machines: images, ideas and myths in the diffusion of non-traditional housing in Britain, 1942–54', *Twentieth Century British History*, 10:3 (1999), 282–309; B. Finnimore, *Houses from the Factory: System Building and the Welfare*

State (London, 1989).

12 *Manchester Guardian* (1 November 1954).

13 TNA, HLG 71/2293, Letter from Evelyn Sharp to the Minister, 20 January 1955. Evelyn Sharp remains one of the most influential figures in post-war housing policy. See Kevin Theakston, 'Evelyn Sharp', *Contemporary Record*, 7:1 (1993), 132–48.

14 A. J. Kidd, *Manchester* (Keele, 1996), p. 205.

15 *1945 Manchester Redevelopment Plan*, p. 4.

16 Minutes of the Housing Committee, p. 568.

17 Ibid.

18 Glendinning and Muthesius, *Tower Block*, p. 172.

19 Ibid.

20 Ibid.

21 Ibid.

22 *Manchester Evening News* (29 March 1946).

23 Ibid.

24 TNA, HLG 71/2293, Report on Lymm / Mobberley from Evelyn Sharp, 29 October 1954.

25 Ibid.

26 *Daily Telegraph* (28 September 1965).

27 Ibid.

28 Manchester Housing Committee minutes, 8 May 1937.

29 *Manchester Evening News* (17 November 1952).

30 'The Langley social survey', *The Surveyor*, February 1957.

31 Egerton interview.

32 See, for example, R. J. Moore-Colyer, 'From Great Wen to Toad Hall: aspects of the urban–rural divide', *Rural History*, 10:1 (1999).

33 *Manchester Evening News* (15 March 1946).

34 *Evening Chronicle* (23 March 1950).

35 *The Times* (1 June 1949).

36 *Cheshire Life* (November 1953), p. 16.

37 *The Times* (7 September 1953).

38 Ibid. (13 January 1954).

39 Ibid. (17 June 1959). They reported that "it has been suggested more than once that the Government have been keeping Manchester away from Lymm and Mobberley in deference to the Conservative voters of Cheshire."

40 *The Times* (15 October 1954).

41 *Manchester Evening News* (4 April 1957).

42 Ibid.

43 *Manchester Evening News* (8 April 1957).

44 Ibid.

45 Ibid.

46 Ibid.

47 Ibid.

48 *North Cheshire Herald* (16 December 1955).

49 *Manchester Evening News* (26 April 1957).

50 TNA, HLG 71/2293, Letter to Duncan Sandys, 18 October 1954.

51 Ibid., 19 October 1954.

52 TNA, HLG 71/2293, Report on Lymm / Mobberley from Evelyn Sharp.

53 TNA, HLG 79/1126, Letter from Evelyn Sharp to the Town Clerk, Manchester, 15 July 1958.
54 TNA, HLG 79/1126, Draft minute to the Prime Minister.
55 TNA, HLG 79/1126, Letter from W. Ogden to Ministry for Housing and Local Government, 9 May 1958.
56 *The Times* (17 June 1959).
57 R. Crossman, *Richard Crossman: Diaries of a Cabinet Minister*, Vol. 1 (London, 1975), p. 125.
58 *The Times* (20 February 1963).
59 *Evening Chronicle* (5 November 1956).
60 TNA, HLG 71/2293, Letter from Evelyn Sharp to the Minister, 20 January 1955.
61 *Guardian* (4 January 1962).
62 *Manchester Evening News* (11 March 1966).
63 Ibid. (9 January 1957).
64 TNA, HLG 118/154, Letter from Mrs E. Hill to Sir Keith Joseph, 26 February 1963.
65 *Guardian* (12 August 1965).
66 Ibid.
67 TNA, HLG 71/2293, Letter from Evelyn Sharp to the Minister.
68 TNA, HLG 71/2293, Draft note of a meeting held on 27 January 1955 at which the Minister met a delegation from Manchester to discuss its overspill problem, February 1955.
69 *Guardian* (17 September 1962).
70 Ibid. (29 October 1962).
71 *Horwich and Westhoughton Journal* (15 January 1963).
72 Ibid.
73 Ibid.
74 Ibid.
75 *Horwich and Westhoughton Journal* (12 July 1963).
76 *Bolton Evening News* (6 August 1963).
77 Ibid.
78 *Cheshire Life* (March 1965), p. 40.
79 *Horwich and Westhoughton Journal* (25 October 1963).
80 See N. Hayes, 'Forcing modernization on the "one remaining really backward industry": British construction and the politics of progress and ambiguous assessment', *Journal of European Economic History*, 31 (2002), 559–88.
81 *Horwich and Westhoughton Journal* (12 March 1965).
82 Ibid.
83 Ibid. (21 October 1966).
84 Ibid.
85 Ibid.
86 *Manchester Evening News* (26 January 1967).
87 *Daily Dispatch* (15 September 1965).
88 *Daily Telegraph* (16 September 1965).
89 *North Cheshire Herald* (14 May 1954).
90 Ibid. (18 November 1955).
91 Ibid. (16 December 1955).
92 *Cheshire Life* (March 1965), p. 40.
93 Ibid.
94 *Manchester Evening News* (14 November 1957).
95 Ibid. (28 November 1956).
96 *North Cheshire Herald* (16 December, 1955).

 97 *Manchester Evening News* (2 December 1965).
 98 Ibid.
 99 Ibid. (4 July 1967).
100 Ibid. (3 July 1964).
101 Ibid. (9 September 1964).
102 *Blackley and Openshaw Reporter* (18 April 1957).
103 *Manchester Evening News* (20 July 1964).
104 Ibid.
105 *Wythenshawe, Report of an Investigation*, Manchester and Salford Better Housing Council (Manchester, 1935).
106 M. Clapson, 'Working-class women's experiences of moving to new housing estates in England since 1919', *Twentieth Century British History*, 10:3 (1999), 345–65. Again, for the post-war period see M. Clapson, *Invincible Green Suburbs, Brave New Towns* (Manchester, 1998).
107 *North Cheshire Herald* (4 October 1963).
108 *Hyde Reporter* (4 October 1963).
109 *Manchester Evening News* (20 July 1964).
110 Ibid.
111 *Hyde Reporter* (4 October 1963).
112 'The Langley social survey', *The Surveyor*, February 1957.
113 Ibid.
114 *Manchester Evening News* (20 June 1964).
115 Ibid.
116 Ibid.
117 *East Manchester Reporter* (28 August 1970).
118 *Horwich and Westhoughton Journal* (20 November 1963).
119 *Cheshire Life* (September 1969).
120 *Manchester Evening News* (18 December 1968).
121 *East Manchester Reporter* (10 July 1964).
122 Ibid.
123 Ibid.

Part III

The decline of municipal legitimacy: inner-city developments and tenants' reactions, 1962–92

6   New slums and the rising tide of tenant anger

The failure to produce sufficient houses on overspill estates inevitably placed an unbearable strain on the council's slum-clearance programme. Tenants needed to be moved out before the slums could be cleared on a large enough scale to be effective. Conditions continued to deteriorate and the scale of the problem was daunting. This, together with the land trap and the demands of central government, combined to place intolerable pressure on the council. New solutions had to be found. This led some officials finally to accept that modern ideas, including tower blocks and multi-deck access systems, were the only solution. Large prestigious schemes were now planned for the inner-city belt. These were heralded as the start of a bright new dawn. Some, such as the Hulme Crescents, were trumpeted as examples of quality homes that would enhance the status of the city as a modern European centre. They would be the modern version of Bloomsbury and Bath.

The reality was very different. Old slums were replaced by new ones. Dreams of a new city were shattered. This proved a pivotal moment as it led to a decline in trust between the council and the tenant. By the late 1960s and throughout the 1970s, tenants (individuals and groups) reacted with increasing anger and bitterness towards the council. These campaigns were different from the earlier protest struggles in the 1930s. They emerged around three issues. First, people formed a series of organised responses against rent rises. Second, groups were created to secure resources under the General Improvement Area and Housing Action Area schemes. Third, angry tenants combined in a reaction against conditions in the new developments. The designs of these factory-built homes were bad enough, but problems were compounded by the council's failure to manage the properties and estates efficiently. Damp, bug infested and expensive to heat, the new properties became victims to litter, vandalism, poor lighting and low maintenance standards. Trust had broken down. Previous mistakes and attitudes were tolerated because the council had been perceived as the only institution capable of resolving the city's housing problems. The situation was now very different. The council was now the problem. Many residents were no longer prepared to accept the substandard service, unlike their predecessors who had suffered the slum conditions provided by private landlords. Groups of tenants were ready to voice their complaints and organise protests in an attempt to influence policy. Although they were not in a strictly market-consumer relationship, they were, nevertheless, acting like consumers of housing, as customers of the welfare system. The council struggled to adjust to the demands of the shifting political climate. Its relations with tenants were entrenched in civic culture. It had the grand narrative, the power and was the source of municipal benevolence. Society, however, was changing and hierarchies no longer enjoyed a largely unquestioned position of authority.

Slum clearance

Post-war slum clearance effectively began in Manchester from 1954.[1] This proved to be a prolonged process. Although an estimated 70,000 houses were declared unfit for human habitation in 1955, the city's five-year slum-clearance programme planned to demolish only 7,500 houses. Even this modest objective fell short by 1,000.[2] By 1960, its completion rate had dropped below 1,000 homes per year. However, the need to clear the slums was more pressing than ever. In the 1950s, many houses were still without running water, had holes in roofs and ceilings and were overcrowded. Particularly disturbing cases included Esther Duerden, an eighty-year-old who was deaf and blind. Every window in her house was blown in or smashed and she was forced to live in a single room, the others being totally uninhabitable.[3] She described how she was unable to use the bedrooms because there were holes in the roof as "big as this table", while her fireplace had completely dropped out.[4] Another tenant, Greta Brookes, told of how she shared a house with her husband, three children and four other adults. She lived with her family in a single box room which could only fit one bed.[5] Partial clearance in some areas made conditions even worse for those left behind, with houses suffering from structural collapse and even more vermin than usual.[6]

Despite the efforts of reformers in the inter-war period, these conditions were replicated across the city's inner slum belt. The problem was so bad that Councillor Lawson told delegates at the Royal Society of Health in 1956 that one-third of the total housing stock was unfit for repair and that it would take forty-seven years to clear them all.[7] By 1960, little had changed. Local Labour MP, Harold Lever, pointed out that there were still 60,000 houses scheduled for clearance but the council was only managing to build 1,500 houses a year. At that rate, it would still take forty years to finish slum clearance. In human terms, this was a catastrophe. It meant that, for an average of twenty years, thousands would have to live in conditions which would have been considered a disgrace in the nineteenth century. They would have to continue suffering in houses where the roofs still had holes, the plaster was completely decomposed, the wallpaper peeled off the walls soon after it was put up and the skirting boards were falling to pieces. There were thousands of homes still infested with rats, mice and a range of insects. The floors were in such bad condition that the lino fell to bits and windows were so overshadowed that it was difficult to read during the day without a light. In some houses, pieces of rope replaced stair rails, there were no bathrooms and outside toilets were comparable with those in Jamaican shanty towns.[8]

Lever sympathised with a council which was not only struggling to secure sufficient land for overspill estates but which also did not have the support of the Conservative government. Nevertheless, he still felt that the council could do more by developing small cleared sites instead of waiting to clear huge swathes that would allow it to implement a grand plan. He believed it was "too wedded" to the idea of garden estates and that it needed to think about building flats. Prophetically, he added that this might mean building "the slums of 30 years hence", though even this time-scale was to prove optimistic. Another Labour MP, Frank Allaun, claimed in Parliament that 250,000 people were living in conditions which were a disgrace to "our civilisation", and that 500 houses a year were collapsing because the walls no longer had the strength to stand up.[9]

Although it faced problems that were largely beyond its control, this was still perceived to be the council's problem. The Ministry did not produce or manage houses, that was the job of the council. People were becoming less interested in excuses. Criticism was beginning to escalate and, with it, the pressure to take more extensive action. Although, in retrospect, the council could be censured for some of the decisions it was to take in the 1960s, it was facing an increasing tide of criticism and demand for action whilst, at the same time, the parameters in which it could manoeuvre were increasingly narrow. It still wanted to build a suburban idyll for its tenants, quality homes in green areas, but it was constantly being frustrated and thwarted. Overspill estates would have freed space to clear the inner-city slum belt and build low-density quality homes. There was nothing wrong with the logic or the ambition, but it was becoming an unrealistic one. Even the council's own Health Committee censured the Housing Committee because of the slow rate of clearance and redevelopment. It was struggling to meet half of its target of 3,000 new houses a year in 1960. Alderman Yarwood again blamed the shortage of land as well as scarcity of technical staff (and an inability to recruit new staff), mining subsidence, vandalism and a delay in making design choices.[10] Conservative members intensified the pressure by demanding an inquiry into the reasons behind the slow progress, describing the failure to redevelop cleared sites as a "scandal" and a "disgrace to the city".[11]

In 1961, the council attempted to address the problem with a radical new plan. It announced a £21 million programme, aimed at building nearly 10,000 new homes over four years.[12] The programme was to continue increasing until it was building 4,000 a year. Completions had declined during 1953–60, from

2,634 a year to only 954.[13] This was crippling the slum-clearance programme. Now, the plan was to increase completions and, in so doing, drastically increase slum clearance.[14] The plans were announced in a report from the council's five-man team of officials, which included Philip Dingle (Town Clerk), Dr Metcalfe Brown (Medical Officer), C. Page (City Treasurer), R. Nicholas (City Surveyor) and J. Austen Bent (Housing Director). This team now attempted to force the pace of change. Their radical reforming agenda was extremely ambitious, big and bold. Slum clearance and rehousing was made the focal point of all council thinking.[15]

Besides the council's failure to attract new technical experts, it also claimed that the government was responsible for some serious delays. Whitehall red tape was blamed for a twelve-month delay in the biggest post-war slum-clearance programme, a fifty-three-acre site around Chorlton-on-Medlock.[16] The atmosphere between central and local governments became strained as one side blamed the other in a round of recriminations. Council officials pointed the finger at the Conservative government, suspicious as it already was because of its support for Cheshire in the overspill row. Attacks did not go unanswered. One of the city's Conservative MPs, James Watts, launched a scathing attack on the city's officials because of their failure to develop land near Hulme. He wanted the council to build tower blocks on a four-acre site, which, he claimed, would allow it to deal with the chronic slum problem across the area.[17] Henry Brooke, the Housing Minister, also refuted the criticism. He told local Labour MP, Will Griffiths, that he was not responsible for delays in the slum-clearance programme and that it was the council who had asked for extensions to its plan, resulting in it having the third largest number of slums in the country.[18] Brooke decided to visit the area. Accordingly, relations began to thaw. Brooke agreed to support the city in finding technical staff to supervise the clearance schemes, increase the size of the workforce and help secure suitable land.[19] By 1962, both the council and government had agreed to clear and build 4,000 houses a year. Evelyn Sharp wrote to the Town Clerk, Philip Dingle, telling him that the government would deal with all compulsory purchase orders quickly, though she did ask him to keep the schemes at a manageable level. Manchester had always liked to do things on a visibly big scale, but, she argued, it was difficult to cope with these "mammoths".[20] Dingle agreed and Manchester's slum-clearance programme was about to increase dramatically.

The new housing drive from the mid-1960s to the early 1970s did have an impact on the total municipal housing stock. Somewhat ironically, this coincided with a brief stint in power for the Conservatives. They gained control of the council in 1967, remaining in office until 1971. From the outset, the Conservative council expressed a determination to introduce radical changes. The Housing Committee was reorganised, with responsibility for designing and processing construction transferring to the City Architect. This, it believed, was responsible for a significant increase in the number of homes demolished under slum-clearance programmes. During 1945–60, an estimated 46,000 homes were cleared, at an average of 3,600 a year. Over the following seven years, this fell to 16,700, or 2,800 a year. However, the Conservative council claimed that its reorganisation led directly to a further increase to 6,800 a year during 1967–70.[21] In reality, many of the plans were in place before the Tories gained power. Nevertheless, the Conservative council did oversee a boom in production. The Town Clerk reported to government in 1972 that the number of homes owned by the council had risen from 69,207 in 1965 to 88,640 by 1972.[22] The figures were impressive, but the results were bordering on catastrophic as the price of adopting the system-built developments began to emerge virtually as soon as they were completed.

The system-built developments

The pressure to increase completion rates inevitably led the council to adopt modern designs. Bill Egerton claimed that the council was forced to turn to modern techniques because "we were running out of reasonably big sites in these other local authorities … we were starting to build in the city itself, and of course to get the maximum usage of any particular site, if you go up you get more personnel in per acre".[23] Like other local authorities, Manchester was being compelled to act by governments, professionals, architects, planners and designers. In September 1962, the Assistant Secretary at the Ministry of Housing and Local Government announced that a special group of technical officers (architects and surveyors) would be established in the city to give advice and assistance to local authorities in Manchester and other areas throughout the north and midlands.[24] The group was to co-operate with local authorities, not only in preparing slum-clearance programmes but also in promoting standardised system-built programmes. Both Conservative and Labour governments promoted the modern solutions of tower blocks and system-built designs as offering a quick and affordable solution to the continuing problems of inner-city slums. Designers had promoted new modern ideas from the late 1940s.[25] Governments believed they offered a chance to fulfil the promises of the welfare state. Crossman thought that the new modern building techniques were part of a wider commitment to national efficiency, part of the emerging 'white heat' culture.[26] Government actively sponsored industrialised systems. Even housing subsidies favoured the new large-scale building techniques.

Nevertheless, Manchester's Housing Committee continued to regard tower blocks with reluctance. The cottage culture remained the primary point of reference. Unlike other cities such as London and Liverpool, there was an absence of any production-minded group promoting the case for tower blocks.[27] However, the five-man team of officials who had unveiled their blueprint for increasing slum clearance and rebuilding in 1961, was determined to continue its programme for radical change. Inevitably, this meant new industrial methods. It was a decision which had little to do with the idealism of the inter-war Modern Movement. The new designs were the most cost effective way of increasing completion rates and developing the city's gap sites. The first flats built by industrial methods were opened at Heywood in 1963.[28] Led by Austen Bent and his team of architects and designers, together with J. S. Millar, who was appointed City Planning Officer in 1966, the council was pressed towards a grudging acceptance of tower blocks and other modern designs, especially the deck-access system. The Housing Committee was forced to accept that slum clearance was taking too long and new methods had to be employed. It agreed to bulk buy materials, use standardised fittings and equipment and employ semi-skilled or unskilled workers by using factory-made, mass-produced units. This would all cost less and be far quicker.

Yet, even here, civic culture, so hostile towards high-rise, could be distinguished. The deck-access systems were a compromise to the city's cottage culture. They were meant to provide Manchester with streets-in-the-sky, traditional rows of 'terraced' homes placed on top of each other to provide a community spirit but with modern facilities and a greater sense of space. Councillor William Egerton described them as "highways in the sky, safe from cars … it was the future of housing now".[30] Local MP for Gorton, Gerald Kaufman, explained they were a "planning concept, streets in the sky instead of having lots of little houses in narrow streets, you keep the street concept in order to keep communities but you have streets in the sky".[31] Bent's Chief Assistant Architect, Robert Stones, was responsible for one of the first schemes built at Gibson Street in Longsight by Bison (Concrete Northern) in 1968. The pessimism about clearance and completion rates of the early 1960s was gradually replaced by a return to the bold optimism and pride that had characterised other housing schemes. In 1964, the *Manchester Evening News* described how the city's architects and planners were full of designs to build a "new city" that would be a "fine place to live in".[32] Slum clearance targets were being met and recriminations were replaced by a picture of "energy and drive", as the council successfully cleared huge slum areas whilst also building up to 6,000 homes a year. This programme was so impressive that it attracted the attention of a deputation of MPs from Tanzania. The visiting MPs were interested in employing new methods to clear the slums of Zanzibar and Dar-es-Salaam, and Manchester provided the inspiration.[33] In Parliament, Alf Morris, MP for Wythenshawe, claimed that Manchester was tackling its slum problem with more "vigour, credit and compassion than any of the great provincial cities", while the Parliamentary Secretary to the Ministry of Housing, R. Mellish, added that Manchester's record was "outstanding".[34]

The positive climate of opinion was a direct reaction to the rapid pace of clearance and rebuilding. Politicians and sections of the press were swept away on a new tide of optimism. Finally, it appeared that the human misery that had blighted the city since Victorian times was at an end. The council was at last delivering. In one six-week period alone, the Housing Minister Richard Crossman held five public inquiries into different clearance programmes across the city. When Crossman visited the clearance site at Hulme, he was extremely impressed by what he described as the "the largest hole ever created in a big city in the history of modern conurbations".[35] Had he returned in the late 1970s he might well have used similar terms to describe the area. Significantly, although Crossman expressed his admiration for the city's housing programme he was also depressed by the standard of replacement houses.

Nevertheless, Crossman's visit to Hulme highlighted the way the whole process of change was symbolised in the redevelopment of the area. Despite limited slum clearance in the 1930s, the social problems in Hulme were as bad as ever. The local parish priest Rev. Harold Lees, Chair of the Hulme community council, claimed in 1953 that the area contained "more misery to the square mile than any other in the city". He described "a world of mean streets and wretched houses, of broken marriages and unwanted children, a world of general darkness without even the blessing of bright lighting".[36] Like many parts of the city, the chronic problems dragged on throughout the 1950s. However, by 1962 the council was at last ready to unveil its vision for a better and brighter Hulme. Plans were revealed at a Public Enquiry, held on 29 May 1962. The deputy Town Clerk, C. A. Marsh, recognised that the area, laid out more than a hundred years previously, was so badly arranged that houses were crumbling away and were totally unfit for habitation. The district was worn out and in desperate need of comprehensive redevelopment.[37] Over 700 houses were issued with CPOs and a twenty-seven-acre site was earmarked for development. Building would include 128 maisonettes, 57 houses, 63 flats, a number of schools and various road schemes, all at a cost of £1 million. The number of pubs was reduced from fourteen to two.

The Inquiry marked the first part of a huge plan to rebuild the entire district. Plans were approved by government in November, and in October of the following year the council unveiled plans for the next stage. Marsh announced proposals to CPO a further 1,800 houses for demolition and to develop a large sixty-six-acre site. There was a feeling that exciting transformations were taking a grip of the city. Marsh claimed that "great social changes are taking place", and that "one area after another is being swept away by a tremendous wave of clearance".[38] The next of the five phases of development was announced in 1964. The total cost increased to £20 million. Large-scale rebuilding commenced in August 1964 with the construction of 5,000 new homes, which included a series of thirteen-storey flats, the first time the city had built such concentrated numbers. John Laing's Sectra system of industrialised building was employed and, much to the delight of the council, they were successfully finished in record time. The Mayor, Dr W. Chadwick, opened the first block with a golden key, proudly claiming that while earlier blocks of flats were monstrosities to be ashamed of, the new blocks had improved beyond all recognition.[39] Manchester was still doing things big. The entire programme was so vast it was to take seven years to complete.

Civic culture remained at the centre of the process. The council boasted that it was building high-status homes to create an exciting new city. Sir Philip Dingle told the North-West Economic Planning Council in March 1966 that the standard of building had to be high and that "the building of today must be suitable for the needs of tomorrow".[40] The centrepiece developments were to be the Crescents. The council was confident that these would be a source of civic pride that would enhance the status of the city. With echoes of Simon and the Wythenshawe plans of the 1920s, it claimed it was providing an "example of good planning to the rest of the country".[41] Local discourse had changed little. The Chairman of the city's Town Planning Committee, Eric Mellor, claimed that the Crescents would be "one of the finest schemes in Europe".[42] The council's Town Planning Committee passed the plan in November 1965. Again, Mellor claimed that the idea presented the city with a unique opportunity.[43] Plans were eventually presented to the council in 1966. The Report of the Housing Committee explained that it was proposing to create an urban environment on a city scale that would involve building continuous blocks of maisonettes, no more than six storeys high in a few bold and simple forms, enabling them to develop large open spaces.[44] While it was admitted that this scheme would be more economical in building costs and would enable them to increase density levels, it was also optimistically hoped that it would provide social advantages, including "greater choice of friends amongst neighbours", whilst also giving elderly people the advantage of "easy contact with the passing world".[45] The scheme involved building 924 homes at an estimated cost of £3,810,955. This meant that the average cost was £3,500 per dwelling, £300 more than the average cost under the Hulme II development. The report explained that additional costs had been incurred because of extras such as the balconies, heating system and insistence on high-quality finishes and fittings.[46] Planning consultants Hugh Wilson and Lewis Womersley were responsible for designing the plans.[47] Womersley had been employed as City Architect by Sheffield city council and was responsible for multi-deck access developments at Park Hill and Hyde Park. They claimed that they were using Georgian planning methods, though in reality they were deploying Scandinavian-style industrial building techniques.[48] The architects maintained that the plans would achieve a solution to the problems of twentieth-century living, which they believed would be the "equivalent in quality of that reached for the requirements of the eighteenth century in Bloomsbury or Bath".[49]

The support of the press was important. They were instrumental in promoting this new vision to the public.[50] The press helped to create a new sense of optimism. The plans for Hulme V were outlined by the *Manchester Evening News* under the wildly optimistic headline 'A Touch of Bloomsbury'. The report claimed that, of all the redevelopment schemes designed to rejuvenate modern

Britain, Manchester's £20 million plan for Hulme "stands out boldly". It was described as "unique" and as a "fascinating concept that should make proud not only the planners but the citizens". The design for a thousand maisonettes in long curved terraces would give a "touch of eighteenth century grace and dignity" to municipal housing, and it believed that the plans showed "both imagination and common sense in planning homes".[51] Even the *Guardian* applauded the promise that there would be "no tower block", just "Georgian elegance".[52] It waxed lyrical about the creation of a new Hulme which would give Manchester high-status value in both Britain and Europe. The newspaper described how the new Hulme would be characterised by grass lawns, flower beds and hundreds of trees. The old 300-acre Slumland was going to be replaced by a development scheme of "superlatives", the biggest of its kind in Europe and by far the "most imaginative housing project in the city, many will say the most imaginative city scheme in the country".[53] Similarly, the *Manchester Evening News* described how the Regency-style terraces would be as attractive as the terraces of Bath and Bloomsbury.[54]

The role of the architects and designers was vital in selling the new vision. Neither councillors nor members of the press were construction experts. Councillors made decisions based on the pressure to cut the waiting lists and on the desire to use high-status projects. The architects sold them an ideal that apparently answered their problems. Bill Egerton claims that the most important people in selling the vision were "clever architects, clever officials, clever planners who convinced the councillors ... the big departments exerted influence ... they sold the various plans". Contractors convinced the council that they had the solution to all its problems. According to Egerton, the Bison Group had a "good sales pitch". Bison was also employed to build the deck-access flats at Wellington Street (Fort Beswick) in east Manchester and Egerton recalled how "with the houses in Beswick we were told that this was the future of housing ... everyone was sold on the pitch". The council had ultimate decision-making powers, but it was always "based on advice and professional expertise".[55]

The final cost of the Crescents was estimated at £4 million and the final topping-out ceremony took place on 14 January 1971. Hulme and Beswick were not the only areas to benefit from the new designs. Two other large deck-access developments were built at Coverdale Crescent in Ardwick and Turkey Lane in Harpurhey. Plans to rebuild Beswick were initially proposed in 1944. Under the 'Better Beswick' plan it was hoped to develop 290 acres, which the mayor believed would be make the area as attractive and convenient as anywhere.[56] However, it was not until 1969 that substantial rebuilding occurred with a £5 million programme that included 1,000 deck-access flats and maisonettes. Payments were to be spread over fifty years. The estate was finally completed in 1973. What became known as Fort Beswick (because of its uncanny likeness to a Wild West frontier fort), was at the centre of the plan. The same company also built Coverdale Crescent (Fort Ardwick), a 500-unit deck-access development completed in 1972. Bison Concrete had gained a strong reputation throughout the 1960s, winning the Queen's Award for industry. Its chairman, Sir Kenneth Wood, became adviser to the Ministry of Housing in 1966. Little wonder, then, that the council trusted them. As will be seen, by the early 1980s it was trying to sue them.

Tenant anger I[57]

While the post-war housing programme stuttered between periods of limited activity and radical change, little attention was paid to tenant ambitions. They remained on the periphery of the entire policy process. However, as problems mounted, some of them became increasingly angry and frustrated. The welfare state promised them rights as citizens, including decent accommodation. These rights were not being fulfilled. Rent increases, the slow pace of slum clearance, the desire to secure resources for house improvements and the poor conditions which emerged in the new concrete homes, provided the motivation for tenant action. Proposed rent rises were always potential grounds for conflict. In 1951, the Wythenshawe federal council threatened to organise a demonstration at the Town Hall and called on all 38,000 council tenants to join in a protest against proposed rent increases.[58] Six years later, the Communist Party, led by Len Johnson, appealed to tenants in the city to reject the government's Rent Act. They asked tenants to organise themselves into associations and make protests to their MPs and the council. People were urged to apply for a Certificate of Disrepair so they would be able legally to withhold any rent increase.[59]

Protests continued in the early 1960s. The Wythenshawe federal council again led the resistance to proposed increases in 1961, organising a 2,000-name petition and a protest march on the estate. Other marches were planned for Langley. The chairman of the Wythenshawe federal council, George Taylor, claimed "we are angry people", and that feelings were "running high against the rent increase".[60] He hoped that the protests at Wythenshawe and Langley, together with the threat of a total rent boycott, would force the council into a rethink.[61] Taylor also became Vice-Chairman of the Manchester and Salford council of Corporation House Tenants Associations. By 1963, they had gathered 23,000 signatures for a petition opposing rent rises. When a delegation from the eighteen Tenants Associations met local authority officials, they hired buses to ferry a crowd outside the Town Hall to make a vociferous protest.[62] Wythenshawe tenants also sent delegates to a national demonstration in London.[63]

Although rent rises were only a means of balancing the books, and not an attempt to make profits, tenants were angered at any proposals to make what they perceived to be unfair increases. They were not interested in the council's increasing financial burden. H. R. Page, the City Treasurer, reported that during 1959–60 the city's housing debt increased by 64 per cent compared with 30 per cent for other boroughs. He claimed that Manchester's total housing debt was £140m and that it was about to increase to a staggering £179m by 1966.[64] Once again, the council found itself under increasing pressure. But residents only looked at the quality of service and its cost. Although not in the same market structure that existed between producers and consumers, they were, nevertheless, using the language of consumers. Most tenants preferred council accommodation. It was seen as infinitely superior to houses in the private rented sector. However, rent increases were not the only source of frustration. Irritation grew at the slow pace of slum clearance and rebuilding. In 1956, for example, a group of residents in Harpurhey, a district of north Manchester, sent two spokeswomen to meet council officials. Dreading another winter in their rain-soaked homes, they met local councillors and the Deputy Medical Officer to present a 112-signature petition from local residents.[65] Similarly, a group of tenants in Miles Platting organised a campaign, gathering a petition with 800 names, to speed up the slum-clearance programme, while a group of thirty mothers in Collyhurst were so angry at their filthy living conditions that they organised a protest march on the Town Hall.[66] Tenants trapped in slums were demanding council action. This was a right, not a privilege. Angry residents in Greenheys, for example, gathered a petition with 2,000 names, and held a meeting attended by 1,000 residents, to force the council into declaring the district a slum-clearance area. Their homes, many of which were literally collapsing around them, were described as an affront to decency and human dignity and they demanded council action as an entitlement not a favour.[67]

Although not obvious at the time, this marked the beginning of a shift in perceptions and relationships between tenants and local government. It was only in the 1980s that the council began to adjust to the shifting political climate, and even then it was often with reluctance. From the turn of the nineteenth century, it had treated tenants as recipients of municipal generosity. Increasingly, however, groups of tenants were demanding a better service, more action and decent homes. The tension between these different perceptions was compounded in the late 1960s when local government came under national pressures to consult tenants. Initial impetus was given by the 1969 Skeffington Report, which suggested that local authorities should develop consultation schemes for future planning proposals. Legislation reinforced the changes. However, this is not to deny the importance of tenant groups, which placed pressure on the council by highlighting its shortcomings and by trying to influence policy.

Although local authorities held public inquiries after unveiling plans to redevelop an area, the council did not bother itself with what it really viewed as the encumbrance of a consultation process. William Egerton accepted that "one of the main problems was the lack of consultation", and that "there was minimal consultation with the local population".[68] There was even limited discussion within the local Labour Party. Gerald Kaufman claimed that "never ever, ever has the local party either at city or constituency level taken an interest in these matters",[69] while Egerton confirmed that "within the party, there was minimal consultation". He added that "the alternatives were slower and more expensive", and claimed the council was simply under too much pressure, pointing out that "there were targets for the number of houses built, and there was political pressure to get out-turns quicker". The council reached its own conclusions and then attempted to sell its ideas. Tenants felt excluded and powerless. The 1969 Town and Country Planning Act and the Skeffington Report were supposed to herald a new dawn, but not for tenants in slum-clearance areas. This allowed the council conveniently to side-step tenant consultation. Its approach was highlighted when plans were made public for a large slum-clearance programme in Newton Heath. There was a preliminary meeting in March 1970 between Newton Heath councillors and Planning Department officials, but the public were not included. In September, a meeting took place at the behest of the Newton Heath Community and Civic Association, a type of tenants group. It involved planners, councillors and members of the public but, although residents were able to voice their concerns, it produced nothing of any meaning. The main issue was whether tenants could be rehoused in the area, but this was dismissed by the Deputy City Planning Officer who told them "it would involve a lot of time and cost more money".[70] By the time of the Public Inquiry in January 1971, the plans for Newton Heath were supposed to have been made public for comment and suggestions, but they were only revealed at the Inquiry.[71] A few weeks later, a private meeting was held between the Planning Department and the Newton Heath Civic Association. The meeting only took place after constant lobbying from the Association. Promises of a public exhibition on the redevelopment of the area were made by officials, but, again, did not materialise. It was felt that the council was making a mockery of the idea of participation and public denunciation of its actions increased.[72] A public debate was finally held in March, but this was effectively an opportunity for local Labour candidates to indulge in some electioneering for the local elections.[73] Attempts at participation with tenants were little more than a cosmetic exercise. Newton Heath underlined the complete lack of partnership between people and planners in the creation of redevelopment plans.

This increased the growing sense of frustration. Groups in neighbourhoods across the city joined to voice their dissatisfaction and demand action. Like the consumer groups that had emerged in Britain and the USA, tenants were attempting to protect their individual rights. Women were especially keen to make their protests at meetings and demonstrations.[74] Several groups in Moss Side were characterised by multi-racial membership. People joined together, black and white, to secure common goals and promote common interests that were not directly related to race or ethnicity. Slum clearance gave everyone a set of common interests.[75]

Besides slum clearance, a number of tenant groups were formed from the late 1960s because of government proposals to establish General Improvement Areas (GIAs) and Housing Action Areas (HAAs). The Labour government moved away from expensive rebuilding schemes to gradual improvement of individual homes or entire districts. The 1969 Housing Act marked an important shift in policy. Local authorities could offer grants to homeowners and provide environmental improvements to designated areas. Assistance included wide-ranging grants for substantial private home modernisation. Labour was actively supporting working-class families who had managed to buy their homes. Many would now enjoy the benefits of indoor toilets and bathrooms for the first time. These were houses which were structurally sound. The worst of the slums, the houses which were beyond salvation because of their rotting fabric, had either been demolished or were scheduled for demolition. Large-scale demolition and development was no longer necessary or desirable. In Manchester, national pressures were reinforced by local electoral defeats in 1967–68. Once in power, the Tories embarked on a different policy path. In July 1970, the Conservative council adopted nine resolutions following the *Report on Housing Needs and Resources*, prepared by the Chief Officers. They agreed that the council was budgeting for more houses than it actually required, that slum clearance would be completed by 1975 and that it would finally put an end to overspill.[76] Land was to be sold off to private developers and it decided to extend the number of GIAs and to provide grants for large homeowners to allow them to carry out quality conversions. Political wrangling, and reticence from a returning Labour council in 1971, led to a series of delays. Despite pressure from some Labour activists who were well aware of the problems, the Labour council's response was grudging at best. Only in the late 1970s did it abandon new building developments in favour of improvement.[77] The council's Chief Officers argued that the financial case for improvement was compelling. They estimated that while the cost of a new two-bedroom house was around £5,000, rising to £33,000 with interest over thirty years, the cost of improving a house was only £2,200 rising to £7,600 over the same period.[78] Tenants would also save. A new house would cost them £11 per week, but an improved house would add only £1 per week to the rent. Older houses would benefit the poor and new tenants because of their low cost, while many of the facilities and amenities needed to build a community already existed. There would be no break up of communities, an issue that had created problems for tenants since the 1920s. It now officially recognised that many people "prefer their own, old house".[79] In what seemed to be a startling change of attitude, it admitted that "above all, it is essential to find out what people want".[80] However, it was now convenient to acknowledge what tenants preferred because it suited official strategy. A policy of improvement was cheaper, quicker and easier. There were no other available options.[81] By 1980, the Director of Housing, R. G. Goodhead, reported that the council had implemented thirty-eight HAAs and nine GIAs since starting the programme in 1974.[82] An estimated 40,000 privately owned homes were still in need of repair and modernisation. Phase I continued until February 1977 (seventeen HAAs and six GIAs). Phase II started in 1978. Over 18,000 houses had been modernised, providing a boost to low-cost housing in the city. The scheme was mainly benefi-cial to owner-occupiers or housing associations. Besides grants for house improvements, the council was involved in wall cleaning, paving, tree planting and other environmental improvements. Large areas such as east Manchester enjoyed a makeover. The scheme helped saved money and, according to Goodhead, had a dramatic impact on the worst areas in the city.

Areas of Moss Side were the first districts to be identified as GIAs and the first areas to witness concerted tenants' action. The late 1950s saw the emergence of the 'Moss Side Image'.[83] It became perceived as a poor and dangerous area. From the 1960s, it was associated with drugs, prostitution and crime.[84] By this time, many of the ageing Victorian buildings were in a state of decay and new buildings were no better.[85] The area already had a number of organisations to provide a platform for local discontent. For example, the Moss Side Peoples Association had been formed to discuss improvement issues with residents. Like many groups, it was led by a mixture of local clergy alongside social and community workers as well as residents. Other groups included the Housing Action Group and Housing Unions. Civil society flourished. Internal structures and personnel differed. Besides local social leaders and actual residents, member-ship included professionals and politically active students. Such diversity, together with regular internal divisions, meant that no exclusive language of consumerism was developed. Nevertheless, tenant action was to leave its mark on the local political landscape. Although central government was giving them positive encouragement and even impetus, tenant groups were taking action because they were wary of the possible consequences of policies imposed by the council. It was an implicit acceptance of the limited trust they had in their local political leaders. Manchester's Labour council, so used to dictating policy, was slow to appreciate the shifting climate. Now, rather than assume a change of heart, tenants wanted to have their own say.

Similar fears about slum-clearance programmes, and the subsequent break-up of communities, together with a desire to influence the distribution of resources under GIA schemes, led to the formation of Manchester and Salford Housing Action (MASHA), one of the most prominent organisations to emerge in the region. MASHA, established in March 1973, shared many of the charac-teristics of the US consumer groups. It was formed as a reaction to the declining legitimacy of the council as a service provider. Volunteers worked at grass-roots level and aimed to co-ordinate local groups in their opposition to Manchester's slum-clearance programme. Members also provided technical resources and collated and disseminated information as and when required. According to its Chair, Dave Ward, the group was created because of "general dissatisfaction" at the unwillingness of local authorities to devote more attention to housing improvements. They aimed to achieve their objectives through "increased community control at all levels of local politics".[86] Although Ward's claims were over-ambitious and tinged with grandiose posturing, they reflected the depth of feeling and disillusionment about the lack of meaningful engagement with tradi-tional bi-partisan politics at the local level. They offered a new discourse that cut across left, centre and right-wing political language. Ward claimed that local people were prepared to fight to prevent their homes and livelihoods being threatened by plans that had no relationship to their own wishes.[87] MASHA, which represented a distinct group of highly organised and motivated individ-uals, was trying to empower tenants in the face of inadequate services. It was an expression of the principle that the "poor people of Manchester should have the indisputable right to be able to take the decisions that affect their everyday lives, their homes, the nature of their community, and the shape of their city".[88]

The tenant view needed to be articulated. It required an organisation and a strategy. A primary objective was to provide information, enabling it to increase public awareness of the problems and intensify pressure on the council.[89] This was part of the process of empowerment – knowledge was seen as power. MASHA conducted its own building and social surveys, recognising that detailed facts had to be provided to build a convincing case.[90] Disseminating information to the public was equally important. It tried to raise the consciousness of residents by making people aware of their rights as consumers. Various strategies were employed, including the publication of a newsletter, hiring a float to parade around Manchester city centre, distributing leaflets to publicise its aims and placing adverts in the local and national press.[91] It tried to establish an informa-tion centre and even proposed to use Manchester Polytechnic to make its own publicity film.[92] Residents were encouraged to get in touch with the organisa-tion about their problems. People were informed of their rights, public inquiries were publicised, and council failings were highlighted. MASHA was trying to mobilise community power and to use it to fight the council.[93] It was an impres-sive exercise in civil engagement, in developing a civil society.

Tactics included organising demonstrations outside local town halls, meeting government ministers and taking local authorities to court if they failed to carry out repairs.[94] In neighbouring Salford, a group of tenants successfully took the council to the high court in 1974 in a bid to get their homes repaired following the postponement of a demolition decision. They were supported by the housing charity Shelter. David Mylan, Shelter's regional organiser in the north-west, claimed that it was a "tremendous step forward", because the judgement meant that a tenant who took his council to court could find out exactly when they would be rehoused or the council would have to carry out repairs.[95] Local authorities were being paid by tenants to provide a service, and the court's decision was an implicit recognition that Salford had failed to fulfil its obligation to the consumer.

While many tenants undoubtedly remained apathetic, some groups achieved impressive levels of popularity. The Moss Side groups held a number of well-attended meetings. They formed a petition with 3,000 signatures and organised door-to-door visits to mobilise support against CPOs taken out against their properties. Members conducted a survey of residents rehousing ambitions, produced a newspaper with a circulation of 1,400 and provided alternative development designs. They even had a Housing Action Group member elected to the council, polling 767 votes from a 1,000 turnout.[96] Monton Street and Carter Street Housing Unions believed that they were responsible for securing equal rights for all residents (including single lodgers).[97] MASHA was also able to claim a number of notable successes. It declared, accurately or otherwise, that it was its campaign that convinced the city council to finally abandon slum clearance across the city in favour of house improvement. Policy changes by central government pushed local authorities into adopting improvement over replacement, but local authorities like Manchester were seen by some to be dragging their feet. Pressure had to come from the community. This is where tenant groups had a tangible impact. They were important pressure groups, revealing housing problems to a wider public, stressing the shortcomings of the council and attempting to influence policy. MASHA boasted that it was because of its campaign and opposition that the council had been forced to make "important, even embarrassing, about facing by officers and councillors alike".[98] One local activist in the early 1970s, Mike Brennan, supported groups of residents in their struggles against clearance orders. Brennan highlighted the illogical rationale at work at the time. He claimed that, in order to obtain a 'rational' area to redevelop, houses had to be cleared in rectangular lots. Entire streets of good houses could be knocked down in order to get a rectangular site. He described one case in Gortoncross Street in east Manchester. A row of twelve houses was included for clearance so that a road could be rerouted. On the morning of the inquiry, he submitted a plan showing the road going through the local Labour Party club instead. The Inspector asked the officials if this was a feasible alternative. Brennan described how they were forced to "smile and say yes".[99] The houses were then excluded.

While the Moss Side groups and MASHA were a reaction to proposed slum-clearance programmes and the policy of using grants for redevelopment, other tenant groups were formed in the mid-1970s because of fear and loathing arising from the disastrous housing development programmes of the 1960s. Beswick and the Hulme Crescents became the most notorious of all Manchester's system-built developments. Poor design and cost-cutting at the Wellington Street flats led to early decay, dampness, vandalism, noise and condensation. Initially, the council blamed bad tenants, governments ignored the problem and Bison chose to keep quiet. In Hulme, after only four years, tenants in the Crescents were demanding to be rehoused. An anonymous local doctor claimed that the whole environment was so bad that it was seriously affecting people's health. His report, *Health in Hulme*, declared that local living conditions were creating high stress levels, marital break-up and even suicidal tendencies, with large increases in neurotic, psychotic and gastro-intestinal illnesses.[100] Problems included broken lifts, which also suffered from poor lighting and the pungent smell of urine, inadequate refuse disposal (with rubbish left rotting on landings), litter, excrement, noise and vandalism. The doctor claimed that the deck-access blocks were the main reason for the low-grade ill health and that they were responsible for the spread of transmittable disease.

Whereas newspapers had earlier followed the council's official line, they now produced a series of damning articles. In 1973, Bernard Spilsbury described how the new flats were already proving to be a huge flop with residents in Hulme and Beswick. He claimed that tenants had told him bluntly that they preferred the old slums.[101] Spilsbury described the litter, broken glass, piles of excreta and lifts used as toilets. He spoke to twenty-two-year-old Fay Powell, who told him that "everybody hates it here … it's not all the tenants' fault – the corporation is not as quick at putting things right as it should be". Another resident, thirty-four-year-old Margaret Ogunyemi from Beswick, had a list of structural complaints, including a window that had fallen out because the fastenings were not strong enough to carry its weight.[102] Journalists created an alternative structure of feeling based on anger, frustration and depression at social conditions. Another discourse emerged from the press and tenants based on disillusionment. In 1978, only a few years after trumpeting the Hulme Crescents as the new Bath, the *Manchester Evening News* labelled them as the new "Colditz".[103]

As the extent of these problems unfolded, tenants began to express their anger. Protests came in several forms, including criticism from disgruntled individuals, groups of local residents acting spontaneously and the more formally organised groups that often included professionals and the politically active. Although it should be remembered that most of Manchester's tenants were largely apathetic, reflected in the low local election turnouts, problems in partic-ular areas led to highly motivated groups coming together to make vociferous protests and place organised pressure on the council. Tenant groups emerged from the disappointment at the failure to fulfil the promises of the welfare state. The New Jerusalem gave people a right to decent homes and living conditions. What they were forced to live in were either the same old slums from the nineteenth century or new slums from the 1960s and 1970s. But many were not willing to accept a substandard service. The council might have continued with its top-down approach to tenants, but the groups that emerged from the late 1960s displayed a different attitude. Now they acted like consumers of a public service. They paid rent (and National Insurance) and they expected a better service.

The council, the producer, was attacked for making poor policy decisions and inadequate estate management. People were in little doubt that the local authority had failed them. Candidates in a Hulme by-election campaign were subjected to a series of angry complaints from residents. Fay Powell, who had claimed that the council was not as "quick at putting things right as it should be", pointed out that she had been waiting for a year to have her front door painted. At Beswick, residents complained that their new homes were in a bad state of repair. Not only had windows fallen out because the fastenings were not strong enough, but mould was growing on the ceiling. One resident even described how she had called in an inspector who discovered that the central heating outlet chimney had not been connected up and that it was spewing fumes into the roof space that had become foul and full of water.[104] Some residents were so angry at what they had to live with that they literally took to the streets. In October 1974, residents of the Moss Side District Centre began a campaign to obtain rehousing for people from some of the worst slum flats in the city. Many were involved in a public demonstration, a squat in an empty terraced house and a pram barricade across a busy road during rush hour. Police were called in to break up the demonstration, arresting one man on an assault charge. The pram barricade got out of hand. One foolish motorist decided to drive through the barricade, damaging a pram that still had a baby inside. Not surprisingly, the women smashed his windscreen.[105]

Residents across the city mobilised. In Hulme, the left-wing Manchester Housing Workshop claimed that the major reassessment of the Crescents that took place in 1975 was forced by the Hulme Tenants Association campaign.[106] Members believed that it was their media campaign against the council that forced the Housing Committee to relent to demands to rehouse all families with children above the ground floor in Hulme and four other deck-access estates.[107] Leading Liberals were also involved. Alan Roberts, Chair of the Housing Committee, provided them with a flat for use as a base and advice centre. However, he was to regret his generosity.[108] Roberts was angered at the way the group used the centre for "political purposes". He blamed Peter Thompson, the centre's co-coordinator, for turning the "whole issue of this rights' centre into a political one", and of "conducting a vendetta against the Labour Council".[109] Thompson, a member of the executive council of the Manchester Liberal Party, was accused of using the centre to undermine the local authority. Yet, this was not about the success of any one political group working for the oppressed masses. However much Liberals and the Left wanted to use protests for their own political agenda, this was about the broader issue of people as consumers, the council as a producer and its failure to provide a decent service. It did not belong exclusively to any political group, and attempts to use it otherwise invariably failed. Efforts to hijack the language of consumerism for long-term political gain were destined to be unsuccessful. Consumerism is a shifting concept that could be interpreted by all sides of the political spectrum. Whether politically biased or not, all groups aimed to protect the interests of residents against the 'council'. Local government officials were perceived as the source of the problem. This was about consumers fighting for their individual rights – a political struggle over material consumption.

Some groups were obviously politicised. There was nothing new about political groups using tenants for ideological struggles. However, while several tenant groups became politicised, others attempted to avoid association with party politics. MASHA was concerned that the council would attempt to smear them as dangerous left-wing radicals. One member was worried that criticising it as inept and inadequate was the type of emotive language that would "alienate councillors and officers". Another member of the group claimed that a proposed letter voicing opposition to council policies would be seen as coming from a "bunch of raving Reds".[110] They did not want to be seen as a minority activist group, but as a truly representative organisation working on behalf of all sections of society.

The council moved falteringly towards accepting tenant participation, despite the fact that as early as 1966 local party activists were warning councillors that residents complaining over maintenance were losing them votes.[111] It failed to understand fully the profound nature of the challenge, but some councillors and officials in the 1970s and 1980s did begin to express sympathy and broad support for tenants. As early as 1972, the council approved a motion expressing sympathy for the principle of encouraging the "maximum participation by the people of Manchester", but the Town Clerk, G. C. Ogden, admitted that participation was actually very limited.[112] The council constantly paid lip service to the idea of consultation whilst doing as little as possible to turn it into a concrete policy. In the following year, it produced a paper, *Housing Action Areas: Suggestions for Public Participation Strategies*, which made a series of recommendations, but little else. In 1975, the Labour Group Policy Committee acknowledged that more thought should be given to establishing tenants' associations.[113] Later in the year, the council produced its own newsletter for Moss Side residents to keep them in touch with issues affecting the area and provide them with any information which might be helpful.[114] It also announced plans to open a local office, run by the Housing Department, and gave details of an Open Day to 'meet the team'. In reality, this was little more than a superficial PR exercise. Although some members of the party, and the council, wanted greater levels of consultation and participation, it was still on their terms.

While these initiatives suggested a shift in attitude and relations between the council and tenants, the scope was limited. It was confined to improvement schemes, but there was a much bigger problem with the management and maintenance of existing housing stock. Recognising the need for a shift in the political climate was a tortuous process for some councillors. It meant their power and authority were being challenged. They struggled with the fact that the language of old-style political dogma was no longer entirely relevant. The language of consumerism cut across traditional political lines, presenting a challenge at a time when suburban expansion was creating a new Conservative base. Here, a Conservative language of rights played differently, but it meant Labour was pressed from several sides. In 1977, Alan Roberts admitted that the council had made mistakes and openly stated that "Manchester has not been doing its job". Even the Head of Direct Works, Ken Wilson, claimed that the whole area was badly managed, confessing that there was a "general inability of management to cope with the unusual and abysmal conditions in which they found themselves".[115] The problem was complicated further by the fact that, while tenant groups were not confined to party or local authority loyalties, councillors and their supporters were. They had to support each other. This was underlined in 1977 when the Labour Group Policy Committee agreed to "close ranks" behind Alan Roberts following criticism of his handling of a site contract.[116] While some were sympathetic to tenant problems, party loyalties confined criticism from within the council.

Although the early 1960s finally ended the deadlock over slum clearance, leading to impressive completion and demolition rates after a crippling impasse, the council's policies and management of its new estates sowed the seeds of future discontent. In fairness, the council had been forced down a path with which it had never been entirely comfortable. The failure to secure enough land outside the city, the seemingly endless problem of a huge stock of overcrowded Victorian slums, together with pressure from central government and reformist officials within the council, led them to accept that flats and multi-deck access systems were the only solution. Time, money and physical space were conspiring against a council that, to its credit, only wanted to build quality homes in green surroundings. Even when it decided to accept the new modern systems, it was still reluctant to build flats over twelve storeys high. In addition, it attempted to be innovative and to adapt its own belief in cottage-style homes and the restoration of community through deploying multi-deck developments in Hulme, Harpurhey, Beswick and Ardwick.

By the late 1960s, early policy directives and financial restriction were pushing the council away from large-scale developments in favour of modernisation of existing housing stock. But it was also coming in for increasing criticism from its own tenants. Trust was eroded as tenants sought to influence policy decisions, to secure funding for their own areas and to demand rehousing as the reality of life in the multi-deck access systems began to dawn. Some members of the council tried to embrace the shift in the political landscape as groups of tenants increasingly adopted the language of the consumer. By the late 1970s, it was being forced into considering tenant views. The Conservative government's new Housing Bill included the Tenants Charter and, with it, rights to security of tenure, the right to improve decorations, the right to take in lodgers, the right to be informed about tenants' rights and the "right to consultation". Tenants were supposed to be consulted about changes in policy, new programmes, maintenance, demolition, improvement or any management issue affecting them.[117] The Housing Committee believed that this did not present any problems and thought it was all "consistent with the development in the relationship in recent years between the city council and its tenants".[118] Yet the council still had a long way to go before it fully embraced consultation and participation as a part of policy.

Nevertheless, while the 1980s were to prove a difficult time, they were also to witness the start of a new approach.

Notes

1 For a national overview see J. Yelling, 'The incidence of slum clearance in England and Wales 1955–85', *Urban History*, 27:2 (2000), 235–55.
2 *Manchester: Fifty Years of Change*, pamphlet (HMSO, 1995), p. 23.
3 *City and Suburban News* (9 November 1956).
4 Ibid.
5 Ibid.
6 *City and Suburban News* (3 August 1956).
7 *Evening Chronicle* (11 January 1956).
8 *Manchester Evening News* (27 January 1960).
9 *Evening Chronicle* (27 April 1961).
10 *Guardian* (24 March 1960).
11 Ibid. (13 April 1960).
12 *Evening Chronicle* (26 January 1961).
13 *Manchester Evening News* (8 April 1961).
14 Ibid. (27 January 1961).
15 *County Express* (16 February 1961).
16 Ibid. (23 February 1961).
17 *Manchester Evening News* (8 April 1961).
18 *Evening Chronicle* (10 May 1961).
19 *Guardian* (31 May 1961).
20 TNA, HLG 118/154, Letter from E. A. Sharp to P. Dingle, 3 May 1962.
21 TNA, HLG 118/1591, Speech on slum clearance and re-housing by Alderman Fieldhouse, 3 November 1971.
22 TNA, HLG 159/428, Figures from Manchester Housing Department to Department of Housing and Local Government, 4 April 1972.
23 Interview with Councillor William Egerton, 25 January 2002.
24 TNA, HLG 118/154, Letter from W. A. Wood, 27 September 1962.
25 M. Glendinning and S. Muthesius, *Tower Block: Modern Public Housing in England, Scotland, Wales, and Northern Ireland* (New Haven, 1994), Section I.
26 TNA, CAB 129/120, 'The housing programme'.
27 Ibid., p. 255
28 *Manchester Evening News* (24 July 1963).
29 *The Times* (13 March 1962).
30 Egerton interview.
31 Interview with Gerald Kaufman, 14 February 2002.
32 *Manchester Evening News* (1 December 1964).
33 Ibid. (28 June 1965).
34 *Guardian* (23 November 1965).
35 R. Crossman, *Richard Crossman: The Diaries of a Cabinet Minister* (London, 1975), p. 125.
36 *City and Suburban News* (27 February 1953).
37 *Manchester Evening News* (29 May 1962).
38 *Guardian* (4 September 1963).
39 *The Times* (11 May 1965).

40 Minutes of North-West Economic Planning Council, Housing Committee, 25 March 1966, p. 2.

41 *Manchester Evening News* (9 April 1965).

42 *Daily Telegraph* (10 November 1965).

43 *Manchester Evening News* (10 November 1965).

44 Report of the Housing Committee, No. 5201, May 1966, p. 1.

45 Ibid., p. 2.

46 Ibid., p. 3.

47 Both were also responsible for the city's Arndale shopping centre.

48 *Manchester Evening News* (10 November 1965).

49 Ibid.

50 For an examination of the role of the press see P. Shapely, 'The press and the system built developments of inner-city Manchester', *Manchester Region History Review*, 16 (2002–3), 30–9.

51 *Manchester Evening News* (22 October 1965).

52 *Guardian* (24 October 1966).

53 Ibid. (22 April 1968).

54 *Manchester Evening News* (17 March 1969).

55 Egerton interview.

56 *Manchester Evening News* (25 February 1944).

57 See also P. Shapely, 'Tenants arise! Consumerism, tenants and the challenge to council authority in Manchester, 1968–92', *Social History*, 31:1 (2006), 60–78.

58 *Evening Chronicle* (3 February 1951).

59 *Fight the Landlords' Rent Increase*, Communist Party leaflet, Local Studies Unit, Manchester Central Reference Library.

60 *Wythenshawe County Reporter* (16 March 1961).

61 Ibid.

62 *Manchester Evening News* (31 July 1963).

63 *Wythenshawe County Reporter* (21 October 1965).

64 *The Times* (13 January 1965).

65 *City and Suburban News* (31 August l956).

66 Ibid. (3 August l956); *Evening Chronicle* (17 October 1962).

67 *County Express* (19 January 1961).

68 Egerton interview.

69 Kaufman interview.

70 *East Manchester Reporter* (25 September 1970).

71 Ibid. (5 February 1971).

72 C. T. Davies, 'Citizen participation in redevelopment with special reference to Newton Heath' (MA dissertation, University of Manchester, 1971), p. 334.

73 Ibid., p. 335.

74 Again, the involvement of women in tenants' groups demands separate study.

75 R. H. Ward, 'Where race didn't divide', chapter, full source unknown, p. 205.

76 TNA, HLG 118/1591, Speech on slum clearance and re-housing by Alderman Fieldhouse, 3 November 1971.

77 Even then, councillors wanted to press ahead with occasional schemes such as Openshaw village, a project of 386 homes that cost £4 million. See Labour Group Policy minutes, March and April 1976.

78 'Housing Needs and Land Resources and General Housing Policies in the City of Manchester: Manchester: Improvement or Clearance – The case for Improvement', report of the Chief Officers (Housing Committee, June 1973).

79 Ibid.

80 Ibid.
81 City Planning Officer, 'Slum Clearance and Re-housing Progress', report to the Chief Officer's Meeting (Housing committee, 1 April 1974).
82 Manchester Housing Committee minutes, 2 October 1980.
83 G. A. Wheale, 'Citizen participation in the rehabilitation of housing in Moss Side East' (PhD dissertation, University of Manchester, 1979), p. 7.
84 Ibid.
85 R. H. Ward, 'Residential succession and race relations in Moss Side, Manchester' (PhD dissertation, University of Manchester, 1975), p. 206.
86 Minutes of Manchester and Salford Housing Action Meeting, Manchester University Community Action, 2 April 1973. All MASHA material is deposited at the Local Studies Unit, Manchester Central Reference Library.
87 MASHA newsletter, 16 April 1973.
88 Ibid.
89 See also B. Natton, 'The future for housing associations', in L. Hancock, 'Tenant participation and the housing classes debate' (PhD dissertation, University of Liverpool, 1994).
90 See for example MASHA minutes, 24 April 1973; 'Haykin Residents Association Survey', August 1974.
91 Ibid.
92 MASHA minutes, 29 January 1974.
93 Ward, 'Where race didn't divide', p. 208.
94 Ibid.
95 *Guardian* (20 December 1974).
96 'Moss Side People's Paper', Manchester Central Reference Library, November 1970.
97 Ward, 'Where race didn't divide', p. 210.
98 MASHA newsletter No. 2, February 1975.
99 E-mail correspondence to author from Mike Brennan, 25 September 2003.
100 *Manchester Evening News* (25 October 1975).
101 Ibid. (23 June 1973).
102 Ibid.
103 Ibid. (24 February 1978).
104 Ibid. (23 June 1973).
105 MASHA newsletter No. 2, February 1975.
106 Manchester Housing Workshop, *Hulme Crescents* (Manchester, 1980), p. 18.
107 The decision was finally made by the council in 1978. See Manchester Labour Group Policy Committee minutes, 4 April 1978.
108 Tenants occupied the Hulme Project office for seven weeks. See A. Ravetz, *Council Housing and Culture: The History of a Social Experiment* (London, 2001), p. 230.
109 *Manchester Evening News* (6 September 1977).
110 MASHA minutes, 24 April 1973.
111 Labour Party minutes, Ardwick Branch, 8 September 1966.
112 Ibid.
113 Labour Group Policy Committee, Manchester Council minutes, 17 October 1975.
114 'Newsletter for the Moss Side Housing Action Area', No. 1, December 1975.
115 Manchester Housing Workshop, *Hulme Crescents* (Manchester, 1980), p. 17.
116 Labour Group, Manchester Council minutes, 1977.
117 Manchester Housing Committee minutes, 9 November 1979.
118 Ibid.

7 New slums, New Left and new partnerships

Tenant dissatisfaction continued throughout the late 1970s and into the 1980s. Problems escalated as the council was faced with internal strife that eventually led to the rise of the New Left. This set it on a collision course with the Thatcher government that was itself determined to introduce a series of radical reforms designed not only to cut back on public expenditure but to change the role of local government. Compounding the council's problems was severe economic decline, the collapse of local industry, concentrated levels of unemployment and rising crime rates. All of these factors had an adverse impact on managing the city's housing stock. Moreover, the deterioration of the stock itself was a growing problem. The sins of the 1960s, already evident in the 1970s, provided a terrible legacy for the council. New developments, designed finally to bring an end to the slums and chronic overcrowding, started to crumble, creating at least as much human misery as the Victorian slums they had supposedly replaced. Now, however, the council had fewer resources to deal with the problem than at any time since the war. In addition, the government was determined to force local authorities into selling their housing stock.

Eventually, the council was able to demolish some of its system-built developments, replacing them with a mixture of private and housing association schemes. It was no longer a producer. The reality of the new political order forced a gradual change in policy and attitudes. From 1987, the New Left approach was replaced by a more pragmatic modernising approach, though the personnel largely remained. Manchester became a model entrepreneurial city. Confrontation with central government was replaced by a more practical third way. This impacted on all policy areas, including housing. Changes to the way the council operated were underlined by the rebuilding (yet again) of Hulme. The council now had to compete for resources and work in partnership with housing groups. It was central to the redevelopment process. Civic culture remained influential in the creation and implementation of the plans. Equally significant, however, was the fact that it was now forced to work in full participation with tenants. This was not a challenging process, but it marked an important change in relations between local government and tenants.

Rising costs, crumbling homes and cut-backs

In the mid to late 1970s, housing policy was facing an uncertain future. The national economic crisis placed severe financial restrictions and uncertainties on all local authorities. The 1970s were deeply affected by the underlying problems of spiralling inflation, a balance of payments deficit and rising unemployment. Both the Heath and Wilson governments failed to combat the chronic economic problems. From 1976, under James Callaghan, the Labour government was forced to introduce a series of deflationary measures to meet IMF demands. Public spending cuts of £1 billion for 1977–78 were followed by further cuts of £1.5 billion for 1978–79. The national economic crisis and local underlying industrial decline placed even greater restrictions on the council. It sparked both a budget and political crisis in the city. In January 1976, the Labour Group discussed the implications of the government decision to cut expenditure increases above inflation.[1] Proposed increases to the base budget would have involved a 20 per cent rates increase. It considered cutting all housing and other public building improvement bids, staff cuts and further reductions to other departments, especially education, but this still left a £3 million shortfall.

It was not only concerned about the impact on services but also the possible loss of votes in the May elections.[2] The crisis continued in 1977. Again, the council resolved to resist cuts in services, but although it opposed rent increases it did not rule out a rent rationalisation policy which might have led to an increase in rent revenue by charging higher rents for better properties.[3] It was willing to increase rates and to consider the new rent scheme in 1977 because there were no imminent elections, but it still feared losing power for four years.[4] In 1978 the Chair of the Policy Committee, Ken Eastham made it clear that "we have the vitally important elections and we must not prejudice our chances by being forced to raise rents".[5] The council found itself juggling between continual financial pressures and pressing political imperatives.

By 1979, its difficulties were further intensified. It had to deal with two other problems that were to cripple its ability to produce an effective pro-active housing policy. The new Conservative government introduced a range of restrictions, financial and legislative, which eventually ended the council's ability to build new homes. Alongside this were a series of mounting troubles with the system-built developments. By the late 1970s, it was clear that the flats had a number of serious structural faults. Problems arose at the Turkey Lane development in Harpurhey only six years after its completion in 1973. The 399 homes suffered either because they did not get enough heat or because the fuel costs were huge. Condensation produced mould, but a new gas-fired heating system would cost an estimated £1.6 million and an updated electrical system at least a further £1 million.[6] In the end, it decided to spend £1.3 million on curing the condensation and mould problems and improving the heating systems.[7] In an ironic twist, the council was awarded the Electricity Council's Civic Shield Award for the new heating systems at Turkey Lane.[8] High notes such as this were short-lived and rare. This was only the start of the council's problems. The deck-access systems at Beswick and Hulme, already the focus for tenant dissatisfaction, also had serious problems with heating, structural defects and vandalism. Water penetration at Fort Beswick was so bad that the council was forced to spend £60,000 to commission a report from Campbell, Reith and Partners, structural engineers, to see what could be done and whether it could sue the builders, Concrete Northern Limited.[9] It reported that a further £3million was needed to stop water penetration through building a pitched roof and relaying the asphalt.[10]

Repair costs on developments across the city were huge. Simple downspouts, for example, were needed for Hulme V, but would cost £55,000.[11] At Beswick, another £500,000 was spent on infill grills and safety barriers, while a further £123,922 was spent to help counter vandalism. Design faults with the heating systems at Forts Ardwick and Beswick meant that each flat was heated by electric under floor pads with tenants only having a simple on/off switch. Heating charges were included in the rent, and rising prices had led to rent increases. The council decided to switch the system off in the summer unless temperatures dropped to 56 degrees for three days.[12] This was despite a survey of tenants in 1979 which had shown a substantial majority in favour of keeping the system running. They were ignored in a bid to save costs. Poor weather in the summer led to a series of protests. It took two days for the pads to heat up, so flats remained cold for at least five days. The council decided to ask tenants for their views, even though they had already made them clear in 1979.

This followed a large number of complaints about the flats, including rainwater seeping through the walls. A further survey, carried out in 1981 by the city architects, revealed hairline cracks in the roof, water penetration on the lower decks, condensation, 320 out of 400 supports to fire escape balustrades were cracked (some exposing the metal core), nine structural failures on bridge supports, unsatisfactory repairs to concrete wall panels and stair towers which were starting to lean away from the main blocks. The City Architect, S. A. Heppell, highlighted the continuing problems with dampness caused by barrier blocks, while the Director of Housing claimed that ninety-eight homes were so bad that it was unfair to expect families to continue living in them and he was authorised to offer voluntary transfers. A further £100,000 was provided for other remedial work, excluding the barrier block problems. It had already spent £4.3 million on construction of the 1,020 homes during 1969–73, and a further £500,000 on improvements, £250,000 on new windows and £13,650 on a pilot heating system. Normal maintenance costs had risen from £74,500 in 1975–76 to £296,185 by 1979–80. It was estimated that further remedial work would cost another £3 million and heating improvements £2.5 million. The council would have to pay off the initial costs for a further fifty years. Repayment costs in 1980–81 alone totalled £643,100. The Housing Committee was urged to knock down three blocks immediately and the rest of the site over the following years.[13] However, the cost of demolition and replacement was put at £20–22 million, rising to £35–40 million in four years. This would cost an extra £3.25 million a year to pay off over sixty years.[14] Nevertheless, in a Joint Report of the City Architect, City Treasurer and Director of Housing to the Housing Committee, phased demolition of Fort Beswick was finally recommended. It listed the huge number of defects and structural problems and, although it had spent £5.2 million since building started in 1969 (and it still owed £4.8 million), and further repairs and part demolition would increase costs to £9.3 million, the council now accepted it had to consider the long-term phased demolition of the entire site. It hoped to rehouse everyone within two years, though the extra costs meant that final demolition would not be complete until the mid-1980s at best. It was a bitter pill to swallow. Millions of pounds had been pumped into the development, but it realised that spending money on continued maintenance would be even more wasteful.[15] Neither was it just the new developments that were causing concern. *The Housing Condition Survey*, which looked at older housing stock, concluded that the overall scale of the problem of disrepair and unfitness within the city's older housing stock was substantial. Nearly half of it – around 25,000 dwellings – was described as unfit or substandard.[16]

The problems were compounded by two political and economic problems. First, the city was plunged into recession. Traditional industries, such as engineering, had collapsed and unemployment increased. Concentrated levels of unemployment usually affected council estates, multiplying the problem further. Crime and vandalism increased. The Moss Side riots of 1981 highlighted the plight many faced in the city, not to mention the problems facing the council. Second, just as the council needed more resources to help it cope, the new government decided to impose financial constraints on all spending and to introduce a moratorium on new building. Early in 1980, the council unveiled an optimistic housing investment programme that would have cost £65 million and which included building 1,000 new houses as well as a modernisation programme.[17] A few months earlier it had requested an additional £4.5 million because of overspending on new capital schemes.[18] It was soon forced to face up to political and economic realities. The impact of government policy was highlighted later in the year when the Director of Housing, Graham Goodhead, reported that the moratorium made it impossible to carry out the recommended modernisation of housing stock in the North Central Area.[19] The Consultative Committee for the area had hoped that the improvement scheme for the district could be carried out over the following twelve months, but this was now impossible. The cut-backs were starting to bite. Tenants would be decanted from walk-up flats, but these would remain empty and, as such, targets for vandals. In addition, a report from the City Engineer, Geoffrey Read, claimed that the costs of existing repairs had risen from £3,069,878 to over £3.5 million due to increased charges.[20] However, it was unable to even sanction repairs worth £43,000 to a mere nine houses. The budget for 1980–81 had to be revised to £13.4 million, saving just over £1 million on the original figure.[21] In the following year, all committees were again asked to review budgets. The Housing Department agreed to further savings of £142,000, but it was not enough.[22] New cuts were demanded and the Housing Committee was forced to consider more reductions in expenditure. The council as a whole had to trim £4.3 million from its budget, but could only identify savings worth £3 million. It was made clear to the Housing Committee that if it failed to make sufficient cuts then reductions would be forced on them by the Budget Resources Sub-committee.

The council had to face up to the shifting political scene. New housing programmes were rapidly becoming a feature of the past. It had to cut future house building to a short priority list. The Housing Needs and Resources Sub-committee accepted that the reduction in the Housing Investment Programme allocations, and the need to allocate resources to the crumbling stock, meant there would be a severe reduction in new house-building schemes. Council building was finally winding down.[23] Some respite was given by the Urban Programme scheme, which allowed local authorities to bid for money for different schemes, including housing improvements. It hoped to acquire £500,000 under the programme, but this was never going to have a serious impact given the growing scale of the problems it was facing.[24] Coupled to this was the mounting repair bill that was beginning to bite deep into its beleaguered resources. The six months during October 1980 to March 1981 underlined the growing severity of the problems. In October, it agreed to spend £42,258 on environmental improvements to the John Nash Crescent,[25] while in February it had to spend a further £575,450 on combating condensation at Turkey Lane and another £178,848 for additional electrical work.[26] By March, S. A. Heppell requested an additional £2,333,445 to pay for the capital schemes programme agreed in 1976.[27] Costs had risen due to increased labour and materials, administrative charges, site conditions and contractual claims. This was all placing an unbearable strain on a council already facing a financial crisis. The Housing Committee was asked to inform tenants that, because of the cut-backs, Direct Works was not going to carry out low-priority repairs. In addition, more expensive modernisation was needed, with £226,000 required for thirty flats at Miles Platting, £205,000 for twenty-four flats at Wythenshawe, £400,000 for forty-eight flats at Portway, £546,470 for the old Victoria Square flats, £520,500 needed for sixty flats at Blackley and £442,000 for the seventy homes at Barrack Street, the site of one of the earliest council developments. Problems were even emerging on the overspill estates. At Langley, money was needed to carry out repairs to concrete balconies, while in Hattersley a large piece of concrete fell from under one of the balconies leading to an investigation into the condition of the flats. It revealed that many balconies in the estate's seven tower blocks had cracked or loose pieces of concrete which represented a real danger to the public. The cost of repair was nearly £200,000.[28]

Financial problems and mounting costs were threatening to cripple the council. It was a vicious circle. Lack of money meant lack of investment that led to further deterioration of an already crumbling housing stock. By 1983, the council had incurred a £5 million overspend on house repairs.[29] Councillor Frances Done pointed out that it was caught between a rock and a hard place, with huge government cut-backs on the one hand and, on the other hand, complaints about the appalling state of repairs.[30] Members of the Hulme Repairs Committee believed the impact of cut-backs on essential maintenance across the city would fall most heavily on them. It was so worried that it circulated leaflets to members of the council warning that further cuts would turn the estate into a ghetto.[31] The situation was so dire that, although some homes had new windows fitted, it could not afford to paint them.[32] Part of the problem lay with the tenants. By the mid-1980s, it was revealed that nearly half of its tenants were in rent arrears. In 1984, they owed £8 million while the following year it increased to more than £9.5 million, compounding an already difficult situation.[33]

It was no coincidence that rent arrears increased in proportion to rising unemployment. The economic crisis created even more problems. Homelessness became a major issue.[34] Initially, figures were relatively stable, with 1,013 homeless families being admitted to temporary accommodation during 1978–79, 1,025 the following year and 1,012 during 1980–81.[35] This contrasted with increasing levels in many other cities. Family disputes, not economic hardship, remained the main reason for homelessness. A strategy was developed for single homeless people, though, again, this was the result of lifestyle changes rather than unemployment.[36] By the mid-1980s, the situation had started to change. High unemployment and changes to the benefits system intensified the problem. In 1984, the council appointed a Co-ordinator for Housing Benefit in response to proposed rule changes and cuts by government.[37] Seven new members of staff were employed to develop a strategy for single homelessness.[38] By the end of the year it agreed to spend nearly £700,000 on two new thirty-three-bed emergency hostels to replace old hostels.[39] However, the growing scale of the problem continued to worry the council. It developed a 'Strategy for Housing Single People in Need', but admitted that growing numbers of homelessness were a real cause for concern. In 1984, it was reported that there would be a 40 per cent increase in homelessness over the following two years. In fact, it increased by 60 per cent. During 1983–84 it was investigating 1,372 applications, but by 1986-87 projected figures pointed to a total of 2,318 applications, with an increase in admissions of 65 per cent. This combined to place even greater pressure on staff and resources.[40] By the end of the decade it had become an acute problem. A report by Shelter, *A Bad Start in Life*, highlighted the difficulties facing many families living in basic and overcrowded hostels and hotels, many of whom were suffering from subsequent ill health. The council was actually praised for its efforts to move the homeless out of substandard properties. Shelter claimed it was "trying very, very hard", but the scale of the problem posed huge problems.[41]

The new slums

Homelessness added to the growing list of problems. The housing situation throughout the 1980s was always at crisis point. Manchester council's system-built homes had turned into a human nightmare. It compiled a dossier of major structural faults affecting flats across the city and published its own booklet, *Housing Defects in Manchester*, in which it claimed that defects were running through the stock of deck-access, tower blocks, post-war maisonettes and traditional-style housing.[42] Besides Beswick, the list included 300 four-storey maisonettes in Ardwick and Wythenshawe, a number of high-rise flats in Hulme III and the flats in Turkey Lane. In many cases, steel links were rusting and cracks had started to appear in the concrete.[43] The council again decided to sue Bison Concrete for negligence and breach of contract.

Problems continued to mount. Vandalism on some of the balconies had exposed asbestos. Loose pieces fell onto the decks below the balconies. Asbestos cement panels had been used throughout the Crescents. The potential crisis was so worrying that the council established an Asbestos Advisory and Action Panel to deal with the issue. In 1984–85 alone a total of £300,000 was approved for asbestos removal.[44] Bison Concrete was not the only villain. Structural problems with four-storey balcony-access maisonettes on twelve sites around the city were so bad that the council started offering tenants voluntary transfers. It did not have the money to make the necessary repairs, so it decanted tenants and deferred making a decision to a later date.[45] Goodhead submitted a report into the four-storey maisonettes in which he highlighted a long list of serious problems. An initial £2 million was allocated for repairs in 1982–83. Ceilings and both internal and external walls had fractures, concrete beams were cracked and most units suffered from condensation. The majority of the maisonettes were a product of 1960s non-traditional schemes. It was decided to demolish some and carry out extensive repairs to others.[46] The scale of human misery was underlined in 1985 in the *Guardian* by Michele Hanson. Once again, the press provided an important conduit in the housing debate. She described how Beswick had become a "desolate looking place". The problems that had been highlighted in 1981 were now multiplied because it was a condemned estate and, therefore, resources were unavailable for repairs, even though it would still have tenants living in it until the final stage of demolition. Hanson claimed that the decision to demolish the flats "was only the beginning of a whole new crop of horrors for tenants".[47] The estate had deteriorated rapidly. Lighting, heating, plumbing and general repairs were ignored. Gypsies were blamed for stealing pipes, tanks and fittings. The lifts were either broken or "full of drunks, vomit and excrement (human and dog)". Drug addicts and prostitutes moved into the empty flats. One family she interviewed had stopped asking friends and family to visit because they were too embarrassed. Their flat was plagued by cockroaches, maggots, bugs and fleas.[48]

The depth of the city's problems inevitably meant that the Housing Committee itself came under investigation. In November 1982, the Policy Committee agreed to form an all-party group of members to examine the Housing Committee's working systems, to look at the potential overspend of £1 million on housing repairs, the homeless families budget, estates management, the number of void properties and repairs and sale of properties. A Housing Examination Panel was created to look at the whole service, not just the Housing Department.[49] Goodhead's response to the Panel was a nineteen-page report, in which he claimed housing management had been historically underfunded. He stated it had reached crisis point as early as 1973 when it had faced a rent strike, caretaking services had broke down at Hulme and rent accounting was poor (some areas were sixteen weeks behind in their accounting). He believed that subsequent restructuring had led to huge improvements and a "first class housing management service". Re-housing and rent accounting were now efficient, though he admitted that the administration of repairs was not as advanced. Also, relations with other departments, employees and unions were strained. The Housing Department and Direct Works were at loggerheads, while a dispute with Housing staff had led to accusations of heavy-handed management resulting in industrial action.[50] Staff at the Moss Side Estate Management offices complained that they were continually falling victim to street crime in the area. The unions, NUPE and NALGO, wrote to Goodhead demanding alternative secure accommodation for all estate management staff, but were ignored. The strike took place and workers were docked a day's pay. The dispute threatened to spiral out of control until the Housing Committee instructed Goodhead to reverse the decision.[51]

Goodhead believed that new technology would make them more efficient and lead to a better service.[52] His recommendations could not mask or stop the underlying rot. Although in 1984 the council started to consider the future of the Hulme Crescents, it still had to continue making repairs until a decision had been made or the estate would decay at an even greater rate. Like Beswick, it was throwing good money after bad. The council also agreed to hold a national conference on defects in system-built housing in Manchester. This followed a similar conference held in London in May 1984, after which Goodhead had reported that all delegates agreed that almost all of the non-traditional housing stock built in the 1960s was an absolute failure and that the people living in the developments did so "in a great deal of misery". He claimed that "we came away from the conference not thinking if the deck access housing should be demolished but when". The answer would not come for another eight years. In the meantime, the problem had to be managed with ever-decreasing funds. There was little respite. Still the disastrous news continued. In 1985, it was revealed that Fort Ardwick had followed Fort Beswick with a series of structural faults. A private firm of consultants surveyed the estate. They found rainwater leaking through the roof, corroded steel fixings and concrete breaking away. The council had to spend £60,000 immediately to bolt 1,100 panels back to the internal skin of the building. The City Architect, David Johnson, claimed that the report highlighted the rapid deterioration of the building's fabric.[53] The discourse of civic pride was devoid of meaning when confronted with the growing mountain of problems. In 1985, the *Manchester Evening News* published a full-length report on the appalling conditions at Hulme. It detailed the "horrors of the concrete jungle", and how the heady dreams of the 1960s had "turned into a human nightmare". The whole area was a "housing disaster" that had entered the mythology of post-war planning. Complaints included dampness, condensation, fungus on the walls, poor ventilation, vermin, cockroaches, shoddy workmanship, serious structural faults, crumbling concrete panels, cracked walkways and rotting window frames. The report graphically illustrated the problems facing the same flats which had once been hailed (by them) as the new Bloomsbury:

> 'I never had dis problem in Saigon' screamed the graffiti. The blood red letters were splashed across a metal door panel in William Kent Crescent in Hulme. The warzone imagery is everywhere. On William Kent Crescent, named after the great architect, a broken washing machine blocks the first floor walkway like some discarded military hardware. The 'streets in the sky' walkways are minefields of dog excrement decomposing under spadefuls of treated council sand.[54]

Importantly, Graham Goodhead blamed the problems on the council's departure from low-rise housing and well-understood practices. The principles of Manchester's civic culture still underpinned local discourse. He believed that the "sins of the sixties" were being visited on the 1980s.[55] The faith in cottage houses was embedded as a part of the council's culture. It had strayed, sinned against conventional wisdom. Now it was decided to return to traditional homes with garages and gardens. David Ford, Chairman of the Housing Committee, unveiled the plans that included a new "village" with 750 homes and community facilities.

However, the financial problems continued to restrict its scope for action. Even at the end of the decade the council was forced to make a 25 per cent cut in its Housing Investment Programme. The government announced it was clamping down on Manchester's "creative accountancy", but the Housing Director Bob Young believed that it was "starving" them of resources and preventing them from carrying out basic maintenance and repairs.[56] His report to the Housing Committee warned that the government's "pitiful" help could decimate the city's housing stock. At least 10,000 homes built during the inter-war period were in need of urgent repair. Sam Darby, the Chair of the Housing

Committee, believed that government cut-backs could lead to such deterioration that it would have to reintroduce "massive slum clearance".[57]

Tenant anger II

Tenants again expressed indignation at the mounting crisis. People living in a 1950s block of flats in Ardwick were so desperate that they handed a petition to Gerald Kaufman begging to be rehoused. They were unable to sleep because of the noise, suffered from vandalism and felt that they existed as "aliens on a forgotten planet".[58] Tenants in the Bradford area formed their own Jobling Street Action Group to protest against conditions. They had been waiting for eight years for a decision about the future of the area based on the withdrawal of an agreement to build a new school (named, ironically, after Lady Shena Simon). In the meantime, the whole area had deteriorated, with empty properties and vandalism leading to an increase in the poor health of residents. Goodwin demanded direct action and a firm decision and exclaimed, "we are fed up with being put off by feeble excuses".[59] Similarly, the Warders Tenants Association, created by residents of former prison warders' flats, petitioned the council as part of a sustained protest about living conditions. The flats had been condemned ten years previously, but, despite some council improvements, they were still living in "terrible bad living conditions".[60] There was no play area for children, mothers "are on valium" and one had had a complete nervous breakdown. All the children had asthma or bronchitis because of the damp and two had dysentery because of the drains. They demanded demolition and rehousing, but the issue was difficult to resolve. The housing budget was already overspent. No money could be made available for the suffering tenants.[61] Vandalism increased the misery and the danger, with flats falling victim to arsonists. One of the flats was still inhabited by a mother and baby. The council was unable to make a firm financial commitment.[62] In the end, it was decided to sell the flats to private developers.

Tenants had to bare the brunt of the cut-backs. But it was not just about expenditure. Criticism continued about the basic efficiency of services. One woman in Hulme claimed she had been waiting six-and-a-half years for the Direct Works to carry out house repairs.[63] Even the former Chairman of Rochdale Housing Committee, Labour councillor, John Carroll, was forced to complain about the poor service in his Langley home. He was left waiting for over six weeks for repairs to the U-bend in his bathroom sink, forcing him to use the kitchen sink, which he found to be an unpleasant experience "particularly after the wife has been peeling spuds".[64] On a more serious note, Carroll believed that the huge rent arrears owed to the council was partly due to the anger at the poor service. The standard of provision offered by the Housing Department (as well as Direct Works) was criticised throughout the 1980s. At the end of the decade, angry tenants in north Manchester claimed they had been left waiting for a month just to talk to officials. Crumpsall councillor, Roger Bullock, complained that tenants were left hanging on the end of a telephone and that the housing management office was "uncommunicative and unsatisfactory". Phone lines were either engaged or left unanswered. Even when people turned up at the offices, they were often unable to see anyone.[65] The council was also condemned for leaving properties empty. Fred Silvester, Conservative MP for Withington, said that his constituents were angry that the council had bought houses from private owners only to leave them empty.[66] Residents were annoyed at the depressing impact it had on the area. Similarly, Shelter joined forces with local residents in Cheetham Hill to complain about seven houses that had been left empty for two years, despite there being 36,000 people on the waiting list. As a result, the whole area had deteriorated, something which Shelter condemned as "absolutely criminal".[67]

The council, however, insisted that it was pursuing an active policy of consultation with its tenants. But the extent to which it was a meaningful exercise remained uncertain. It did discuss the idea of tenant consultation, but it was obliged to do so under Section 43 of the 1980 Housing Act. This required landlords to inform tenants of any proposals and demanded that tenants should be able to make their views known within a specified time. All landlords had to consider "any representations made".[68] Arrangements had to be published and made available. This covered all management issues except rent. The council admitted that, although it published plans through the local media, carried out small surveys, had the occasional public meeting and attended some tenant group meetings, there was a clear "shortfall" in its relations with tenants. The duty to consult compelled them to refer to tenant views before a final decision was reached. It used its own *Mancunian Way* newsletter to publish consultation arrangements, to discuss the future use of a Tenants Consultative Committee, to invite tenants for occasional meetings with the Housing Committee and to publish a housing supplement twice a year. No final decisions were made on these proposals. It agreed to produce *The Policy of the City of Manchester on Consultation with Council Tenants*, which accepted that tenants should be consulted either individually by letter or through public meetings, and it promised that views expressed by tenants would be taken into consideration where appropriate on housing matters which were brought to the Housing Committee "from time to time". It also agreed to listen to existing tenants' groups "with interest". This was as far as it was prepared to go. It would meet and listen, but this fell a long way short of active consultation and participation demanded under the Housing Act. It even claimed that it welcomed the new legislation because it helped to formalise a procedure that it had adopted for "many years", but the substance was clearly lacking.

The extent of its consultation process was highlighted when Goodhead met tenants in the Gamesley and Hadfield overspill estates to discuss a proposed transfer of the estates to the High Peak council. He met two groups, one with

150 tenants and the other with 80. A pre-paid questionnaire was sent out to all tenants. Three-quarters supported the move, but Goodhead was disappointed with the fact that so few of the 1,400 tenants had bothered to get involved, which he believed was "not good participation". He concluded that participation in the exercise was less than hoped for, though he was happy with the result.[69] Yet what Goodhead failed to acknowledge was that if people were generally happy with a policy there was no need to voice an opinion. He was looking for confirmation that the policy proposal was acceptable and not for dissent and debate. In this respect he succeeded, though not as he had wanted. He had chosen an issue that was never going to be controversial – do you want to be part of the Peak District or Manchester? This was hardly contentious. All he wanted was public endorsement so he could tell the government that the council was involved in active participation. There was no such attempt at Hulme, Beswick or Ardwick. Similarly, in 1986 tenants were allowed to address the Housing Committee about proposals to replace the roofs of their maisonettes in Collyhurst. But, again, this was hardly contentious. They were told that the council was already reviewing the strategy of decapitation for the flats, assessing the feasibility of replacing the roofs with new pitched roofs.[70]

Tenant relations were complicated in the 1980s by a growing realisation that there was now an ethnic dimension that could no longer be ignored.[71] The council's ethnic minorities working group admitted that it needed to examine all policies, practices and procedures as a provider of services, including housing.[72] Riots in Moss Side during the summer of 1981 underlined the growing problems facing the council. Although tenant action groups in areas like Moss Side had been multi-racial in composition, the council had not considered the racial dimension to housing policy. It decided to hold an Open Day/Forum for representatives from the ethnic minority communities in March 1982 to enable them to view and gain an understanding of how the city's housing service worked and to communicate their concerns about the provision of housing services.[73] Goodhead's ten-page report highlighted a number of race-related problems. These included the absence of black officers working in multi-racial areas, the need to train staff to take account of cultural needs, the necessity of monitoring anti-discrimination policies, the concentration of black communities in a few inner-city estates, the lack of effective consultation by housing managers and the need for a race-relations advisor and two tenant-liaison officers to work on multi-racial estates together with four reception liaison officers.[74] In a Joint Report of the Town Clerk and Director of Housing into 'Tenant Consultation and Participation in Moss Side and Hulme', it was reported that tenants in both areas had asked for greater involvement in the management of their estates. There were no tenants' associations in either area and the report recommended the creation of a working party between councillors, officers and tenants in the Alexandra Park estate. The area was chosen because it was thought to be safer than some of the other estates that were plagued with problems. The Housing

Committee agreed to the working party as a pilot scheme. Once more, the council had opted for a soft option to show its willingness to engage with tenants in a meaningful way.

Barriers in the council–tenant relationship still existed. But tenants needed council help more than ever to support them in the face of growing social problems. Anti-social behaviour was becoming an increasing problem. Manchester, which was to become the pioneer of the Anti-Social Behaviour Order (ASBO), was acutely aware of the trouble created by disruptive tenants. It had received a number of complaints from tenants in Miles Platting and asked the Director of Housing to report on the extent of the problem across the city. It was decided to take all necessary steps to prevent letting houses in the area to families who had a bad reputation for anti-social behaviour. An increased programme of anti-vandalism measures costing £1 million over two years was also agreed.[75] However, by the mid-1980s it was recognised as a city-wide problem. The council decided to form a panel to look into rehousing anti-social households. It was a small gesture. The panel lacked the power and resources to tackle the problem. It was unsurprising, therefore, that, once local authorities were able to issue ASBOs, Manchester was the first to use them extensively.

While the council grappled with the problem, it continued to develop consultation strategies. In the mid-1980s, it recognised that attempts to increase consultation and participation had been unsuccessful and that a number of issues needed to be addressed. A working party was created from across different committees to review its commitment to public participation in all policy areas. Public involvement was one of the key themes in the local party's 1984 policy document, 'Labour's Programme for Manchester'. It wanted to make the council more responsive and accountable and to give people a greater say in how council services were planned and delivered.[76] The working party admitted it had lacked an overall direction and had only achieved partial success. The terms 'participation' and 'consultation' were used loosely and interchangeably. This resulted in confusion. It admitted that it was still at an early stage in developing its approach and recognised that it needed to be clear about the purpose of the exercise, to decide who it was going to involve and to use a variety of methods to reach the public. By 1989, it had formed a new charter for tenants' rights, which promised greater support for victims of racial harassment and nuisance neighbours and to keep vacant properties clean and tidy. The charter came after negotiations between the council and the tenants watchdog group the Federation of Associations on Manchester Estates (FAME).[77] But it was only in the early 1990s that an effective framework was developed, and even then it was compelled to act.

The great sell-off

The council's problems were intensified by a radical Conservative government determined to force through a number of changes affecting the role of local authorities. Financial restrictions were only a part of the problem. Ideologically, the government was committed to restricting local authority powers and to enforcing the Right-to-Buy for tenants. There was nothing new about the policy. Successive Conservative governments had promoted the idea since the 1950s.[78] In Manchester, the only period in which sales became an integral part of policy was when the Conservatives gained control during 1967–71. In the late 1960s, the Conservative council published a pamphlet, *How to Buy a Corporation House*, which provided details about which properties were for sale, how tenants could purchase their homes and what mortgages were available.[79] The policy was curtailed by Labour Housing Minister Anthony Greenwood when over 3,000 tenants applied.[80] Once Labour returned to power in May 1971, the policy was abandoned. However, by this time the Conservatives had successfully sold nearly 4,000 homes, while 15,000 tenants had applied for details of the scheme.[81]

Labour's decision to end the sale of council houses received an angry backlash from tenants who were half way through the purchasing process. Alderman Fieldhouse led the protests. Although he received the full backing of the Conservative Minister for Housing, Julian Amery, the city council remained resolute. Amery wrote to Fieldhouse expressing his great concern over the issue, and, following a meeting between the two, he agreed to consider the whole question of council-house sales.[82] Tenants were so angry that they formed the Council House Buyers Association (CHBA) and organised a petition with 364 signatures which they sent to the Queen. Fieldhouse claimed that the Association had hundreds of members, "many of whom are extremely militant".[83] John Graham, leader of the CHBA, told a meeting of over 400 tenants at Wythenshawe that while the group would remain politically neutral, politics were creeping into the issue, "dirty politics, really dirty politics".[84] It was alleged that some tenants had spent up to £800 on improving their homes, certain in the belief that their purchase would be successful.[85] One tenant, E. Tomlinson, wrote to Graham describing how he had received and signed his Contract of Agreement for the purchase of his house in April 1971, only to be told in May that the council had terminated it. Tomlinson had spent nearly £300 on a series of improvements in anticipation of owning the property.[86] When the Conservative councillors introduced a motion to reintroduce the Right-to-Buy scheme they were supported by a group of tenants who gathered on the Town Hall steps. The motion was heavily defeated by seventy-five votes to twenty-five, but the controversy continued. One Labour councillor, Julian Goldstone, resigned over the issue. It was claimed that 110 tenants had signed up to buy their homes only to be denied by the returning Labour council.[87] By 1974, the group was able to claim victory. An Appeal Court ruling, followed by a report from the council's own Director of Administration, Leslie Boardman, forced the Policy Committee to allow the 110 tenants to complete the purchase of their homes.[88]

Dogma was getting in the way of consumer choice. This was taken to new heights earlier in the year when the council announced its plan to buy back one of its former houses for £8,500, having sold it only five years previously for £1,920.[89] The plan created a political storm, but this was just the start. The council Policy Group decided to negotiate the purchase of the first 900 homes sold between March and August 1969. This followed the end of a five-year clause that prevented the houses from being sold. Gerald Kaufman condemned the plans, openly criticising the council in a speech in April.[90]

With the victory of the Thatcher government there was a new drive and determination to force local authorities into selling homes to tenants. The Tenants Charter emphasised the Right-to-Buy. However, the council was worried about the impact on relets and on the number and quality of remaining houses.[91] Initially, it condemned the policy as immoral and promised to dig in.[92] It produced a six-point plan to thwart the Conservative policy.[93] But it was vacuous political gesturing. Within a month, it decided to start selling houses to sitting tenants and unimproved miscellaneous houses to tenants and housing associations.[94] The pattern of ownership was beginning to shift.[95] Besides, the council had no choice. The Labour Chairman, Norman Morris, conceded that because of the financial constraints and the tremendous loss of income due to government cuts, it had no option.[96] Failure to sell would simply mean the houses would be sold and it would lose the income from the sale. By October, there was already a backlog of over 1,500 applicants, while Graham Goodhead reported in December that he had received 3,400 applications.[97] A strike by two-thirds of the Housing Department staff (due to a dispute about restructuring) delayed further action. The Department was failing to meet the four-week requirement for processing applications under the Right-to-Buy scheme, but it claimed that this was not political reticence but due to the sheer volume of applications. It would take at least another two months to clear the backlog. Some tenants complained to the Secretary of State about the delays and, after meeting a delegation of protestors, the Housing Minister, John Stanley, promised to take action.[98] The 500-strong Manchester House Buying Association handed him a dossier accusing the council of deliberate delaying tactics. One member of the Committee claimed that the council had failed to pre-empt the legislation and make adequate preparations.[99] By this stage it had finally managed to deal with most of the backlog, answering 5,500 of the 5,900 applications.[100] By September, it had cleared the excess applications and by the beginning of 1982 a total of 6,801 had applied to buy their own homes, of which 6,520 had been accepted.[101] However, by the late 1980s the council was again seen to be dragging its feet. A backlog of 2,000 applications had accumulated. Officials blamed the lack of staff. The average waiting time between receiving the application and confirmation of the tenants' Right-to-Buy (not the actual purchase) had risen to twelve months. An amendment to the Housing Bill meant that tenants had the right to a rent rebate taken from the final price of the house as compensation.[102] This was no longer about ideological differences. The sale of at least some properties was now not only seen as a tenants' right but also a policy option to ease the council's chronic financial problems. A report to the Housing Committee recommended selling thirty blocks of flats and maisonettes at Langley to private developers. The homes were in need of modernisation, were being targeted by vandals and were impossible to let. The only answer was private investment, ownership and management. Some blocks had already been transferred to the Collingwood Housing Association and this, it seemed, was now the only long-term solution.[103] The council had started to shift its own political stance. It had been a painful and troubled journey.

The New Left[104]

Besides the impact of government policy and restricted finances, the move towards a more pragmatic housing policy was punctured during 1984–87 by the domination of the council by the New Left. Under the leadership of Graham Stringer, this radical group, many of them young graduates, wanted to push the council towards adopting a series of left-wing policies which, they hoped, would involve high levels of public spending and continued local authority control over all public services. They deliberately followed a path that would lead to overt confrontation with the government. Even before taking power, the group had tried to pressure the council into leading an open revolt against the government. Faced with a cash crisis in 1982, Stringer urged Labour councillors to introduce a rent freeze and minimal rates increase and to "cut nothing".[105] He believed that confrontation was the "best solution" to the council's £35 million deficit. When his New Left group gained power, it was determined to take the fight to Whitehall. The Housing Committee decided to bid for housing investment resources totalling £90.5 million for 1985–86, even though it had been set at £60 million in previous years. It also made further representations about the debt charges it had to pay on demolished non-traditional estates which the government already recognised should no longer be a burden on ratepayers. Goodhead pointed out that, in reality, this was a wish list of work that should ideally be commissioned.[106] It was never going to be accepted, but the council wanted to use it as a tool to attack the government.

The mid-1980s were characterised by a series of anti-government posturing. The language was confrontational, but there was no hiding from the fact that it had little room for independent action. In 1984, when it discussed the Housing and Building Control Act, members were quick to condemn the legislation as "the right to rip off".[107] The Deputy Chair claimed that the legislation was "another confidence trick by the Thatcher government" which would lead to the transfer of repair work to "cowboy builders or DIY enthusiasts". Somewhat dramatically, he claimed the government's legislation would increase complaints and deaths by tenants attempting to do repairs.[108] He even condemned the Family Housing Association for circulating a newsletter to tenants stating that the legislation did not pose a threat to tenant safety, objecting to its "clear political bias". The Housing Committee reported them to the Housing Association Working Party and referred the Act to the Campaign and Information Sub-committee to consider further action. But there was little else it could do. Its lack of power was underlined by the continuing cut-backs. When the government announced that its Housing Investment Programme for 1985–86 was being reduced to £36.05 million, the Chair of the Housing Committee, Nicholson, blasted the budget as "totally inadequate", but could do no more. This constituted a large reduction on previous years. In 1981–82 it had been £44.92 million, in 1982–83 it was £53.33 million and then it decreased in the following two years to £44.53 million and £40.50 million.[109]

This was the problem. The council spent a great deal of time in the mid-1980s making political statements and complaining about the government but there was only minimal policy creation. In 1986, it was decided to keep a detailed record of all damage sustained by the police when carrying out searches on council-owned property. It demanded that the Police Authority should bear the costs incurred, except in life or death cases. This may have been a case of best economic practice, but there was an element of deliberate confrontation.[110] Opposing government policy was a core element of council policy. It even gave the tenants' group, FAME, £350 towards its travel costs so it could lobby Parliament in opposition to the Housing and Planning Bill.[111] With one housing disaster coming after another, together with the underlying problem of a crumbling stock of old houses and the shrinking budget, the Housing Committee devoted time to a number of sectional reports, some more understandable than others. It discussed a series of papers concerning issues such as working women, equal opportunities, immigration, race relations, the Chinese community and the possibility of using the City Engineer and Surveyor's Department to assist local authorities in the Third World.[112] Also, it appointed a representative to sit on the Aids Working Party. More controversially, the Housing Committee gave its support to three housing initiatives in Nicaragua. It expressed huge sympathy for a country that had not only successfully overthrown a "cruel dictatorship" but which, it was keen to point out, faced a counter-revolutionary movement backed by the USA. It was eager to give its "moral support and encouragement" to the schemes and to support fund-raising initiatives.[113] How the tenants of Hulme, Beswick, Ardwick and Turkey Lane related to the oppressed workers of Nicaragua is unclear, but it was support for this type of cause which undermined backing for the council.

Besides confrontation with the government, the New Left defined itself by focusing on the politics of single-issue causes and groups, including tenants. The council promised to take consultation and participation to another level. When the Langley Estate Residents' Association sent a petition complaining about conditions at Lakeland Court flats, the Committee agreed to meet a deputation at the next meeting, though it later changed its mind.[114] It did, however, allow a representative from the Platt Lane tenants' association to address them. He told them improvements in contacts between the council and tenants' groups were long overdue. Goodhead also issued his report on 'Tenant Participation and Housing Service' in which he claimed that tenant involvement was widely accepted to be fundamental to securing effective housing management. He reported that over the previous three years they had considered a number of issues and possible schemes that touched on tenant participation. The current position was outlined in Manchester Labour Party's own manifesto for 1984, which included a section on 'Tenant Participation'. However, he admitted that the council still had a long way to go. The Housing Committee agreed to encourage the participation of tenants in the decision-making process and it asked the Housing and Social Services directors to hold a one-day conference with tenants' groups to examine the issue and make detailed arrangements for the future. A total of fifty-six groups, including the names and addresses of contacts, were identified and a grant of £150 was approved for FAME to support its activities.[115] It was also decided that any future plans for Hulme should involve "extensive consultation with the local community".[116] Yet attempts to form a consultation strategy for Hulme were met by a series of frustrating delays. Although it agreed to appoint a clerk to help, there would be no tenant participation in making the appointment.

Despite a series of good intentions, there was still a question over the extent to which the council really wanted to engage in a meaningful process. A few local surveys of tenant feelings were carried out, including a brief review of attitudes in the low-rise homes in Wellington Street. Unremarkably, this concluded that a proportion wished to be rehoused from the area whilst others wanted to remain but be compensated for the discomfort endured during the demolition of Fort Beswick.[117] This was far from being a contentious issue. As one member of the Committee remarked, "the consultation exercise with tenants had been superficial in that tenants had not been asked to give their views on all the options which had been before the Housing Committee".[118] It was paying lip service to the consultation process. Eventually, it resolved to defer the issue altogether. Similarly, in 1984 it consulted tenants on the Turkey Lane estate on the question of whether it should be demolished and, not surprisingly, it was discovered that the majority were in favour of the proposals. Again, this was not a controversial issue. While some officials appeared to be genuinely keen on the idea of developing a meaningful dialogue with tenants, and while there existed a great deal of references to consultation, in reality there was a lack of substance to the process. When, for example, it proposed to include tenants in a pre-inspection of properties prior to a programme of replacement floors on the Anson estate, it was little more than a ploy to record the content and condition of fittings to avoid "alleged damage caused during the contract period".

Towards New Labour and partnership

Answers to the council's long-term problems took it in new directions. Profound changes occurred that influenced every aspect of policy. Following the Conservative victory in the general election of 1987, Manchester's Labour council began to shift its ideological stance.[119] The New Left agenda was gradually replaced. Municipal socialism gave way to the entrepreneurial model of managing and developing the city.[120] After years of largely fruitless confrontation, the Conservative victory underlined the reality of the new political order. It was now a case of swim with the tide to acquire real benefits for the city or continue to resist central government with little hope of securing the resources needed for social and economic development. Graham Stringer and the council opted to move towards greater co-operation. It would work with the government, the private sector, community groups and the local Quango, the Central Manchester Development Corporation. It would have to compete for resources under a series of development schemes.[121] The council successfully applied for resources that allowed it to make the Olympic and Commonwealth Games bids. It also secured funding under the City Pride initiative.[122] In housing, this shift in approach was highlighted with the City Challenge. The council remained at the centre of all new initiatives. With Stringer at the helm, it abandoned attempts to decentralise power and enfranchise disadvantaged groups through council initiatives such as the Gay and Lesbian sub-committee. The city needed investment and a programme of urban regeneration if it was going to recover from the years of decline. Political processes gave way to a desire to get a concrete outcome by working in partnership with groups that could secure tangible results.[123] The new approach was pre-empted in 1986. The council was already working with other agencies, housing trusts and housing associations, to develop a housing strategy. For example, it agreed to meet the Guinness Trust about the possibility of using council land in Smithfield to build hostels. Both saw this as part of their wider strategy for homelessness.[124] Partnership was now the key.

Limited finance continued to restrict its scope for action. The first priority was to demolish the remaining system-built developments. Following the phased demolition of Fort Beswick, attention turned to Fort Ardwick. In 1988, a report to the Housing Committee underlined the expensive problems of water penetration, corrosion of steel fixings, condensation, poor heating, lack of security and vandalism.[125] Repayment of loan charges on the flats would increase to £9 million over the following forty-three years, but, as with Beswick, refurbishment would be a waste of money. In 1989, Graham Stringer told tenants and union officials at a conference in the city that the system-built developments were crumbling and the older housing stock was continuing to deteriorate, but the government had taken away nearly £1 billion from the council over the previous ten years.[126]

Officials realised they needed a co-ordinated approach, linked to the wider issue of urban regeneration – the creation of sustainable communities. Even when Fort Ardwick was finally demolished, the subsequent development of the area was seen as a lost opportunity. Houses were built to replace the flats, but David Lunts, Chair of the Housing Committee, claimed that while the redevelopment of Ardwick provided an exciting opportunity for urban regeneration, the fact was that "we wasted it – we just replaced one unsuitable estate with another". Hulme provided the focal point for the new approach. Unlike other deck-access estates, such as Byker Grove and Broadwater Farm, Hulme was an utter failure. While these estates had their problems, Hulme was totally beyond redemption. It was uniquely bad. The government wanted to introduce a Housing Action Trust, the brainchild of Nicholas Ridley. Under the 1988 Housing Act, it proposed to transfer estates to an unelected trust which would improve it before passing it over to a different landlord. However, the council and the tenants opposed the policy. Tenants carried out an anti-HAT campaign.[127] The policy failed to address the area's serious social and economic problems. Such was the level of their opposition that the Housing Minister, William Waldegrave, was forced to withdraw the proposal. The government decided to commission its own survey into the area, the 'Hulme Study'. At a cost of £200,000, the consultation document looked at the whole issue of how to develop a viable community. Housing was seen as one factor in the social and economic regeneration of inner-city areas. Again, time and money were being spent on research and debate, but nothing was actually done. Ultimately, the study was criticised as being vacuous and was abandoned in 1990.[128]

Both government and the council agreed to fund a more focused study. The consultants, Price Waterhouse, were employed to formulate limited plans for small-scale redevelopment. A new regime was created between the council, government and the private sector. It included housing associations, which the report believed provided the best solution for social housing. There was a growing recognition inside the council that this was the reality of the new world. Swimming with the tide meant it could be at the centre of the decision-making process whilst also giving it greater potential to secure funds for real change.

Civic pride and the City Challenge bid

In 1991, the significance of the study increased as the Secretary of State for the Environment, Michael Heseltine, unveiled the City Challenge. The scheme guaranteed £7.5 million a year for five years, given to ten pacemaker local authorities with the purpose of regenerating a run-down inner-city area. Fifteen cities competed with each other for the money. Once again, local authorities would have to work with the government and the private sector. Manchester did not hesitate to make an application. This was a golden opportunity to resolve the chronic problems at Hulme. In August 1991, Heseltine announced that the city had been successful. Hulme was given another chance.

Its application meant that the council could take centre stage in the redevelopment process. Civic culture was important in shaping its approach. It continued to promote a grand narrative. Hulme was part of the 'new' Manchester – modern, bold and exciting. Like Wythenshawe and the Crescents before them, this was going to be a high-status project, a flagship. Graham Stringer drove the new vision. Allegedly inspired by a visit to Barcelona, where he was impressed by the transformation of the city following its successful Olympic bid, he became committed to developing a sustainable urban environment with quality as the watchword. Manchester was portrayed as a truly great European centre and as a rival to Birmingham as Britain's second city.[129] The Olympic and Commonwealth Games bids were part of the new strategy. It secured considerable investment from government and the private sector, including the largest indoor arena in the country and the national Velodrome. Michael Heseltine started to spend more time in Manchester than Liverpool, with which he had developed a close relationship since the early 1980s. He put himself in the frontline of the Olympic bid and was so impressed with the many regeneration schemes that he described them as "projects of historic significance and lasting value".[130] The City of Manchester Stadium, the Bridgewater Concert Hall, the Urbis centre and the large multi-million pound expansion of the City Gallery followed. Other schemes, such as becoming the City of Drama and the promotion of the Gay Village and the Northern Quarter, were aimed at reinventing the city as a thoroughly post-modern and exciting European centre. The success of Madchester music and of Manchester United as the biggest sports club in the world, together with neighbouring schemes such as the Trafford Centre, the Lowry Centre and the Imperial War Museum in Salford and Trafford, all supported Manchester's image, its grand narrative as the city of firsts.[131] Hulme provided another opportunity to develop a high-status project. Prestige was a central source of motivation. In 1994, Hulme Regeneration Limited produced its guide, *Rebuilding the City, a Guide to Development in Hulme*. The Chair proudly boasted that "here in Manchester we have achieved major successes in recent years", including the expansion of the international airport, the investment from the Olympic Bid, the Metrolink system, the hosting of Global Forum 1994 and the new international concert hall. All of this pointed to Manchester's "emergence as a leading European city". Hulme was a part of this new image as it gave them a "unique opportunity to pursue this vision".[132] Heseltine described it as the "most striking" of all the City Challenge schemes.[133]

Fundamental to this approach was the creation of partnerships between central and local government, private investors, housing associations and tenants. The council had already been involved in public-private initiatives such as the Phoenix initiative, an attempt to regenerate part of the city centre. Heseltine insisted that the private and public sectors had to converge. They would provide a 'joined-up' approach, a new pragmatic and holistic way of addressing the chronic problems of inner-city decline. He proudly claimed that the area was transformed by "a dynamic partnership between the public authorities and the private sector".[134] This was underlined after a meeting between Local government and Housing Minister, David Curry, and Graham Stringer. After the meeting, Stringer observed that it was a sign of how much things had changed as he now agreed with "95 per cent of the minister's presentation".[135]

The council formed new companies to develop and implement plans. Together with the construction company AMEC, it established Hulme Regeneration Limited, while Hulme Community Homes Limited was formed between the council, the housing associations (including North British Housing Association, Guinness Trust, Manchester and District Housing Association, Mosscare Housing, Family Housing Association, Arawak Walton Housing Association, People First Housing Association) and local tenants. The council had to work with the Central Manchester Development Corporation, but Stringer found it to be a relatively passive group which he was able to use to promote his own agenda.[136] Some in the government may have believed that its ideologically driven changes would sideline the 'council' in managing the city, but the reality in Manchester was that the council adapted and reinvented itself as the dynamic agent for development and reform.

Forging effective partnerships was not without its difficulties. Different sides often lined up as if they were in opposition.[137] The council did not have a history or culture of co-operating with other institutions. It liked to be in sole control. For some within the council, this new process constituted a loss of power, but most worked through their reservations as they realised that it remained the central agency. Indeed, in many respects it found power was returned to them.[138] Housing associations and the private sector proved largely compliant. Future business prospects were too great for the private sector to rock the council boat, while many of the voluntary groups involved relied on the council for funding. The council was also unwilling to make any disagreements public, fearing the negative publicity and the possible loss of future funding if it was seen to be unable to work in partnership with others. There was too much to lose on all sides. Besides the government funding of £7.5 million, private-sector investment in Hulme by the end of the initial period was £81.5m and expected to exceed £200m by the end of the decade.[139]

The council's aims for Hulme were, in cultural terms, typically bold. This was not just about demolishing and rehousing people. It was designed to rebuild completely the entire fabric of one of Britain's worst inner-city districts. The aim was to develop the economic base, return people to work, transform the area's housing stock by rebuilding or refurbishing the entire housing stock, offer tenants a choice of accommodation, promote tenant participation and improve the entire physical environment. It wanted to develop a balanced community, catering for people of all ages, and to build or facilitate the creation of all the necessary services to make any community work, including shops, schools, workshops, restaurants, health centres, post offices and a cinema.[140] People would be able to rent or buy low-cost flats and houses. The buildings were designed by different people, including tenants. The entire community would be fully integrated.

A central aim was the implementation of the Urban Design Code. The Code was partially influenced by Jo Berridge, a Canadian urban design specialist, and drawn up by George Mills, a local architect, and David Taylor of AMEC. The objective was to avoid the design mistakes of the 1960s. Planners were looking beyond the planning culture of the post-war world to see what had actually worked. Streets, previously closed off, would now be opened up. Public spaces with squares and parks would be created. Street fronts would be designed to highlight the virtues of each building. The whole area was to be become inviting and accessible, creating a sustainable community.[141] The new design code would also take full account of the traditional working-class culture that characterised the historical development of the area. Architects used overlays of the old network of streets to provide an initial template for planning. George Mills claimed that they were showing an understanding of working-class culture.[142] As such, it was an attempt to appreciate what the customer actually wanted in a new home.

Hulme contained 5,375 social housing units, all owned by the council. Achieving its aims meant the initial demolition of 2,900 deck-access homes, the building of over 1,000 new homes for rent, 1,500 new homes for sale and the improvement of 600 council homes. North British Housing Association and the Guinness Trust were responsible for the majority of the new homes. Private-sector housing would also make a significant contribution. There was to be a mixed economy of housing, avoiding an over-concentration of rented property and the threat of ghettoisation that had characterised the previous Hulme. The four Crescents, the centre of the new 'Bath' in the 1960s, were to be demolished. They symbolised the dreams and failures of the 1960s and 1970s. Pushed into making a quick-fix solution, attempting to avoid tower blocks by developing streets in the sky, persuaded by the experts, utterly failing to manage the estate and to meet the demands of tenants – they were the epitome of all that was wrong with inner-city housing in the city. Equally, the announcement of their demolition, and the plans and structures that were established to replace them, symbolised the new approach and attitudes.

Another key departure from the past was the level of tenant consultation and participation. Central government continued its policy of encouraging participation. It was part of its commitment to empowering the consumer as an individual capable of making informed choices. This was an important element in the idea of partnership. However, building a new relationship between council and tenants took time. There was a great deal of distrust. Tenants were so angered at cut-backs to the workforce in the area in 1987 that they had occupied the local project offices for seven weeks. The sense of distrust was entrenched. Tenants became organised into the Hulme Tenants Alliance. Initial consultation about redevelopment had been greeted with cynicism and anger. They were deeply suspicious of both the council and the Department of the Environment and felt they were in danger of again being overlooked. Activists erected a large signboard declaring, 'Manchester City Council, Cutting Jobs, Destroying Services, Selling your Home'. Some were convinced that the council had a hidden agenda. Parodying a council advert, they declared that it had "democratically decided that your homes are not important", and that tenants would "not be able to come to the city and spoil our chances of attracting big business and the Olympics".[143] People were deeply scarred by the council's poor management record and were still complaining bitterly that the service offered was shoddy and that council staff made living in Hulme hard work.[144] The main focus for discontent was the Direct Works Department. One tenant commented that the relationship between tenants and Direct Works was one of "mutual disrespect".[145] Tenants were determined to voice their opinions on the future of the area. When Michael Heseltine flew to the city to meet the council, he was confronted on the return flight by two tenants, Genni Flynn and Elizabeth Holland. Although most of the tenants involved were unemployed, the Alliance had had a quick collection, raising £300 to pay for the tickets. They presented Heseltine with their own document, *Hulme City Challenge – a Response From the Community*, in which they expressed their views on the future redevelopment of the area.[146] Peter Marcus, a spokesman for the group, stressed that this was not a stunt to antagonise or annoy Mr Heseltine but an honest attempt to get "30 seconds of his time to present our case so that the needs and wishes of Hulme residents are not overlooked".[147]

Tenant responses were themselves problematic. The Alliance consisted of twelve different groups who did not always agree. There were also a number of informal associations, including head teachers, voluntary workers and a local business support group. When they did meet the council, they often felt they were wasting their time. Apathy began to creep in and the council was accused of making real decisions behind their backs.[148] Initially, the groups had their own office and funded workers, but, by the mid-1990s, the number of groups had declined and the funded support dwindled.

Despite these problems, tenant participation emerged to become a successful part of the City Challenge-funded redevelopment of Hulme. Tenant groups were not fixed, institutionalised organisations. They came and went, shifting according to the changing circumstances. During their life span, tenant groups provided valuable input into the development plans. The bidding process stressed the requirement for tenant involvement. Tenants participated in a number of ways, including house design, housing management, schools, shops, open spaces, and planning other facilities. Participation was promoted through the Tenant Participation Project, the Community Architecture Group and an arts group that was used to help people understand the details of the different designs. Public meetings were held that encouraged tenants to make their own suggestions.

Weekly design workshops took place and plans were presented to the public at every stage of the design process. Architects even made personal visits to people in their own homes. Newsletters, giving regular updates, were distributed on a regular basis. Some tenants were far more active than others. Three tenant co-operatives, comprising a number of professionals, promoted their own vision of what should happen to the area. The Housing Associations were also keen that participation should go beyond the design and development stage. They promoted tenant involvement in the management of the new homes. The government also wanted to develop self-help schemes by funding organisations such as the Priority Estates Project. One of the central concepts was to make people feel responsible for the upkeep of their community. All sides had to be involved to make it a long-term success. Tenant participation did not only apply to those who would move into new properties. All Hulme tenants were consulted about future priorities. Tenant choice was taken to a new and largely unprecedented level. Not only did they have a say in the design process, in choosing facilities and in managing properties, but they were even offered a choice of properties, who they wanted as neighbours and in which direction they would like their new homes to face. They were given up to £1,500 for new furnishings and helped with removal expenses. Whereas the redevelopment of Hulme in the 1960s was planned in offices by professionals and politicians removed from the district, the new Hulme was designed in a far more public arena, even leaving some professionals feeling susceptible and bemused.[149]

The redevelopment of Hulme was intended to be more sensitive to the demands of the tenant than any other housing scheme involving the council. It did not end with the physical rebuilding of the area. Two extensive surveys were carried out by the Independent Monitoring Project. In the first, the European Institute for Urban Affairs employed MORI to gauge tenant satisfaction before the end of the City Challenge project. The second was carried out by MORI after the project had finally been completed. They aimed to assess the scale of the development, the popularity of the changes, how effectively change was being managed and what needed to be prioritised in the future. The survey showed a high level of satisfaction and a generally strong level of future commitment to stay in the area.[150] Significantly, despite the history of fractious relations between Hulme tenants and the council, half of all residents believed the council was responsible for the improvement.[151]

The changes, which saw over 2,200 new homes being built by housing associations and private developers, and which included the symbolic Hulme Arch spanning Princes Road, were generally heralded as a success.[152] During 1992–97, the council was able to attract over £200 million of investment into the area. All remnants of the 1960s developments, including the notorious concrete walkways and Moss Side shopping centre, were demolished. Hulme, so often a barometer of housing across the twentieth century, was unrecognisable. Houses built by North British Housing Association and the Guinness Trust were so successful that they were awarded three Royal Institute of British Architects awards. The five-year project was finally ended in 1997 when Hulme Regeneration Limited was officially closed down.

Further housing schemes were developed with housing associations and the private sector. The council became particularly keen to promote developments in the city centre. It still views them as part of the process of economic regeneration for the entire city. Many of these have been high-status projects, expensive and affordable only by the professional community. Nevertheless, the lessons learnt through the City Challenge were carried into the regeneration of other areas. In neighbouring Moss Side, for example, officials were active in door-to-door consultations and conducting surveys using local residents. Despite its success, the City Challenge was not repeated. In the end, thirty-one areas across the country benefited. But the lasting impact was on the approach and method. Partnership and participation continued at the centre of urban regeneration schemes. This was highlighted by the redevelopment that took place in the aftermath of the IRA bomb. Central and local government again worked in a highly successful partnership with the private sector to create a huge building programme.[153]

However, although there was a gradual change throughout the 1980s in relations between the council and its tenants, there remained an underlying tension. In certain respects, attitudes had not changed as much as would appear. Council policy in 1994 had echoes of pre-war attitudes. Its vetting system for new tenants applying for homes in Collyhurst was condemned by Shelter as a "sinister step too far".[154] Adverts asked for mature people over twenty-five years old. All applicants needed a National Insurance number, proof of address, proof of ability to pay the rent, proof of "willingness to be a good neighbour" and two written references. Everyone would be thoroughly checked and the Housing Department even warned that police records would be inspected. This was a response to the growing problem of anti-social behaviour, but it still had parallels with the 1920s attitudes towards slum dwellers. Poverty and homelessness were not the criteria. Tenants had to be trustworthy and properly managed.

Nevertheless, the political landscape shifted dramatically across the 1980s and, with it, approaches to housing. At the start of the decade the old Labour council struggled with biting cut-backs and a growing list of problems. Old housing stock needed modernising, while the new developments were crumbling and draining slender resources. The city suffered economic and social upheaval, as traditional industry collapsed, unemployment rose and crime and social unrest increased. Coupled to this was the electoral victory of a Conservative government determined to cut public spending, to challenge Labour strongholds and to change the role of local government from producer to enabler. The Labour council of the early 1980s was not overtly confrontational. Generally, it was politically pragmatic and willing to accept initiatives such as the Tenants Charter and even the sale of council houses. This, however, frustrated the young and more radical members of the local party. By the mid-1980s the New Left group had control and was far more willing to confront the government. However, it was eventually forced to rethink its approach, especially after the Conservative election victory in 1987. By the late 1980s it had changed direction. The city was starved of investment and in danger of going into terminal decline. Despite some reservations, the change in policy direction brought a new lease of life to the city. Civic culture, civic pride and status, again formed a framework for action. Manchester was actively promoted as the city of firsts. It went for the big and the bold. This was reflected in the redevelopment of Hulme, a project that still acts as a beacon for people entering the city.

Notes

1 Manchester Labour Group Policy Committee minutes, 13 January 1976. These hand-written minutes have been generously loaned by Councillor William Egerton.
2 Manchester Labour Group Policy Committee minutes, 18 and 20 January 1976.
3 Ibid., 1 February 1977.
4 Ibid.
5 Ibid., 3 January 1978.
6 Manchester Housing Committee minutes, 9 November 1979.
7 Ibid., 23 April 1980.
8 Ibid., 14 February 1983.
9 Ibid., 10 December 1979.
10 Ibid., 8 September 1980.
11 Ibid.
12 Manchester Housing Committee minutes, 8 June 1981.
13 *Manchester Evening News* (9 November 1981).
14 Manchester Housing Committee minutes, 3 October 1980.
15 Ibid., 9 November 1981.
16 Ibid., 3 November 1982.
17 Ibid., 14 March 1980.
18 Ibid., 12 November 1979.
19 Ibid., 10 November 1980.
20 Ibid.
21 Manchester Housing Committee minutes, 12 January 1981.
22 Ibid., 13 July 1981.
23 Ibid., 9 March 1981.
24 Ibid., 8 December 1980.
25 Ibid., 3 October 1980.
26 Ibid., 9 February 1981.
27 Ibid., 9 March 1981.
28 Ibid., 8 June 1981.
29 *Manchester Evening News* (17 February 1983).
30 Ibid.
31 *Manchester Evening News* (27 July 1983).
32 Ibid.
33 *Manchester Evening News* (29 March 1984); (8 June 1985).
34 Homelessness, like race and gender issues, and its many related topics, needs to be examined in a separate study.

35 Manchester Housing Committee minutes, 9 March 1981.

36 Ibid., 13 September 1982.

37 Ibid., 9 April 1984.

38 Ibid., 30 May 1984.

39 Ibid., 9 November 1984.

40 Ibid., 16 October 1986.

41 *Manchester Evening News* (20 September 1989).

42 *Housing Defects in Manchester*, report to the Housing Committee (Manchester, 1982), p. 1.

43 *Manchester Evening News* (20 April 1982).

44 Manchester Housing Committee minutes, 17 July 1984.

45 Ibid., 11 January 1982.

46 Ibid., 8 March 1982.

47 *Guardian* (5 November 1985).

48 Ibid.

49 Manchester Housing Committee minutes, 13 December 1982.

50 Ibid., 20 February 1984.

51 Ibid., 10 January 1983.

52 Ibid., 19 March 1984.

53 *Manchester Evening News* (22 February 1985).

54 Ibid.

55 Ibid.

56 Ibid. (10 December 1988).

57 Ibid.

58 Manchester Housing Committee minutes, 8 January 1980.

59 Ibid., 8 December 1980.

60 Ibid., 9 February 1981.

61 Ibid., 14 September 1981.

62 Ibid., 9 November 1981.

63 *Manchester Evening News* (23 October 1975).

64 Ibid. (15 October 1981).

65 Ibid. (17 October 1988).

66 Ibid. (1 July 1979).

67 Ibid. (15 December 1981).

68 Manchester Housing Committee minutes, 14 September 1981.

69 Ibid., 8 March 1982.

70 Ibid., 4 July 1986.

71 See R. H. Ward, 'Residential succession and race relations in Moss Side, Manchester' (PhD dissertation, University of Manchester, 1975); H. Flett, 'Black people and council housing: a study of Manchester' (PhD dissertation, Bristol University, 1979). Like the gender dimension, race is an issue which justifies a separate study. See also I. G. Law, 'White racism and black settlement in Liverpool: a study of local inequalities and policies, with particular reference to council housing' (PhD dissertation, University of Liverpool, 1985).

72 Manchester Housing Committee minutes, 14 July 1980.

73 Ibid., 14 December 1981.

74 Ibid., 14 June 1982.

75 Ibid., 13 September 1982.

76 Ibid., 11 September 1986.

77 *Manchester Evening News* (16 June 1989).

78 See above, Chapter 1.

79 *How to Buy a Corporation House*, Housing Department pamphlet (July 1968).
80 *Manchester Evening News* (4 September 1968).
81 TNA, HLG 118/1591, Notes for J. Amery by Alderman R. A. Fieldhouse, 6 September 1971.
82 TNA, HLG 118/1591, Letter from J. Amery to Alderman R. A. Fieldhouse, 29 September 1971.
83 TNA, HLG 118/1591, Notes for J. Amery by Alderman R. A. Fieldhouse, 6 September 1971.
84 *Wythenshawe Express* (5 August 1971).
85 *Manchester Evening News* (4 April 1973).
86 TNA, HLG 118/1591, Letter from E. Tomlinson to J. Graham.
87 *Manchester Evening News* (3 April 1973).
88 Ibid. (26 October 1974).
89 Ibid. (27 March 1974).
90 TNA, HLG 118/1591, J. Winder, 'Proposed purchase of former council houses by Manchester Corporation'.
91 Manchester Housing Committee minutes, 9 November 1979.
92 *Manchester Evening News* (21 December 1979).
93 Ibid. (29 September 1980).
94 Ibid. (28 October 1980).
95 Manchester Housing Committee minutes, 10 November 1980.
96 *Manchester Evening News* (28 October 1980).
97 Manchester Housing Committee minutes, 8 December 1980.
98 *Manchester Evening News* (27 February 1981).
99 Housing Committee minutes, 14 September 1981.
100 Ibid., 9 March 1981.
101 Ibid., 11 January 1982.
102 *Manchester Evening News* (17 October 1988).
103 Ibid. (6 September 1989).
104 For the rise of the left in the Labour Party see S. Fielding and D. Tanner, 'The "rise of the left" revisited: Labour Party culture in post-war Manchester and Salford', *Labour History Review*, 71:3 (December 2006).
105 *Manchester Evening News* (26 January 1982).
106 Manchester Housing Committee minutes, 11 June 1984.
107 Ibid., 9 November 1984.
108 Ibid.
109 Ibid., 11 January 1985.
110 Ibid.,16 October 1986.
111 Ibid., 3 June 1986.
112 Ibid., 21 August 1985; 17 January 1986.
113 Ibid., 25 October 1985; 11 April 1986.
114 Ibid., 11 June 1984.
115 Ibid., 17 July 1984.
116 Ibid., 11 June 1984.
117 Ibid., 14 September 1984.
118 Ibid.
119 S. Lansley, S. Goss and C. Wolmar, *Councils in Conflict: The Rise and Fall of the Municipal Left* (London, 1986), p. 186. See also D. Cooper, *Sexing the City: Lesbian and Gay Politics within the Activist State* (London, 1994); A. Eisenschitz and J. Gough, *The Politics of Local Policy* (London, 1993).

120 S. Quilley, 'Manchester first: from municipal socialism to the entrepreneurial city', *International Journal of Urban and Regional Research*, 24:3 (2000), 601–15. See also T. Hall and P. Hubbard, *The Entrepreneurial City* (Chichester, 1998).

121 Quilley, 'Manchester first', p. 610.

122 See, for instance, A. While, A. Jonas and D. Gibbs, 'The environment and the entrepreneurial city: searching for the urban "sustainability fix" in Manchester and Leeds,' *International Journal of Urban and Regional Research*, 28:3 (September 2004), 549–69; J. Peck and K. Ward (eds), *City of Revolution: Restructuring Manchester* (Manchester, 2002).

123 Quilley, 'Manchester first', p. 606.

124 Manchester Housing Committee minutes, 16 October 1986.

125 *Manchester Evening News* (27 June 1988).

126 Ibid., (14 October 1989).

127 Nationally, tenants won the right to be balloted before a Housing Action Trust was enforced.

128 R. Ramwell and H. Saltburn, *Trick or Treat? City Challenge and the Regeneration of Hulme* (Manchester, 1998), p. 12.

129 Ibid., p. 17.

130 M. Heseltine, *Life in the Jungle* (London, 2000), p. 406.

131 Quilley, 'Manchester first', pp. 605–12.

132 *Rebuilding the City, a Guide to Development in Hulme, Hulme City Challenge*, Hulme Regeneration Limited (Manchester, June 1994).

133 Heseltine, *Life in the Jungle*, p. 396.

134 Ibid.

135 Ramwell and Saltburn, *Trick or Treat?*, p. 17.

136 Quilley, 'Manchester first', p. 610.

137 Ramwell and Saltburn, *Trick or Treat?*, p. 25.

138 H. Russell, *Town and Country Planning* (April 1998), 102–3.

139 Ramwell and Saltburn, *Trick or Treat?*, p. 114.

140 Hunt Thompson Architects, *City Challenge: Creating the New Heart of Hulme* (Manchester, 1993), p. 64.

141 Ibid., p. 65.

142 Ramwell and Saltburn, *Trick or Treat?*, p. 75.

143 Ibid., p. 12.

144 Hunt Thompson, *City Challenge*, p. 68.

145 Ibid.

146 *Manchester Evening News* (18 June 1991).

147 Ibid.

148 Ramwell and Saltburn, *Trick or Treat?*, p. 25.

149 Ibid.

150 A. Harding and P. Garside, *Hulme City Challenge: First Residents Survey*, report (April 1996), pp. 2–15.

151 Ibid., p. 6.

152 K. Jacobs, *Town and Country Planning* (November 1998), p. 338.

153 Heseltine, *Life in the Jungle*, p. 517.

153 *Manchester Evening News* (30 November 1994).

Conclusion:
consumers, locality and discourse

Housing histories highlight the necessity of focusing on locality in analysing the dynamics of the decision-making process. Contemporary national overviews are often oversimplified.[1] There were broad similarities, common features and common claims made by different local authorities. This was partly inevitable because of shared experiences and ambitions and partly because of central government involvement. But, while the state provided the legislation, an ideological lead and the money, it did not have its own central production or administrative network to implement policy itself. Under a number of guises, government had a ministry responsible for housing, but it was never intended to make specific plans and build houses. It relied on local authorities to create and manage their own policies within the broad framework. This provided plenty of scope for individual choices. Each local authority reacted not only to govern-ment legislation but to its particular circumstances. Councils created and managed policy in their own urban environment, shaped by cultural, traditional as well as political circumstances. This produced a variety of policy outcomes across time and across the country.[2] Slum clearance and completion rates varied wildly at times. Local authorities displayed a range of responses to house designs, the use of overspill and the willingness to embrace modern designs.[3] Equally diverse were their relations with the tenants. Some local authorities, especially in London, were far more receptive than others to the idea of consultation and participation. Eventually, all had to realise that the political climate was shifting. Greater levels of tenant involvement were becoming inevitable in the 1980s. Pressure from above and below was to leave a lasting mark on local governance across the country.

National government, local authorities, professionals and ideologies had the most obvious impact on local politics and policy. But there was a range of other issues in this complex interplay underpinning government and governance. Policy studies need to take full account of the multifarious interaction of factors underpinning their creation, implementation and management. This means appreciating not only national factors but also each local environment. National legislation across the twentieth century encouraged a range of interpretations and different policies. Attempts at making generalisations and commonalities are problematic and raise more questions than answers. The process of policy creation and implementation can only be understood by making detailed individual studies *and* by placing them into a broader framework which demands studies of comparable depth.[4] Overviews can only be made where broadly similar policies were produced, but cannot be imposed on all towns and cities at all times. Besides, the factors that direct the production of policy might not be the same. Alongside national and local government, ideological, financial and economic factors, any understanding of politics, policy production and management needs a detailed appreciation of cultural and social factors that influence local authorities. J. B. Cullingworth's 1969 *Report of the Housing Management Sub-Committee of the General Housing Advisory Committee* emphasised that it was impossible to talk about a single national housing problem and, therefore, a single solution. There existed a series of local housing problems and, as such, it was vital to produce local policies based "on the problems of individual areas and the context in which they arise".[5]

The politics of housing can only be fully appreciated by looking at the social and cultural context in which policy was implemented across the twentieth century. In Manchester, once the ideological struggle between conservatives and progressives had been overcome, then reformers like Horsfall, Marr and Simon were to leave an indelible mark on the city's civic culture across the twentieth century. Manchester created its own discourse that shaped outlooks and policies over the period. Although it might not have been repeated in the later part of the century, it had, nevertheless, become deeply embedded in civic culture and was clearly evident in policy ambitions. The council's principles and guiding beliefs were based on an unswerving commitment to clearing the slums creating the city beautiful. There was an inextricable correlation between the two. In cultural terms, it entailed an unequivocal belief in the value of cottages and working–class suburbs in green and pleasant areas and a rejection of flats wherever and whenever possible. It also meant doing things on a big and grand scale – the culture of urban grandeur. Wythenshawe was to be the finest example of planning and quality homes in the country, slum clearance was to be bold and dramatic, overspill estates were to be the biggest and best in Britain, and system–built designs would create a grand new world which would reflect the elegance of Bath. Its aim was to provide quality homes that would reflect civic pride. The new Hulme of the 1990s was not only about creating a sustainable community, it was also a triumphant entrance into the city, symbolised by its great arch.

The efforts of Manchester's social reformers and many local politicians are in many respects to be applauded. They created a discourse that served the people and the city's grand ambitions. But they also had to battle against major problems, not least of which was the sheer scale of slum housing. While some have concluded that local discourse, and the values emanating from civil society, was a primary issue in policy creation, civic leaders could not always fulfil their aims and ambitions.[6] Across the century, different leading figures had a broadly shared idealistic vision which was meant to clear the slums and create a bright new world for everyone. Yet it was fraught with problems. Discourse could be rendered meaningless in the face of financial and physical barriers. Resources were a constant obstacle in virtually every decade and the land trap was a relentlessly difficult issue. Even in the 1930s, it had to build some low-level flats to meet demand. Manchester struggled to find sufficient land to develop its vision. It liked to produce the grand narrative, but implementation of the big plan was not always possible. Overspill seemed to be the only solution. But this highlighted another problem – there was more than one discourse at work. Cheshire had its own values and ambitions. This led to a major political upheaval between neighbouring authorities, resulting in yet more disappointment. Its failure meant that the council was being pressured from government and tenants alike to improve on its faltering slum-clearance programme and increase the number of completions. Inevitably, it was pushed towards system-built designs. It made a number of policy choices that it was deeply to regret. But what choice did it have? Ironically, the problem was that now it was the one seen as being responsible for adopting policies with which it had never been entirely comfortable. The result was more frustration and disappointment. Once again, the grand vision had failed and it was left with an expensive legacy that troubled it throughout the 1970s and 1980s.

The legacy of the factory developments, and of a crumbling old housing stock, was obviously most acutely felt by the tenants. They produced an alternative local discourse developed around anger and frustration. Tenants began to organise and voice their grievances at what they perceived to be the council's failure. But they had never been a part of the political equation. This was the second element of the city's civic culture inherited from the late-nineteenth century. Housing reformers, linked as they were to the progressive wing of the council, adopted a top-down approach to tenants. There was a prevailing belief in the Octavia Hill model of tenant management and control. The very notion of working-class housing, of social reform and of creating working-class suburbs, came from middle-class reformers.[7] Tenants were simultaneously perceived as both victims of the slums and in need of careful management. They were not seen as being capable of producing or articulating their own wishes and desires and, as such, they were never sought. Reformers knew best. The likes of Horsfall, who had studied the issue at length at home and in Germany, could provide expert advice. What would a slum dweller know? The same attitudes crossed over into civic culture. The council would provide homes paid for and subsidised by the tax and ratepayers. This gave it the moral upper hand. It produced the plans, taking advice from the experts. Once they had moved into their new homes and experienced the benefits of their foresight, tenants would be sold on its vision.

Only in the later part of the century did it begin to consult tenants. Yet, by this stage, tenant anger had already bubbled over the edge. In the first part of the century, tenants were generally content that the council was a guarantee against the exploitation of the private slum landlord. Their houses were infinitely superior and they enjoyed greater rights and protection. But tenants were not an entirely passive group. A few were willing to organise and protest against perceived mismanagement. This was evident in the 1930s with the Hulme slum-clearance programme. Once the council became the main landlord in the city, and the welfare state offered promises of a better world, then protests and dissatisfaction increased. They were willing passively to accept the council's discourse, its vision, until it proved to be a disaster. Then the discourse of the angry, active citizen consumer emerged. They were part of a wider consumer movement engaging not only in economic choices but also public policy and, later, in environmental discourse.[8] By the 1970s, trust between council and tenant was, in some areas, on the verge of collapse. Tenants adopted the language and the organisational structure of the consumer movement. Council reactions varied. Some inside the council were willing to appreciate the value of the tenants but others were really only paying lip service to the idea of consultation. It was an imposition on their power and authority. However, government policy was also forcing the council towards greater levels of tenant participation. Public service reform under New Labour has been partly determined by what Frank Field described as the demanding "citizen-consumer".[9] Inevitably, the council was pushed into changing its attitude, but the extent to which this has successfully altered civic culture, by providing a lasting and universal change in council outlook, remains to be seen.

Studying housing policy in Manchester highlights three important points about urban governance. First, locality is important. Politics and policy cannot be understood in isolation from the community. There is an undeniable link between traditional interpretations, which emphasise the role of government and party politics on the one hand, and the influence of civic culture and social groups on the other hand. These factors are specific to each town and city and commonality cannot be assumed. Local discourse, understanding the cultural structures of feeling, assessing the role of social groups (reformers and tenants), as well as local party and council officials, also affected to varying degrees the politics of housing. Civic culture, civic pride, local jingoism, and the role of local government in promoting and boasting about their own cities – in claiming to build not simply a better place but the best place – characterised, shaped and moulded housing policy across the century. The creation of national social policy and directives did not lead to a single, homogeneous and exclusively government-dominated series of policies. A sense of locale and the creation of a local discourse, with all its tradition and bristling pride, continued to impact on policy. This study of housing offers a unique and challenging evaluation of the urban context, of civic culture. The twentieth century did not witness the emergence of a single urban society. Each urban arena remained a distinct place, characterised by its own culture.

Second, despite the value of studying local culture and discourse, these factors were not always successful in shaping policy. Studying the urban context and the discourse of housing politics highlights the stresses and strains underpinning policy. The picture was fragmented and full of disappointment. Local government was constantly frustrated about the disparity between what they wanted to achieve and what finance and legislation would allow them to do. Barriers existed that did not allow local civic discourse to be played out. Grand narratives failed because of the lack of land and resources. Also, it was essentially meaningless for tenants suffering due to slum conditions, remote overspill estates, system–built hovels and a general inability to keep estates clean and safe and to maintain even the most basic repairs.

This had an impact on the third important point, the role of the tenant. Analysis of traditional political discourse, whether it is at the national or local level, provides a partial insight into what was being played out at the local level. In many respects, the language of established political ideologies did not have relevance in the everyday lives of most tenants. Their anger, worries and concerns were articulated through a discourse that increasingly paralleled the language of consumerism. This absorbed and cut across the politics of the left, liberal and conservatives. Tenants were not as interested in these political solutions as they were in more fundamental issues. They wanted repairs completed in a reasonable time, retention of their communities and refurbishment of their homes. Some wanted slum clearance, others wanted improvement. All wanted a clean, affordable and safe home in a decent environment. For them, this had less to do with traditional politics and much more to do with securing a good service from the policy producers. Deference for traditional political authority declined as the demand for a quality service and decent homes increased.[10]

This has implications on the way we view local politics. Without an understanding of the complex interchange of locality, local discourse, tenants, civic culture and social groups, policy analysis remains in a vacuum. Even this study does not go far enough. The race and gender dynamics need further research. This is not to dispute the fact that national government and above all finance were central factors. But to understand the politics of housing demands an appreciation of the exchanges between social reformers, tenants and the council. Moreover, there are wider political implications arising from the discourse between tenants and council officials. What was happening in Manchester reflected a growing disinterest in traditional political language and solutions. It did not mirror their worries and concerns. The language of consumerism provided a relevant expression of their needs. Local politics, and local political authority, failed to satisfy their hopes and aspirations. Only by studying the urban context is it possible really to appreciate these vital influences shaping the politics of housing across the twentieth century.

Notes

1 The point is emphasised in D. Byrne, 'Working-class owner occupation and social differentiation on inter-war Tyneside', in W. Lancaster (ed.), *Working-Class Housing on Tyneside, 1850–1939* (Whitley Bay, 1994), p. 109.

2 M. Glendinning and S. Muthesius, *Tower Block: Modern Public Housing in England, Scotland, Wales, and Northern Ireland* (New Haven, 1994).

3 B. Finnimore, *House from the Factory: System Building and the Welfare State* (London, 1989); A. Power, *The Crisis in Council Housing* (Suntory Toyota International Centre for Economics and Related Disciplines, 1987); A. Power, *Council Housing: Conflict, Change and Decision Making* (Suntory Toyota International Centre for Economics and Related Disciplines, 1988); C. L. Andrews, *Tenants and Town Hall* (London, 1979).

4 J. Nasr, 'Comparisons across reconstructions', P. J. Larkham and J. Nasr (eds), *The Rebuilding of British Cities: Exploring the Post-Second World War Reconstruction*, working paper series No. 90 (University of Central England, 2004), p. 70.

5 TNA, HLG 117/99, Ninth Report of the Housing Management Sub-Committee of the General Housing Advisory Committee, 1969, p. 118.

6 J. Lawrence, 'The complexities of English Progressivism: Wolverhampton politics in the early twentieth century', *Midland History*, 24 (1999), 147–66.

7 A. Ravetz, *Council Housing and Culture: The History of a Social Experiment* (London, 2001), p. 5.

8 F. Trentmann, 'Knowing consumers', in Trentmann (ed.), *The Making of the Consumer: Knowledge, Power and Identity and the Modern World* (Oxford, 2006), p. 2.

9 F. Field, *New Ambitions for Our Country: A New Contract for Welfare* (London, 1998), cited in Trentmann (ed.), *The Making of the Consumer*, p. 2.

10 See also F. Mort, 'Competing domains: democratic subjects and consuming subjects in Britain and the United States since 1945', in Trentmann (ed.), *The Making of the Consumer*, p. 225.

Bibliography

Secondary sources

Books

Andrews, C. L., *Tenants and Town Hall* (London, 1979).

Banton, M. (ed.), *Anthropological Approaches to the Study of Religion* (London, 1966).

Binfield, C., Childs R., Harper, R., Hey, D., Martin, D. and Tweedale, G. (eds), *The History of the City of Sheffield* (Sheffield, 1993).

Black, L., *The Political Culture of the Left in Affluent Britain, 1951–64: Old Labour, New Britain?* (Basingstoke, 2003).

Blunt M. and Goldsmith, M., *Housing Policy and Administration: A Case Study*, Occasional Paper (University of Salford, July 1969).

Burnett, J., *A Social History of Housing 1815–1985* (New York, 1986).

Burt, S. and Grady, K., *History of Leeds* (Derby, 2002).

Cherry, G. E., *Town Planning, Britain Since 1900* (Oxford, 1996).

Chinn, C., *Homes for People* (Birmingham, 1991).

Clapson, M., *Invincible Green Suburbs, Brave New Towns* (Manchester, 1998).

Clapson, M., *Suburban Century, Social Change and Urban Growth in England and the United States* (Oxford, 2003).

Cohen, L., *A Consumer's Republic: The Politics of Mass Consumption in Post War America* (New York, 2003).

Collison, P., *The Cutteslowe Walls: A Study in Social Class* (London, 1963).

Colls, R. and Rodger, R. (eds), *Cities of Ideas: Civil Society and Urban Governance in Britain 1800–2000* (Aldershot, 2004).

Cooper, D., *Sexing the City: Lesbian and Gay Politics within the Activist State* (London, 1994).

Cullingworth, J. B., *Housing Need and Planning Policy: Problems of Housing Need and Overspill in England and Wales* (London, 1960).

Cullingworth, J. B., *Housing and Local Government* (London, 1966).

Daunton, M. J., *House and Home in the Victorian City: Working-Class Housing, 1850–1914* (London, 1983).

Daunton, M. J. (ed.), *Councillors and Tenants: Local Authority Housing in English Cities, 1919–1939* (Leicester, 1984).

Daunton, M. J. (ed.), *The Cambridge Urban History of Britain*, Vol. 3 (Cambridge, 2000).

Daunton, M. and Hilton, M. (eds), *The Politics of Consumption, Material Culture and Citizenship in Europe and America* (Oxford, 1990).

Dunleavy, P., *The Politics of Mass Housing in Britain, 1945–1975: A Study of Corporate Power and Professional Influence in the Welfare State* (Oxford, 1981).

Eisenschitz, A. and Gough, J., *The Politics of Local Policy* (London, 1993).

Englander, D., *Landlords and Tenant in Urban Britain* (Oxford, 1983).

Fielding, S., *The Labour Governments: Labour and Cultural Change*, Vol.1 (Manchester, 2002).

Finnimore, B., *House from the Factory: System Building and the Welfare State* (London, 1989).

Frances, M., *Ideas and Policies under Labour, 1945–1951: Building a New Britain* (Manchester, 1997).

Fraser, D., *A History of Modern Leeds* (Manchester, 1980).

Fraser, D. (ed.), *Municipal Reform and the Industrial City* (Leicester, 1982).

Fyrth, J. (ed.), *Labour's Promised Land* (London, 1995).

Gabriel, Y. and Lang, T., *The Unmanageable Consumer* (London, 1995).

Gauldie, E., *Cruel Habitations: A History of Working-Class Housing 1780–1918* (London, 1974).

Gibson, M. S. and Langstaff, M. J., *Urban Renewal* (London, 1992).

Glendinning M. and Muthesius, S., *Tower Block: Modern Public Housing in England, Scotland, Wales, and Northern Ireland* (New Haven, 1994).

Gordon, G. (ed.), *Regional Cities in the UK, 1890–1980* (London, 1986).

Goss, S., *Local Labour and Local Government* (Edinburgh, 1988).

Grant, C., *Built to Last: Reflections on British Housing Policy* (Nottingham, 1992).

Grayson, J., *Opening the Window – Revealing the Hidden History of Tenants' Organisations* (Leeds, 1996).

Gunn, S., *The Public Culture of the Victorian Middle-Class: Ritual and Authority and the English Industrial City, 1840–1914* (New York, 2000).

Gyford, J., Leach, S. and Game, C., *The Changing Face of Local Government* (London, 1989).

Haesagwa, J., *Replacing the Blitzed City Centre: A Comparative Study of Bristol, Coventry and Southampton, 1945–50* (Buckingham, 1992).

Hall, P., *The Containment of Urban England* (London, 1973).

Hall, T. and Hubbard, P., *The Entrepreneurial City* (Chichester, 1998).

Harloe, M., *Swindon: A Town in Transition* (London, 1975).

Hayes, N., *Consensus and Controversy: City Politics in Nottingham, 1945–1966* (Liverpool, 1996).

Johnson, P., *Land Fit for Heroes: The Planning of British Reconstruction 1916–1919* (Chicago, 1968).

Kidd, A. J., *Manchester* (Keele, 1996).

Kidd, A. J. and Roberts, K., *City, Class and Culture* (Manchester, 1985).

Lancaster, W. (ed.), *Working Class Housing on Tyneside, 1850–1939* (Whitley Bay, 1994).

Lansley, S., Goss, S. and Wolmar, C., *Councils in Conflict: The Rise and Fall of the Municipal Left* (London, 1986).

Larkham P. J. and Nasr, J. (eds), *The Rebuilding of British Cities: Exploring the Post-Second World War Reconstruction*, working paper series No. 90 (University of Central England, 2004).

Lees-Marshment, J., *The Political Marketing Revolution: Transforming the Government of the UK* (Manchester, 2003).

Lowe, R., *The Welfare State in Britain Since 1945* (Basingstoke, 1993).

Manchester: Fifty Years of Change (HMSO, 1995).

Marshall, T. H., *Social Policy in the Twentieth Century* (London, 1970).

Marshall, T. H., *The Right to Welfare and Other Essays* (London, 1981).

Mathieson, D., *The St. Pancras Rent Strike* (London, 1987).

Mayne, A., *The Imagined Slum, Newspaper Representations in Three Cities, 1870–1914* (Leicester, 1993).

McKibbin, R., *Classes and Cultures, England 1918–1951* (Oxford, 2000).

Meller, H., *European Cities 1890–1930: History, Culture and the Built Environment* (New York, 2001).

Meller, H., *Cities of Ideas: Civic Society and Urban Governance in Britain, 1800–2000* (Aldershot, 2004).

Mitchell, P., *Momento Mori: The Flats of Quarry Hill* (Otley, 1990).

Monti, D. J., *The American City: A Social and Cultural History* (Malden, 1999).

Newton, K., *Second City Politics: Democratic Processes and Decision-Making in Birmingham* (Oxford, 1976).

North Shields: Working Class Politics and Housing, 1900–1977, North Tyneside CDP (London, 1978).

Morris, R. J. and Trainor, H. (eds), *Urban Governance: Britain and Beyond Since 1750* (Aldershot, 2000).

Nove, A., *The Economics of Feasible Socialism* (London, 1983).

Olechnowicz, A., *Working Class Housing in England Between the Wars* (Oxford, 1997).

Peck, J. and Ward, K. (eds), *City of Revolution: Restructuring Manchester* (Manchester, 2002).

Pooley, C. G. and Irish, S., *The Development of Corporation Housing in Liverpool, 1869–1945* (Lancaster, 1984).

Power, A., *The Crisis in Council Housing* (Suntory Toyota International Centre for Economics and related Disciplines, 1987).

Power, A., *Council Housing: Conflict, Change and Decision Making* (Suntory Toyota International Centre for Economics and related Disciplines, 1988).

Ravetz, A., *Model Estates: Planned Housing at Quarry Hill* (London, 1974).

Ravetz, A., *Council Housing and Culture: The History of a Social Experiment* (London, 2001).

Reed, A., *Brentham: A History of the Pioneer Garden Suburb, 1901–2001* (Brentham, 2000).

Rhodes, R. A. W., *Control and Power in Central-Local Government Relations* (Farnborough, 1981).

Roberts, N., *Homes for Heroes: Early Twentieth Century Council Housing in the County Borough of Swansea* (Swansea, 1992).

Rodger, R., *Housing in Urban Britain, 1780–1914: Class, Capitalism and Construction* (London, 1989).

Skern, B. C., *Housing in Kingston Upon Hull* (Hull, 1986).

Spiegel, H., *Citizen Participation in Urban Development* (Washington, 1968).

Stearns, P. N., *Encyclopaedia of European Social History* (New York, 2001).

Swenarton, M., *Homes Fit for Heroes* (London, 1981).

Taylor, I., Evans, K. and Fraser, P., *A Tale of Two Cities: Global Change, Local Feeling and Everyday Life in the North of England* (London, 1996).

Tiratsoo, N., *Reconstruction, Affluence and Labour Politics: Coventry 1945–60* (London, 1990).

Tiratsoo, N., Hasegawa, J., Mason, T. and Matsumura, T., *Urban Reconstruction in Coventry and Japan, Dreams, Plans and Realities* (Luton, 2002).

Towers, G., *Shelter is Not Enough: Transforming Multi-Storey Housing* (Bristol, 2000).

White, E., *A History of the Manchester and Salford Council of Social Service 1919–1969* (Manchester, 1969).

Trentmann, F., *Paradoxes in Civil Society: New Perspectives on Modern German and British Society* (New York, 2000).

Trentmann, F. (ed.), *The Making of the Consumer: Knowledge, Power and Identity and the Modern World* (Oxford, 2006).

Wohl, A., *The Eternal Slum* (London, 1977).

Young, K. and Garside, P., *Metropolitan London: Politics and Urban Change, 1837–1981* (London, 1982).

Young K. and Rao, N., *Local Government Since 1945* (Oxford, 1997).

Articles

Bradley, Q., 'The Leeds Rent Strike of 1914', Leeds 1997, at www.freespace.virgin.net/labwise.history6/rentrick.htm.

Bromley, M. and Hayes, N., 'Campaigner, watchdog or municipal lackey? Reflections on the inter-war provincial press, local identity and civic welfarism', *Media History*, 8:2 (2002).

Butler, S., 'Socialism and housing: the British experience', *Journal of Social and Political Studies*, 3:4 (1978).

Cameron, S., 'Housing, gentrification and urban regeneration policies', *Urban Studies*, 29:1 (1992).

Cashmore, H., 'An interesting co-operative venture', *The Woman Citizen*, 20 July (1929).

Clapson, M., 'Working class women's experiences of moving to new housing estates in England since 1919', *Twentieth Century British History*, 10:3 (1999).

Cook, M., 'Council house sales: the rights and wrongs', *Contemporary Review*, 248:1445 (1986).

Cooney, E. W., 'Innovation in the post-war British building industry', *Construction History*, 1 (1985).

Cooper, T., 'Review', *Urban History*, 31:2 (2004).

Dennis, R., 'Room for improvement? Recent studies of working class housing', *Journal of Urban History*, 21:5 (1995).

Doyle, B., 'Mapping slums in a historic city: representing working class communities in Edwardian Norwich', *Planning Perspectives*, 16 (January 2001).

Englander, D., 'Review', *Urban History*, 21:2 (October 1994).

Englander, D., 'Urban history or urban historicism? A response to Alan Mayne', *Urban History*, 22:3 (December 1995).

Farmer E. and Smith, R., 'Overspill theory: a Metropolitan case study', *Urban Studies*, 12 (1975).

Fielding, S. and Tanner, D., 'The "rise of the left" revisited: Labour Party culture in post-war Manchester and Salford', *Labour History Review*, 71:3 (December 2006).

Fitzgerald, M., 'Manchester and Salford Better Housing Council', *Social Welfare*, January (1931).

Fitzgerald, M., 'Problems of new housing', *Social Welfare* (October 1933).

Gaskell, S. M., 'Gardens for the working class: Victorian practical pleasure', *Victorian Studies*, 23:4 (1980).

Hartley, O. A., 'The relationship between central and local authorities', *Public Administration*, 49:Winter (1971).

Heathorn, S., 'An English paradise to regain? Ebenezer Howard, the Town and Country Planning Association and English ruralism', *Rural History*, 11:1 (2000).

Harrison, M., 'Thomas Coglan Horsfall and the example of Germany', *Planning Perspectives*, 6 (1991).

Hayes, J., 'The Association of London Housing Estates and the "Fair Rent" issue', *London Journal*, 14:1 (1989).

Hayes, N., 'Making homes by machine: images, ideas and myths in diffusion of non-traditional housing in Britain 1942–54', *Twentieth Century British History*, 19:3 (1999).

Hayes, N., 'Civic perceptions: housing and local decision-making in English cities in the 1920s', *Urban History*, 27:2 (2000).

Hayes, N., 'Forcing modernization on the "one remaining really backward industry": British construction and the politics of progress and ambiguous assessment', *Journal of European Economic History*, 31 (2002).

Heller, R., 'East Fulham revisited', *Journal of Contemporary History*, 6:3 (1971).

Hilton, M., 'The fable of the sheep, or, private virtues, public vices: the consumer revolution of the twentieth century', *Past and Present* (2002).

Jacobs, K., *Town and Country Planning* (November 1998).

Jones, H., '"This is magnificent!": 300,000 houses a year and the Tory revival after 1945', *Contemporary British History*, 14:1 (2000).

Lawrence, J., 'Class and gender in the making of Urban Toryism, 1880–1914', *English Historical Review*, 108 (1993).

Lawrence, J., 'The complexities of English Progressivism: Wolverhampton politics in the early twentieth century', *Midland History*, 24 (1999).

Lewis, J., 'Consumer politics and housing', *Bulletin of the Society for the Study of Labour History*, 47 (1983).

Lowe, R., 'Welfare policy in Britain', *Contemporary Record*, 4:2 (1990).

Lowerson, J., 'Leisure, consumption and the European city', *Urban History*, 30:1 (2003).

Macintyre, C., 'Policy reform and the politics of housing in the British Conservative Party, 1924–1929', *Australian Journal of Politics and History*, 45:3 (1999).

Maclennan D. and Gibb, K., 'Housing finance and subsidies in Britain after a decade of "Thatcherism"', *Urban Studies*, 27:6 (1990), 905–18.

Machon, P., 'The sale of local authority houses in Great Britain', *Geography*, 72:2 (1987).

Marsh D. and Rhodes R., 'Implementing Thatcherism: policy change in the 1980s', *Parliamentary Affairs*, 45:1 (1992).

Mayne, A. and Lawrence, S., 'Ethnographies of place: a new urban history agenda', *Urban History*, 26 (1999).

Meller, M., 'Urban renewal and citizenship: the quality of life in British cities, 1890–1990', *Urban History*, 22:1 (1995).

Moore-Colyer, R. J., 'From Great Wen to Toad Hall: aspects of the urban-rural divide in inter-war Britain', *Rural History*, 10:1 (1999).

Murphy, L. R., 'Rebuilding Britain: the government's role in housing and town planning, 1945–1957', *Historian*, 32:2 (1970).

Pelling, H., 'The 1945 General Election reconsidered', *Historical Journal*, 23:2 (1980).

Pepper, S., 'Early LCC experiments in high rise housing, 1925–29', *London Journal*, 7 (1981).

Potter, L., 'The Woodchurch controversy, 1944', *Transactions of the Historic Society of Lancashire and Cheshire*, 150 (2000).

Quilley, S., 'Manchester first: from municipal socialism to the entrepreneurial city', *International Journal of Urban and Regional Research*, 24:3 (2000).

Rodger, R., 'Political economy, ideology and the persistence of working-class housing problems in Britain, 1850–1914', *International Review of Social History*, 32:2 (1987).

Rose, M. E., 'The Manchester University Settlement in Ancoats, 1895–1909', *Manchester Region History Review*, 7 (1993).

Russell, H., *Town and Country Planning* (April 1998).

Shapely, P., 'Urban charity, class relations and social cohesion: charitable responses to the cotton famine', *Urban History*, 28:1 (2001).

Shapely, P., 'The press and the system built developments of inner-city Manchester', *Manchester Region History Review*, 16 (2002–3).

Shapely, P., 'Tenants arise! Consumerism, tenants and the challenge to council authority in Manchester, 1968–92', *Social History*, 31:1 (2006), 60–78.

Shapely, P., Tanner, D. and Walling, A., 'Civic culture and housing policy in Manchester, 1945–79', *Twentieth Century British History*, 15:4 (2004), 410–34.

Sheail, J., 'Interwar planning in Britain: the wider context', *Journal of Urban History*, 11:3 (1985).

Simmonds, A., 'Conservative governments and the new town housing question in the 1950s', *Urban History*, 28:1 (2001).

Skilleter, K.,'The role of public utility societies in early British town planning and housing reform, 1901–36', *Planning Perspectives*, 8:2, (1993).

Smith, R., 'The politics of an overspill policy: Glasgow, Cumbernauld and the Housing and Town Development (Scotland) Act', *Public Administration*, 55 (March 1977)

Swenarton, M.,'"An insurance against revolution". Ideological objectives of the provision and design of public housing in Britain after the First World War', *Bulletin of the Institute of Historical Research*, 54:129 (1981).

Taylor, P., 'British local government and house building during the Second World War', *Planning History*, 17:2 (1995).

Theakston, K.,'Evelyn Sharp', *Contemporary Record*, 7:1 (1993).

Tiemstra, J.,'Theories of regulation and the history of consumerism', *International Journal of Social Economics*, 19:6 (1992).

Tsubaki, T., 'Planners and the public: British popular opinion on housing during the Second World War', *Contemporary British History*, 14:10 (2000).

Tylecote, M., 'Community Associations on new estates', *The Woman Citizen*, March (1937).

Vignozzi, A., 'Urban aesthetic control in Britain: form the Housing and Town Planning Act to the beginning of deregulation', *Storia Urbana*, 17:65 (1993).

Ward, R. H.,'Where race didn't divide', chapter, full source unknown.

Weiler, P., 'The rise and fall of the Conservatives' Grand Design for Housing', *Contemporary British History*, 14:1 (2000).

While, A., Jonas, A. and Gibbs, D., 'The environment and the entrepreneurial city: searching for the urban "sustainability fix" in Manchester and Leeds,' *International Journal of Urban and Regional Research*, 28:3 (September 2004).

White, J.,'When every room was measured: the overcrowding survey of 1935–36 and its aftermath', *History Workshop Journal*, 4 (1977).

Whitehead, C.,'From need to affordability: an analysis of UK housing objectives', *Urban Studies*, 28:6 (1991).

Wohl, A. S., 'The 1880s: a new generation?', *Nineteenth Century Studies*, 4 (1990).

Yelling, J.,'Homes fit for heroes', *Modern History Review*, 9:4 (1998).

Yelling, J.,'Public policy, urban renewal and property ownership, 1945–55', *Urban History*, 22:1 (1995).

Yelling, J., 'The incidence of slum clearance in England and Wales, 1955–85', *Urban History*, 27:2 (2000).

Unpublished dissertations

Adderley, S., 'Bureaucratic conceptions of citizenship in the voluntary sector, 1919–1939' (PhD dissertation, University of Wales, Bangor, 2001).

Backwith, D., 'The death of municipal socialism: the politics of council housing in Sheffield and Bristol, 1919–1939' (PhD dissertation, Bristol University, 1995).

Baldock, P. A., 'Tenants' voice: a study of council tenants' organisations, with particular reference to those in the City of Sheffield, 1961–71' (PhD dissertation, Sheffield University, 1970–71).

Brady, K., 'The development of the Wythenshawe Estate, Manchester: concept to incorporation, 1919–1931' (MSc dissertation, Salford University, 1990).

Cooper, S. M.,'English housing policy, 1972–1980' (PhD dissertation, London School of Economics, 1984).

Cuthbert, R. S., 'Tenant participation in public sector housing: a case study of Glasgow' (MSc dissertation, Stirling University, 1988).

Davies, C. T., 'Citizen participation in redevelopment with special reference to Newton Heath' (MA dissertation, University of Manchester, 1971).

Dunleavy, P. J., 'The politics of high rise housing in Britain: local communities tackle mass housing' (DPhil dissertation, Oxford University, 1978).

Flett, H., 'Black people and council housing: a study of Manchester' (PhD dissertation, Bristol University, 1979).

Hancock, L., 'Tenant participation and the housing classes debate' (PhD dissertation, University of Liverpool, 1994).

Johnstone, C., 'The tenants' movement and housing struggles in Glasgow, 1945–1990' (PhD dissertation, Glasgow University, 1992).

Jones, B., 'Manchester liberalism 1918–1929: the electoral, ideological and organisational experience of the Liberal Party in Manchester with particular reference to the career of Ernest Simon' (PhD dissertation, University of Manchester, 1997).

Kay, A., 'Wythenshawe circa 1932–1955: the making of a community?' (PhD dissertation, University of Manchester, 1993).

Law, I. G., 'White racism and black settlement in Liverpool: a study of local inequalities and policies, with particular reference to council housing' (PhD dissertation, University of Liverpool, 1985).

McKenna, M., 'The development of suburban council housing in Liverpool between the wars' (PhD dissertation, University of Liverpool, 1986).

Rao, J. S. G., 'Power and participation: tenants' involvement in housing' (MPhil dissertation, Brunel University, 1983).

Richardson, A. W., 'The politics of participation: a study of schemes for tenant participation in council housing management' (PhD dissertation, London School of Economics, 1978).

Stoker, G. T., 'The Politics of urban renewal in Withington, 1962–83' (PhD dissertation, University of Manchester, 1985).

Walling, A., 'Modernisation, policy debate and organisation in the Labour Party 1951–64' (PhD dissertation, University of Wales, Bangor, 2001).

Ward, R.H., 'Residential succession and race relations in Moss Side, Manchester' (PhD dissertation, University of Manchester, 1975).

Wheale, G. A., 'Citizen participation in the rehabilitation of housing in Moss Side East' (PhD dissertation, University of Manchester, 1979).

Primary sources

Pamphlets

Bendixson, T., speech at a forum on 'Public Participation', unpublished transcript, (London, 1971).

Broady, M., *Planning for People, National Council of Social Service* (London, 1968).

Daniel, G., *Looking to the Future, report of the Seventh National Conference on Social Welfare* (London, 1970).

Government papers

The National Archives, London (hereafter TNA), HLG 117/99, Parliamentary Debates, 1919–1987, Advisory Committee, 1969.

TNA, HLG 157/21, Appendage to Memo on the *Housing Manual*, 27 June 1958.

TNA, HLG 157/21, Confidential note to the Ministry, 21 August 1957.

TNA, HLG 79/1126, Draft minute to the Prime Minister.

TNA, HLG 71/2293, Draft note of a meeting held on 27 January 1955 at which the Minister met a delegation from Manchester to discuss their overspill problem, February 1955.

TNA, HLG 71/2293, Letter from Evelyn Sharp to the Minister, 20 January 1955.

TNA, HLG 79/1126, Letter from Evelyn Sharp to the Town Clerk, Manchester, 15 July 1958.

TNA, HLG 71/2293, Letter to Duncan Sandys, 18 October 1954.

TNA, HLG 79/1126, Letter from W. Ogden to MHLG, 9 May 1958.

TNA, HLG 71/2293, Letter from Evelyn Sharp to the Minister, 20 January 1955.

TNA, HLG 118/154, Letter from Mrs E. Hill to Sir Keith Joseph, 26 February 1963.

TNA, HLG 71/2293, Letter from Evelyn Sharp to the Minister, 20 January 1955.

TNA, HLG 118/154, Letter from E. A. Sharp to Philip Dingle, 3 May 1962.

TNA, HLG 118/154, Letter from W. A. Wood, 27 September 1962.

TNA, HLG 118/792, Letters from J. E. Beddoe to R. Metcalfe, 15–29 January 1968.

TNA, HLG 157/21, Letter to J. L. Womersley, 10 February 1958.

TNA, HLG 47/594, Letter to A. Johnstone, 3 March 1936.

TNA, HLG 47/594, Letter to W. H. Howes, Ministry of Health, 26 November 1936.

TNA, HLG 118/1591, Letter from E. Tomlinson to John Graham.

TNA, HLG 91/565, Letter from K. G. Gunn to W. K. Morris, 5 May 1960.

TNA, HLG 71/2293, Report on Lymm / Mobberley from Evelyn Sharp, 29 October 1954.

TNA, HLG 157/21, Memo on the *Housing Manual 1958*, 27 June 1958.

TNA, HLG 47/594, Ministry of Health Circular 1331, 20 March 1934.

Royal Commission on the Distribution of the Industrial Population (HMSO, 1940).

Report of the Committee on Public Participation in Planning (HMSO, 1969).

Report of the Committee on Local Authority and Allied Personal Social Services (HMSO, 1968).

Report of Royal Commission on Local Government in England 1966–69 (HMSO, 1969).

TNA, HLG 101/815, *Report of the inquiry into the collapse of flats at Ronan Point, Canning Town*, London, 1968, p. 61.

TNA, BD 107/21, 'The Right-to-Buy – a consultation paper', 11 October 1979.

TNA, CAB 129/120, 'The housing programme'.

TNA, HLG 118/2642, draft circular, *A handbook on tenants participation in council housing management*.

TNA, HLG 118/2642, A. Richardson, *Getting Tenants Involved*.

TNA, HLG 91/564, P. R. Tindale, Director of Housing Development Directorate, 'Population recruitment for Cwmbran'.

Political papers

Addison, C., *The Betrayal of the Slums* (London, 1922).

Conservative Party manifesto, 1945–1987.

(All post-war manifestos are taken from www.psr.keele.ac.uk/area/uk/manifesto).

Crossman, R., *Richard Crossman: The Diaries of a Cabinet Minister*, Vol. 1 (London, 1975).

Field, F., *New Ambitions for Our Country: A New Contract for Welfare* (London, 1998).

Greenwood, A., *The Labour Outlook* (London, 1929).

Heseltine, M., *Life in the Jungle* (London, 2000).

Joseph, K., *Stranded on the Middle Ground? Centre for Policy Studies* (London, 1976).

Labour Party, *Up with the Houses, Down with the Slums* (London, 1934).

Labour Party manifesto, 1945–1987.

Macmillan, H., *The Tides of Fortune* (London, 1969).
TNA, HLG 118/258, Memo from E. A. Sharp, 'Slum clearance drive', 9 April 1962.
TNA, HLG 118/258, Memo from E. A. Sharp, 'Northern Housing Office', 23 October 1962.

Contemporary reports

Ancoats Healthy Homes Society, *Annual Reports*, 1894–1905.
Booth, C., *The Housing Question in Manchester: Notes on the Report of the Citizens' Association* (Manchester, 1904).
Chorltonville, A Garden Village of Better Planned Houses (Manchester, 1911).
Disraeli, B., *Coningsby, or, the New Generation* (London, 1911).
Engels, F., *The Condition of the Working Class in England* (Oxford, 1971).
Gaskell, E., *Mary Barton* (Oxford, 1998).
Harding, A. and Garside, P., *Hulme City Challenge: First Residents Survey* (April, 1996).
Hulme Housing Association Survey Section Report (Manchester, 1931).
Hulme Housing Association, Preliminary Report (Manchester, 1932).
Hunt Thompson Architects, *City Challenge: Creating the New Heart of Hulme* (Manchester, 1993).
Inman, J., *Poverty and Housing Conditions in a Manchester Ward* (Manchester, 1934).
Kay, J. P., *The Moral and Physical Condition of the Working Classes Employed in the Cotton Manufacture in Manchester* (Manchester, 1969).
Manchester City News.
Manchester Housing 1926 Ltd (Manchester, 1929).
Manchester and District Regional Survey Society, No. 12, *Some Housing Conditions in Chorlton-on-Medlock* (Manchester, 1931).
Manchester and District Regional Survey Society, No. 12, *Some Social Aspects of Pre-War Tenements and of Post-War Flats* (Manchester, 1932).
Manchester and Salford Better Housing Council, *Report of a Survey Undertaken in Part of St. Michael's and Collegiate Wards of the City of Manchester*, the Red Bank Survey Group (Manchester, 1931).
Manchester and Salford Better Housing Council, *Under the Arches (Behind London Road Station), Report of a Survey Undertaken for Manchester and Salford Better Housing Council in St. Clements Ward in the City of Manchester* (Manchester, 1931).
Manchester and Salford Better Housing Council, *Wythenshawe, Report of an Investigation* (Manchester, 1935).
Manchester University Settlement, *Ancoats: A Study of a Clearance Area, Report of a Survey made in 1937–1938* (Manchester, 1945).
Manchester University Settlement, Diamond Jubilee – Souvenir Brochure (1954)
MASHA minutes, 24 April 1973; 'Haykin Residents Association Survey', August 1974.
Marr, T. R., *Housing Conditions in Manchester and Salford* (Manchester, 1904).
Ramwell, R. and Saltburn, H., *Trick or Treat? City Challenge and the Regeneration of Hulme* (Manchester, 1998).
Rebuilding the City, a Guide to Development in Hulme, Hume City Challenge, Hulme Regeneration Ltd (Manchester, June 1994).
Redford, A., *History of Local Government in Manchester*, Vol. 3 (Manchester, 1940).
Rent Book for 1932, Manchester Central Reference Library.
Scott, F., *Transactions of the Manchester Statistical Society* (Manchester, 1889).
TNA, BT 56/10, *The Seven Cities Housing Trust Limited*.
Shimwell, Canon T., *Some Manchester Homes*, pamphlet (Manchester, 1929).
Simon, E. D., *A City Council from Within* (London, 1926).

Simon, E. D., *How to Abolish the Slums* (London, 1929).
Simon, E. D. and Inman, J., *The Rebuilding of Manchester* (London, 1935).
TNA, RG 19/101, Simon, E. D., *The Anti-Slum Campaign*.
Social Welfare, January–October 1933.
The Surveyor, February 1957.
The Woman Citizen, 1925–37.

Manchester city council reports

Abercrombie, P., 'Report to the Housing Committee', 10 March 1920, included in the
    Housing Committee minutes, 29 March 1920.
Barrack Street Tenement Dwellings, Council proceedings, 8 January 1906.
Heywood, L., '50,000 Houses below a reasonable standard of habitation', Manchester
    Central Reference Library cuttings, 1934.
'Housing Needs and Land Resources and General Housing Policies in the City of
    Manchester: Manchester: improvement or clearance – the case for improvement',
    report of the Chief Officers, June 1973.
Housing of the Working Class, City of Manchester (Manchester, 1904).
'Housing of the Working Classes', report from the Sanitary Committee, 18 October 1899.
How to Buy a Corporation House, Housing Department, July 1968.
Luke, J., City Surveyor, 'Report upon the development of the city', Manchester Housing
    Committee minutes, 9 October 1920.
TNA, HLG 159/428, Letter from Manchester Housing Department to Department of
    Housing and Local Government, 4 April 1972.
Manchester Housing Committee minutes, 1919–1986.
1945 Manchester Redevelopment Plan (Manchester, 1945).
City Planning Officer, 'Slum Clearance and Re-housing Progress', report to the Chief
    Officer's Meeting, 1 April 1974.

Manchester political papers

Ardwick Branch, Labour Party minutes, 8 September 1966.
Fight the Landlords Rent Increase, Communist Party leaflet, Local Studies Unit, Manchester
    Central Reference Library.
Labour Group Policy Committee, Manchester Council, minutes 17 October 1975–77.
TNA, HLG 118/1591, Letter from J. Amery to Alderman Fieldhouse, 29 September 1971.
Minutes of North West Economic Planning Council, Housing Committee, 25 March
    1966.
TNA, HLG 118/1591, Notes for the Rt Hon. Julian Amery by Alderman R. A.
    Fieldhouse, 6 September 1971.
TNA, HLG 118/1591, J. Winder, 'Proposed purchase of former council houses by
    Manchester Corporation'.
HLG 118/1591, Alderman Fieldhouse, Speech on slum clearance and re-housing, 3
    November 1971.

Newspapers

Bolton Evening News, 1963.
Blackley and Openshaw Reporter, 1957.
Cheshire Life, November 1953–March 1965.
City and Suburban News, 1956.
County Express, 23 February 1961.

Daily Dispatch, 1933–65.
Daily Express, 1933.
Daily Telegraph, 1965.
East Manchester Reporter, 1964–71.
Evening Chronicle, 1961.
Horwich and Westhoughton Journal, 1963–65.
Hyde Reporter, 1963.
Illustrated London News, 1933.
Manchester City News, 1890–1920.
Manchester Courier, 1911
Manchester Guardian/Guardian, 1896–1986.
Manchester Evening Chronicle, 1933–61.
Manchester Evening News, 1946–92.
North Cheshire Herald, 1955.
Municipal Journal, 1904–10.
The Times, 1904–92.
Wythenshawe County Reporter, 1961–65.

Tenant papers

Gosling, R., *Personal Copy: A Memoir of the Sixties* (London, 1980).
Hulme Crescents, Manchester Housing Workshop (Manchester 1980), p. 18.
Manchester and Salford Housing Action committee minutes, 1973–75, Manchester
    Central Reference Library.
'Moss Side People's Paper', Manchester Central Reference Library, November 1970.
'Newsletter for the Moss Side Housing Action Area', No. 1, December 1975.
The South Wales Association of Tenants' campaign against damp homes in 1979,
    www.tenant2u.tripod.com/quotes.html.

Miscellaneous

Jenkinson, C., *The Leeds Housing Policy* (Leeds, 1934).
World in Action, 'The System Builder', Granada (20 June 1983).

Index